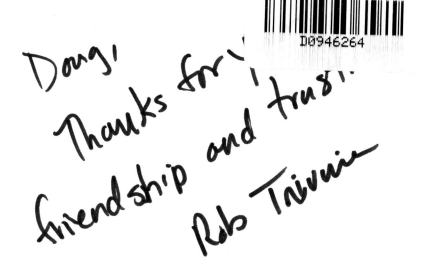

Doug!
Thanks for '
friendship and trust.
Rob Trivino

A Warrior's Path
Lessons In Leadership

ROBERT A. TRIVINO

"Go Forward With Courage"
White Eagle

FOR THOSE WE LOST

AND THEIR FAMILIES

CONTENTS

PREFACE

Shortly after retiring from the military I started to have second thoughts about my decision, like some that retired before me I'm sure. I really missed the people that I worked with and the mission that we all shared, it gave me a focus in life because I believed in what I was doing. During this time of reflection I realized that I learned a lot about myself from my time in the Army, primarily from my failures, specifically dealing with people - following and leading people. I also realized how much I enjoy working with and teaching people and it was from this desire to help and continue teaching that the idea for my book developed.

I wrote this book to help those that lead and have a desire to improve their leadership skills and to learn from my mistakes and successes. This book focuses on leadership lessons that I've learned through my own trials and those of others. You can expect honest evaluations of my performance and decisions during some of my hardest trials as a leader. There is a focus on my failures because I think I've learned more from those than from successes. Lessons learned from one's own mistakes are invaluable.

I have changed the names of the majority of the people in the book in order to protect them while they continue to fight for this great country of ours. I have also deliberately eliminated information about operations in order to protect tactics, techniques, and procedures used in current operations.

I want to thank my wife, Buzzy, for supporting me during this time. When I first approached her with my idea for this book, she immediately understood that I needed to do this. I could not have done it without her help and support.

The next person I want to thank is my mom, Irma. She has inspired me in many ways, most notably through her humanity and strength in the face of adversity. She made me strong because she was and remains one of the strongest people I know.

A special thanks to Nick Kokot and his family for their support and friendship. His insight and feedback were invaluable in the completion of the book. I must also thank Baba Kokot for helping me with the project and ultimately helping me understand and improve my writing weaknesses.

Additionally I would like to thank Brian Voden, Preston Kline, Jerami Summers, Klancey Zubowski, and Dalton Fury for helping me with my writing and giving me, amongst other things, confidence and direction. They all helped me develop my book to the best of my ability and I hope I learned well enough. Lots of folks have helped me by reviewing portions of the book, and I am grateful for their help as well. I have not recognized some by name, as they are still serving our country in some form, but I wish to extend my heartfelt thanks to all who helped me.

I would like to thank all those that served underneath me while I served as your leader. For the majority that I led, I know you essentially had no choice in the position you were placed in. You didn't vote me in to be your leader. I hope I performed my duties well and more importantly I hope I earned your trust and respect. I want you all to know that I trusted and respected each of you.

I want to thank everyone that is serving or has served our great country with honor. Without people like you, our country would not be as wonderful as it is today. I believe one does not have to be in the military to support our country, all you have to do is serve your fellow citizen well and try to be a good American.

Many of the leadership lessons in this book were learned fighting the war on terror and because of that, many were learned through the loss of sweat, blood, and lives. After these experiences, I realized I grew as a person and so did the people around me. Those around me learned and changed based on lessons like mine. In the end I've come to realize that all of my reasons for writing this book have melded into one purpose: to help others and to attempt to ensure that those that lost their lives while we learned would not be lost in vain.

1

LEARNING TO FOLLOW...CORRECTLY

The sound of a mature bull elk's screeching bugle broke the stillness of the early morning mountain air. It was a beautiful, brisk dawn in Northern New Mexico. This late in September it was only about thirty degrees and I was hunting elk with my father. The sun broke over the horizon as the bull elk called a second time. This was an archery hunt, my first, and I was 16 years old and excited like only a teenager can be at times. I'd prepared for months with my bow by practicing after doing my chores and homework. My father also prepared me for the hunt in many ways. He was a great hunter, but liked to hunt with a rifle. I, on the other hand, wanted to try my skills with the bow that my father somehow acquired for me. For a family with very little, it was a tremendous gift.

I knelt about twenty-five meters in front of my father and pulled my wool army scarf away from my face; my breath was freezing in it and the steam was affecting my vision. I looked back at him and he gave me a little nod and I passed a thumbs up back to him. I stood up and moved cautiously through the pine and aspen trees as I tried to close the distance, stalking the herd of elk in front of us. The frost on the vegetation helped lessen the noise of my footsteps. This was important because there was nothing in the silence of the morning to mask my noise. I moved forward at a snail's pace, like my father taught me. Luckily for me there wasn't much deadfall or thick underbrush; in a way it was perfect for stalking. I looked back at my dad intermittently, expecting him to pass the elk's location to me by pointing... nothing. I continued to move forward, filled with excitement. I tried to calm my nerves a bit so I could make an accurate shot if the situation presented itself.

This hunt's preparations began at home over the summer and continued all the way through to the day before my hunting trip. I packed my stuff into the family's truck the evening before and kept just a few items near my bed to be ready for an early morning departure. My dad also showed me how to make a small offering to help us have a successful hunt: a Native American way of preparing for a hunt. We both said a prayer and afterward, my dad gave me what appeared to be a pebble. As he presented the stone to me he said, "This is a hunter's stone. This is mine and I want you to use it for your hunt. It will help you master your hunting skills, give you good luck when you need it and it will help you come home safe at the end of your hunt."

It was meaningful to me and I thanked him. I put his stone into my leather medicine pouch that I kept with me at all times, in my pocket or worn around my neck on a leather strap.

My father ended the conversation by saying, "Remember, you can use this stone until you get your own stone. As a hunter you have to get your own. Who knows? Maybe you'll find yours on this hunt."

The next morning started at 4:00 a.m. The smell of fresh tortillas filled the house. My mom was cooking on the wood stove making burritos for me and my dad for the day. My father came into my room to check my morning progress as I quickly tied my shoes to get rolling out the door. He knew I would be up early and he just wanted to see me filled with excitement, I'm sure. I was happy. I wanted nothing more than to get out of the house, into the truck, and head into the mountains and get after the elk. My family didn't have much and the elk could supply meat for the whole family for most of the winter.

I grabbed our lunches, which were bean, meat, and chile burritos and made my way toward the door with my bow in hand. My mom approached us and passed us some water in an old gallon milk jug and a small thermos of coffee for my dad. I was already out the door when my father said to me, "Hey, *cabron*, haven't you forgotten something?" He motioned for me to come back inside and we both knelt in front of my mother to receive "the blessings." As we knelt down we removed our knitted hats. My mom proceeded to pray over us asking the Creator for a successful, and more importantly, a safe hunt for both me and my father. After quick hugs with my mom I almost sprinted out the door. I was so excited.

A few hours later, the hunt was on. I was moving in, trying to get a shot on one of the elk in front of us. The meat was important to my family, so I was going to shoot the first elk that crossed my path. My father always said in a half-joking manner, "You can't eat the antlers!" He was definitely not a trophy hunter.

I paused for a few seconds; I still hadn't seen anything, although we knew they were there, we heard them. I was in a rush. I was about to push forward when I heard my dad moving behind me. He tapped me on the shoulder and whispered, "Just wait a few minutes; have patience. Remember to look, listen, and smell before you move. Go slowly and place your foot on the ground before you put your weight on it."

As I knelt there in front of a tree, I was repeating what he told me in my head. He had said the same things to me many times before, but obviously I wasn't doing it. I was sixteen and I was sure I knew what I was doing.

My father motioned me to move forward and I started again, slowly, like he said. He waited until I was about fifty meters away before he used his elk call to mimic the sound of another, younger bull elk. I was approximately seventy-five meters in front of him before I looked back. I swear I could see the frustration in his eyes even at that distance. He motioned at me to stop, so I found a place to set up for a shot. A few minutes passed and at some point I felt I needed to move again. I still hadn't seen an elk and I thought if I didn't get moving I'd miss out on my opportunity. So I moved toward the herd of elk that we knew were in front of us, although we couldn't see them. My father was more than likely shaking his head as I did exactly the opposite of what he wanted me to do. I looked back and realized I couldn't see my dad, which wasn't bad; most times we couldn't see each other when we did this. I moved faster. I thought the elk had moved away because we hadn't seen or heard them in quite a while.

Out of nowhere a strong, musty smell filled my nostrils and the sound of large branches breaking just a short distance from my left flank broke the silence. It was a large, mature bull elk and he was already running away from me. Shit! I screwed up big time! I was moving exactly how my father didn't want me to and now I was seeing my hard work go down the drain. I didn't know what to do, the bull was already way out of bow range. I stood there for a few seconds hoping he would stop and turn around and look or something…not so lucky. I took off after the elk, running as fast as I could. Somehow I thought I'd be able to catch it. What was I thinking? As I sprinted I heard my dad yelling, "Robert! You'll never catch him!"

***

My parents raised their kids in a traditional Mexican and Native American home. We bounced around when I was a young child, living first in Carlsbad, New Mexico, and then traveling to live with my mom's Indian tribe, the Cochiti Pueblo, which is located in the north central part of New Mexico. My mother and all her children are enrolled tribal members (recognized by the United States as being Native American). My father was half Yaqui Indian, one-quarter Mexican and one-quarter Irish. The Yaqui Indians range from southern Arizona into Northern Mexico. Life on Cochiti Pueblo had its ups and downs. Children had a blast and the entire pueblo was safe. It functioned like one big family, with relatives keeping tabs on the kids of the pueblo within their reach. It was great for children because we were able to run as free as the wind. My parents did their best to keep us close to home, but we always pushed the limits. I was a mischievous kid and experienced my fair share of self-induced trouble! Like the time I blew up my hand with some fireworks while pretending they were a hand grenade. I knew I would get in trouble for my swollen, bruised hand, so my brother and I came up with the genius idea to wear a baseball mitt. I snuck by them with a left-handed mitt on my right hand, and thankfully they never noticed. Another time I jumped off a water pipe and into an irrigation canal and nearly drowned. Luckily for me one of the older boys I was with saved my life, diving in to rescue me. I still remember looking up from the bottom of the canal through the water as everything went black.

It is a Cochiti tribal custom for a woman who marries someone outside of the tribe to leave and live with her husband off the pueblo. Because of this, after a short while, my father was asked to leave the pueblo with the entire family. So we headed south to live with my father's tribe, the Yaquis, in Sonora, Mexico. Life in Mexico was much different than life in the United States. There were a lot fewer amenities, like running water and electricity. Most of the people, including my family, lived in bamboo houses with dirt floors. We cooked outside on a fire pit and washed clothes by hand on old washing stones. This was a hell of an adjustment! But we made do. We lived free and ran around with the village kids, but as before, with all of that freedom came many opportunities to get into trouble. None of us spoke Spanish, but we were learning as we made this place our home.

Our little house was a two room structure with a dirt floor and wood stove. The walls were made of bamboo and there were only three little windows in the house, keeping it dark to help keep it cool in the summertime. My father moved a bed into one room for me and my brother along with another, smaller bed for my sister. My parents occupied the second bedroom which encompassed part of the kitchen. The quarters were tight, but it suited my siblings and me just fine.

The following year we moved back to the United States. After bouncing around for a few months from one rental home to another, we finally settled on the Ohkay Owingeh Indian Pueblo, formerly known as the San Juan Pueblo, which is located near Espanola, New Mexico. The next priority for my mom was to get us kids into school because we missed over a year during our stay with the Yaquis in Mexico. We attended school in

Mexico, but the spoken language was Spanish. We weren't fluent speakers, so all three of us were placed in the first grade.

Once the family was settled and we were in school my father looked for work. He became a police officer for the pueblo and did all his work for free. He was a disabled veteran and he believed if he received money for his work then he would lose his benefits.

I remember my father as a fearless individual. He feared absolutely no man...regardless of the situation. When we first moved to the pueblo, we learned that almost every day someone would shoot at the Catholic church bell in the middle of the pueblo. The local police officers were unable to find a suspect. This was somewhat of a serious issue, primarily because of ricochets off of the bell. It took my father about two days to figure out the location from which the shots were being fired. Once he figured that out, he then moved in and put a stop to the shooting.

I always thought of my father as a great police officer. He functioned in an undercover role at times, primarily working counter-drug assignments. He handled himself with steely composure in any situation and many times he was asked for by name to do certain 'buys' or to attend meetings with suspects that were considered potentially dangerous. My father had a reputation for being extremely reliable in a tough situation.

A year later, we moved to another home off the pueblo. My father no longer worked as a pueblo police officer, but would still be called upon for "special jobs." I believe this is where I learned, from an element outside of our culture, of the importance of honor and trustworthiness.

My first leader in my life was my father. There are those who would argue this idea that parents aren't actually leaders, but I disagree. He ruled our home with an iron fist and the last thing I wanted was his hand across my face. My father was what I would consider "old school". My brothers, sister and I were taught at a young age to treat our elders with respect. He taught us that a man of his word was more important than a man who possessed money, material items or status. A man's word was his bond and I still believe this today. My father was very strict, and he believed any negative behavior on the part of his children reflected poorly on him and my mom as parents. He wasn't afraid to discipline us at any time or anywhere. My head and behind can attest to that fact! My father commanded respect and I called him "sir" until the day he died. As you can imagine our relationship was not one of love and mutual understanding.

As I reflect on my father, I believe that he possessed more faults than positive traits with some major behavioral problems as well, but he helped shape who I am today. For that I am thankful, and I focus on learning from the positive traits I observed in my younger years. I hope to pass those positive traits on to my children…his grandchildren.

One of the first things I remember him teaching me and my siblings was not to be afraid of hard work. At an early age we learned that we needed to work for everything in our life. My father would tell us, "People may call you whatever they want, but they will never call you lazy." He always reminded us that nothing would ever be given to us in our lives and if we wanted to be successful we would have to work …and work hard. Our family lived off my father's pension from the military. Most of the time the money didn't go far, so we all worked whenever we could. From a young age, my siblings and I helped my parents with whatever they did. My sister didn't shy away from hard work either and she helped us boys many times too.

Child labor laws don't reach far in a poor, rural environment. Starting at an early age we did all kinds of manual labor whenever and wherever we could get work. I remember, at times, seeing my mother crying because of the family's financial difficulties and I will never forget that feeling. All of the money my siblings and I made went to my mom. Even after I joined the army a significant portion of my paycheck went home to help her. In our teenage years, my brothers and I did exactly what the men did. Sometimes we would help friends of the family and get nothing and, other times, we worked for money, or would take home a small portion of the produce we worked to harvest.

We helped my mother make crafts to sell. A couple of the countless things my mom taught us to make were *ristras* (hand-tied strings of chiles) and dreamcatchers made of willow branches. We would park at the side of the road in front of our house and sell them from the back of the truck, along with produce we picked from nearby farms.

We spent a lot of time cutting wood in the mountains. This served our family for two purposes. First and foremost, it was for sustainment,

...use we heated our home and cooked with wood. Secondly, we would try to cut enough extra wood to sell as this would bring in good money for the family. I still love to cut wood in the mountains. There's nothing like working hard and spending time in the great outdoors.

As a kid, I had a tendency to disobey my parents' directions. Not intentionally, or at least that's how I felt! This was a tendency that taught me what the back of my father's hand felt like upside my head, and what his belt felt like across my behind. Make no mistake about it...as a youngster, I was good at hearing...but not at listening! My parents allowed their children a wide berth when growing up and there are things my siblings and I did that I would never let my children do today. However, I am grateful for the freedom I had as a child, as I believe this allowed me to really grow from an independent perspective.

I was the boy that always tried to push things a little too far. My older brother loved to read, but all I wanted to do was run around outside, playing whatever and getting into trouble. I apparently displayed more audacity as a child than my brother since I was always prepared to do something that my brother might refer to as stupid. I realize now that I may have been an idiot at times and probably did some things that seemed foolish during my youth. But I never really felt fear doing these things or acting the way I wanted.

As a kid, one of my favorite times of the year was hunting season. Whenever fall came around I always got excited because I knew hunting season was just around the corner. To this day I still have those same feelings! My father hunted most of his life; not only out of necessity, but because he enjoyed the whole hunting experience. He helped me to develop a great sense for finding my way around the woods as we hunted. It was fun, and I enjoyed just being in the woods. Little did I realize that my father was teaching me skills that would come in handy in the future.

I remember hunting for deer with him one year when he decided it would be a good idea to split up so we could cover more ground. After a short time, I decided I should head back to the truck because I felt I wasn't going to see anything to shoot. My father showed up about an hour and a half later and we talked about what we saw and the areas we hunted. At the end of the conversation my father asked me how long I had been back at the truck and I said, "I guess about an hour and a half." My father looked at me and said, "Listen, Son, you need to hunt hard, because the license I bought you cost twelve dollars and fifty cents. It may not seem like much, but there have been times when I wished I carried that much money in my pocket to buy food. So you need to hunt hard, 'cause if we each get a deer we will have enough meat for the entire year." I felt crushed, like I let him and the family down. So while I came to love the hunt at a young age, I was also deeply aware of the hunt's serious purpose.

We never wasted a single piece of an animal. We ate most of the entrails, but I must admit I don't like to eat them today. My dad tanned the hides for leather or blankets, and he used the antlers for knife handles and other ceremonial items. Dad even made Indian jewelry out of the elks' ivory teeth. If we were successful on a hunt we honored the animal where he or she fell, and we always thanked it for giving its life for us. At home, the entire family would gather around the animal and give thanks and bless it for its sacrifice, and we gave it a place of honor in our home before we butchered it. This is something that I still do today with my family.

When I was a teenager my father, who was also a great horseman and horse trainer, acquired a horse for me. It was with this horse that I first experienced and understood responsibility. I took care of him as a colt, and more so after he was severely injured by a mare's attack in a friend's pasture. Apparently, the mare separated him from his mother and tried to kill him. His recovery was long and hard, and though he eventually recovered most of his health, his right eye was irreparably damaged and he was blind in that eye. As a young kid I didn't understand why the mare did that, and I'm not sure my father knew why, either. If he did know, he didn't tell me.

Losing an eye didn't seem to bother my colt much after he healed up. I hand-stitched an eye patch for him out of leather, and eventually I named him Patchy. I don't know if all Indians do this, but we commonly didn't name animals until we knew them well. I cared for him throughout his recovery, and worked with him by myself based on my father's guidance. Because of this one-on-one interaction, I was the only person that could get near Patchy, he trusted only me. It was an incredible learning experience for me about trust.

I will never forget the first time I got on his back to ride him. I was by myself in the corral with him and I decided that I would just try getting on him. At first I just laid across his back like a sack, and two days later I was riding him bareback holding onto his mane without issue. He never once got aggressive or tried bucking me off, or running away. It was awesome.

About a month after that I was riding Patchy every day after school. This was a great time for me; I would come home after school, pretend to do my homework, do my chores around the house, then saddle up Patchy and take a long ride into the foothills behind our house. My brother and I would go together most times, which was good, because riding a green broke horse in the mountains can be rough. The horse can easily get spooked and buck or fall, resulting in serious injury to the rider. This was something my brother learned firsthand; fortunately, he didn't get hurt badly when his horse bucked him off. I love any time spent with horses. But I must admit, it's been a long time since I've ridden purely for pleasure.

As a teenager I loved the outdoors and rarely watched television. I'm not sure if it is because we only got four or five channels, or because my siblings and I were always the early remote control for my dad. My favorite show on television was *Wild America* with Marty Stouffer. It aired on the local PBS station. I really enjoyed and looked forward to that show, as well as any shows about the military. I would make any excuse to get outside and run around the mountains, but if there was a good army movie on, I made sure my butt was parked in front of the television set.

***

One great aspect of Native American cultures is that they are all warrior-based societies. This was the way my parents, primarily my father, chose to raise me and my siblings. We were taught early on the aspects of what my parents considered traits of a good person and a true warrior which they tried to teach us more by example than with words. They specifically taught us that a true warrior is one that:

Helps his people when help is needed.
Fights for his people, when necessary, without thought for his own life.
Protects his people, when necessary, without thought for his own life.
Most importantly, puts others before himself.

As I grew older, I came to realize that these were not just traits of a warrior, but also traits of a good leader. The warrior becomes a leader by virtue of his actions, which ultimately results in his people respecting him. One becomes a leader not for egotistical reasons, but rather to provide protection, true guidance, and to facilitate growth. He is not just a fighter; he embodies humility and selflessness as a father, teacher, and loving husband. His people know that he will always place their needs and welfare above his own. I embraced this concept early on, and it became the foundation for me and my growth from a child to a young man.

When discussing warriors and leaders, some would immediately think of a male figure. While there have undoubtedly been many great male leaders, female leaders rarely get the credit due them. I must give my mom a lot of the credit for being my first and best role model. My mom taught me the most important lesson in my life. A true warrior must do things for the betterment of someone else in order to become a great individual. Little did I realize that she was preparing me for a leadership role later in my life. My mom went through a lot of hard times in her life as a young child, and also as a woman, wife, and mother. Her story is much more interesting than mine, and I'll leave that to her to tell. At the end of the day I realize that my mom wasn't perfect, but she always tried hard and loved us. And even though she made mistakes along the way, she always did her best to take care of her children the best way she knew how. I understand now that my mom is one of the toughest people I have ever known... not my father.

Now in my mid-forties and a parent myself, I am beginning to understand the subtle lessons my parents taught me as a youngster that I was blind to in my youth. Being a warrior, and ultimately a leader, did not begin in a classroom for me. It began in the family structure at an early age, and developed as I discovered and internalized the lessons taught by my parents. That was when the embryo of the leader was formed for me. Leader development comes from learning experiences, not only our own but learning from the experiences of others as well. This is why I believe leaders are not born with an innate ability to lead: leaders are created.

When I left home to join the army, I knew that my mom loved me and she did her best and that's all anyone can ask of another person. Later in life, as a leader of specialized operators, I kept this lesson close to my heart, and tried to treat those I led in much the same way.

✳✳✳

My first Indian name given to me by the medicine man when I was a child was Bobcat. As I grew and became a young man, I returned home from my first combat experience and was given my warrior's name, Evergreen Mountain. I am an American, first and foremost, but I am also a Pueblo and Yaqui Indian. I am a former member of the US Army's 18th Airborne Corps, 75th Ranger Regiment, and spent most of my career as an operational member of a Special Missions Unit under the United States Army Special Operations Command. This is my personal journey through one of the greatest warrior and leadership cultures of today, which ultimately provided me with defining leadership characteristics and the skills of a serious warrior.

2

CIVILIAN TO SOLDIER

June 3rd, 1988. Leaving home to join the army.

My stomach was in one large, nervous, freaked-out knot. It was a feeling a friend once unforgettably described to me as, "My guts are bubbling up." I just hoped they didn't bubble *all* the way up, I didn't want to get stinky, dirty, and embarrassed. I was eighteen years old and had graduated from high school just two days before. Now I was heading off to make my own life, and to serve my country. I lived most of my life in a small town in northern New Mexico under the strict rule of my father. I had never flown on an airplane before nor had I ever seen one up close. So it was a big day for me, leaving my family and home to attend US Army Basic Training, and to take my first airplane ride.

My father was a complicated man, proud of who he was and his military service though he was somewhat troubled, and extremely proud to have his children serving as well. It was impossibly hard to leave my mom. I'd never been away from her for more than a few nights in my life; once when she was in the hospital, or when my father, brother and I went hunting. I worried about her, my little sister and brother. We didn't have an easy life. But we were and are a close family; we take care of each other. How would they do without me? I wanted and needed to go, though. I had always wanted to be a soldier and frankly, in a poor family there aren't a lot of other opportunities.

The goodbyes were searing in the way that sadness mixed with fear and excitement can be. My recruiter came to our home, picked me up, and drove the three hours to the Military Entry and Processing Station (MEPS) in Albuquerque on a sunny summer afternoon. The emotion and anticipation in the car were unbelievable. From the MEPS station I boarded a bus to the airport. At approximately eleven thirty in the morning I boarded the aircraft to head south to Ft. Bliss, TX. The excitement and rush of truly being away from home and on my own for the first time hadn't fully hit me yet. It would take me a while to feel and recognize independence. It's a foreign sensation when you grow up in as strict a household as mine.

Boarding the aircraft was really incredible. The inside of the Boeing regional jet was cavernous and futuristic-looking to me. Luckily, I was assigned a window seat. I carried a small bag with some snacks my mom packed. I was seated near the back, and I could smell the pungent, oily jet fuel when the engines revved up and whined. As the aircraft climbed to altitude I felt like I was soaring! It was exhilarating to see the ground from so high up, and feel the turbulence. This sensation, coupled with it being my first flight and landing on a windy, turbulent day made the flight a memorable one.

I was filled with a number of emotions. I was excited to start training and become my own person, yet at the same time I was also sad to leave home. I was unsure of things to come, and it made me more than a little uneasy. The reception station was perfect; it was a good transition from civilian life to army life. We didn't have someone yelling at us 24/7 while we in-processed into the army, but we did get corrected every now and again as we started our paperwork and learned our way around the chow hall and barracks. The craziness was sure to come when we were assigned to our platoons and actually in basic training. The food was an adventure for a boy who grew up largely on beans, tortillas, and wild game, but it was all good. I was forever missing my mom's New Mexican chile.

I slept in a bunk hall with a bunch of other guys, green army blankets, firm mattresses, communal bathrooms, like you might expect. I liked wearing BDUs - battle dress uniforms - army clothes, and worked hard at polishing my boots. When the training started, I tried to do everything to the best of my abilities. For those who never attended the US Army's Boot Camp…let me give you a hint. It is hard to do anything correctly in the first month, and when you do, you rarely receive any accolades.

The first influential leader I looked up to in the army was a drill sergeant in basic training named Staff Sergeant (SSG) Jones. He distinguished himself by being professional and fair, which was noticeably different from the rest of the drill sergeants. He wasn't your typical drill sergeant. Screaming and yelling like the world was falling apart, such as one would see in Hollywood depictions, was not his style. SSG Jones spoke calmly and assuredly and with conviction. When he did raise his voice, we all listened. He carried himself with confidence, and his professional demeanor commanded respect. I was impressed, and found that he motivated me to not only do my best, but also to emulate his calm, confident manner.

Like most young men in the early part of their lives, I was impressionable. I searched for a role model I thought was a complete and total professional. At the time there was no doubt in my mind: I wanted to be like Staff Sergeant Jones. Up to that point, I thought a good soldier was one who kept his gear straight, stayed in shape, and always acted with motivation. So that's exactly how I carried myself. When I look back at my initial military training, I realize the impact leaders can have on young soldiers at certain stages of their lives - both positive and negative. What a huge responsibility that is for those in leadership positions.

After completing basic training, and advanced individual training, I attended Basic Airborne School at Fort Benning, GA. After my training I was assigned to the Headquarters and Headquarters Company, 18th Airborne Corps at Fort Bragg, North Carolina. I was subsequently assigned to the Air Defense Element under the Operations section of the 18th

Airborne Corps Command. I spent my entire life prior to joining the army in the southwestern part of the United States, and I never experienced humidity like the first time I stepped off an air-conditioned bus and into the summer humidity in the South. The hot, moist air literally smacked me in the face. It felt strange and it seemed heavy to breathe. Sweat trickled down my face and back underneath my uniform. Imagine living in a sauna.

The unit I was assigned to was known as the Dragon Brigade because of the dragon's head on the unit patch. During World War II, members of the unit were called the Sky Dragons. This brigade was staffed with every rank in the army, from private, like me, all the way up to the commanding general of the 18th Airborne Corps. Looking back at the leaders I encountered during my first assignment, I realize there were few positive role models for me as a young soldier. Those few good leaders were helpful in shaping my development. And because of them I aspired to be the best at what I did, regardless of the task at hand.

The most significant and influential leader during my time spent in the 18th Airborne Corps was Captain Arthur A. Sobers Jr. Several of Capt. Sobers' character strengths separated him from the other leaders within as well as outside the section. The most important of these for me was that he cared for his subordinates. Let me emphasize: he TRULY cared for his subordinates. From a militaristically accepted leadership perspective, that was a rarity.

Capt. Sobers went out of his way to keep an eye on us young privates. He displayed a genuine desire to aid our personal and professional growth. We felt that he truly cared about us, not because he was *supposed* to, but because he *wanted* to. His genuine caring made us feel valuable and drove us to do our best and, as a group, become a top-notch unit.

He displayed a unique balance of professionalism and a bubbly personality, which made him officially and personally approachable. When he provided his input to the section commander it was humbly taken, and when he provided direction to those of us underneath him it was obvious to everyone that he took his job seriously. All those who served underneath him knew he was in charge; he didn't have to remind us. At the same time, we knew we could ask any manner of personal or professional question and we'd get an honest and clearly thought out answer. He was much more approachable than the other officers I had encountered up to that point in my career.

Capt. Sobers was like the Energizer Bunny when it came to being motivated, which in turn, inspired us to be the same. Once again, it didn't hit me until later in life that motivation and inspiration are somehow intertwined, but they are. They are must-have attributes for good leaders. You simply can't have one without the other. During physical training we sometimes would split into ability-based groups. Capt. Sobers always ran with the fast group of runners, which made me do the same.

On one particular occasion we were on a fast run, and maintaining a formation. The sergeant in charge of the group was having a hard time keeping up, and, eventually fell back and out of the formation. I took this as an opportunity to take charge of the formation of runners, and I did. I was a young private, leading the run with sergeants and officers, and I was in charge of them! For that moment, anyway. When Capt. Sobers saw me do this he went nuts! He called out to the runners, yelling that a private was now in charge of the formation and everyone needed to step up their game. It was a great feeling to see him do that for me.

Under Capt. Sobers' tutelage I was able to attend the first step in the Army's Non-Commissioned Officer's (NCO) educational system, known at that time as the Primary Leadership Development Course (PLDC). This course brought eligible corporals and specialists together from Ft. Bragg, as well as other nearby posts, to learn to become sergeants and ultimately leaders in the army. This type of training was, and still is, mandatory in order to be promoted to the rank of sergeant. After the first week of training my perception was that the course was more concerned with management than leadership.

I learned a lot from PLDC and felt that it gave me the skills to become a better manager, but not necessarily a better leader. In my experience, a leader must present themselves with character and dignity, setting an example on both professional and personal levels. A leader inspires his subordinates to perform beyond their expectations. The end does not necessarily justify the means for a true leader. Great leaders provide guidance while simultaneously creating an environment that encourages teamwork and ensures that all subordinates feel as though they are an integral part of the greater good.

On the other hand, I feel that managers tend to be result and position-oriented, and not necessarily concerned with the attributes of character or the welfare of those underneath them. At times, this management-oriented approach can seem simply selfish. Managers must be obeyed, but are not necessarily respected. True leaders are not only respected, but find that respect motivates those they work with - the foundation for leading by example.

The core focus of PLDC was management, and those who constructed the curriculum entirely missed the importance of true leadership qualities. I assumed that they must have been phenomenal managers and piss-poor leaders, which, at the conclusion of the course, proved to be correct. The majority of students became good managers; however, a lot of them were horrible leaders. Many of them couldn't lead soldiers to the bathroom, let alone lead them in battle. It became brutally apparent that this course was more business-oriented than battle-oriented.

What a kick in the gut! I thought we were soldiers first and foremost. The conflation of *leadership* and *management* bothered me, and I made a mental note to always remember the differences. I kept my personal focus on leadership.

At one point just before Capt. Sobers departed the section, I drove him, the section commander, and the rest of the section officers to the 18th Airborne Corps Headquarters for a meeting. We left our air-conditioned office and went outside into the heat and humidity of a hot July day in North Carolina. As we loaded into the HMMWV (Humvee), the section commander sat in the front passenger's seat and the rest of the officers jumped in the back cargo area of the vehicle. I exited the parking area and started down Longstreet Road, heading towards the 18th Airborne Corps Headquarters. During the drive, Capt. Sobers, who was seated behind me, leaned forward and asked me a question, "Hey, Trivino, what's the speed limit on the road here?" When I heard his question I looked at my speedometer and realized I was speeding almost ten miles per hour over the posted limit.

When the section commander heard this he immediately snapped at me, "Trivino! You'd better slow down before I have the section sergeant write a counseling statement on you!" I slowed down and drove the speed limit, grumbling behind my teeth.

We reached the headquarters and the section leadership got off the vehicle and made their way to the back entrance to the building. Capt. Sobers came to the driver's side, slapped my shoulder and said, "Sorry," as he walked towards the building. I knew that he knew I was speeding, but what separated him from my section commander was how he chose to inform me of my mistake. He asked me a question. He didn't bark at me or threaten me, he merely made me aware of my mistake by asking me a simple question. This was a huge lesson for me; something I would never forget. As I exited the parking lot of the headquarters building I did my best to make the tires on my HMMWV squeal, but I must say I failed miserably.

Capt. Sobers nicknamed me "Ranger" because of my dream of becoming a Ranger. His mentorship didn't impact me as much then as it did a few years later. I needed some personal and professional growth before his guidance came full circle. Even when Capt. Sobers received orders for re-assignment, he was still thinking and caring about me and my goals. Before departing, he wrote me a letter with some guidance and advice for my future. It was so meaningful to me that he cared enough about me to do that. I took everything he said to heart and have always saved it. (The letter can be viewed in the photo section of this book.)

In August of 1990, the Iraqi Army crossed the border of their neighboring country Kuwait to initiate an act of war. The international community took notice, and the United States mobilized its military forces in what was to become known as Operation Desert Shield. I was deployed with the 18th Airborne Corps to Ad Dammam, just outside of an air base in Dhahran, Saudi Arabia. My duties during this deployment were to support my superiors in my section as part of the 18th Airborne Corps Tactical Operations Center.

Days after the start of the US-led coalition air campaign in January of 1991, the Iraqi Army launched several SCUD missiles targeting US forces in our area of Saudi Arabia. This was the most feared threat of the war, as we all believed that Saddam Hussein would use chemical weapons against us, delivered via SCUD missiles. One day, during regular operations, an alarm sounded, indicating a SCUD missile was headed for our location.

Everyone in the Tactical Operations Center (TOC) stopped working and started putting on their Level 4 chemical-protective over-garments and masks, which were the highest level of personal protection available to us. The uniforms contained charcoal to help protect us from airborne chemical weapons. The regular hustle and bustle within the TOC ceased, and an eerie silence filled the immediate area, punctuated by the screech of the alarm. The distinctive smell of charcoal filled the rooms as we all busted into the packages containing our gear. Missiles could arrive anytime. No one spoke a word; everyone was concentrating on getting their protective gear and masks on as fast as possible.

While in the process of suiting up, I looked over at a young soldier in another section and noticed that he was in a panic. I watched him violently pull out his protective mask from his carrier, with pieces falling everywhere. It was completely disassembled. I was a bit nervous because the seriousness of the situation was clear to me. What really concerned me was the fact that this young soldier was so scared and unprepared that it made him dysfunctional. His voice shook me as he half-begged and screamed, "Somebody help me!" He was almost in tears and on the brink of coming completely undone because he realized it was impossible to put his mask together before the missile might hit our location.

I decided I could be a manager, and selfishly mark off my own checklist of duties, or I could bypass some of that and be a leader by assisting and guiding him. I watched in amazement as no one uttered a word or moved to assist him. I placed my mask on my face, cleared it to ensure it was properly sealed, and immediately ran over to assist him. I grabbed several of the pieces and systematically laid them out in front of us. I addressed him by his first name, and spoke to him in a calm and assured manner. Then I explained to him that we were going to assemble the mask together. I felt "in the moment" - calm, alert, strong, and utterly confident in my skills. As more people finished dressing, they made their way over to help.

After several minutes passed we heard an immense explosion in the distance. Damn it! A SCUD landed, and we didn't have the mask together yet. We all worked together to get it assembled. We still hadn't received any indication of a chemical dispersion in the area, as the warning alarms for that were still silent. Several seconds after the explosion we completed the mask and the young soldier was protected. He was very thankful, and I could visibly see him start to relax. We remained in our protective garments for about two hours before we were allowed to remove our masks. Ultimately, we discovered that no chemical agents were used in any of the SCUD missiles that hit near our location.

In the days following that incident, I thought a great deal about the events surrounding the young soldier and his protective mask. What should have been a seemingly simple task for the young soldier turned into an educational experience for me. I've learned that great leaders learn not only from their own experiences, but from the experiences of others as well. There were two failures in leadership I found noteworthy.

The young soldier had a personal and professional responsibility to ensure his equipment was easily accessible and functioning properly. This was critical due to the threat level with the risk of chemical weapons. I had to ask why he was unprepared - was he incapable? Who trained this soldier, and what exactly did they teach him?

I feel that the second failure was clearly his sergeant's fault. Possibly because his sergeant was more of a "check the box" manager, as opposed to an individual in a leadership role that sincerely cared about his subordinates. If that sergeant was a good leader, he would have taken the time to check each one of his subordinates' equipment to make sure it was accessible and functioning properly. Not micromanaging his subordinates, but making sure each one was properly prepared.

Those in classic military leadership positions might argue with me, and stress that the failure rested squarely on the shoulders of the young soldier's sergeant. I disagree. It is my belief that all people need to take personal responsibility for their own successes and failures. I knew that then, and I firmly believe it to this day.

This weighed heavily on me for some time during my assignment in the headquarters element. The younger NCOs seemed to lack a desire to be a total soldier. Don't get me wrong; they were all good at their respective jobs - analysts, typists, administrative assistants, etc., and we needed them. But I wanted to be a fighting soldier. It was at that point that I realized I wanted and needed a change. I decided to leave the headquarters life as soon as I could and search out a unit that embodied the soldier that I wanted to be.

Approximately two weeks after the start of the bombing campaign, I was re-assigned to the 18th Airborne Corps Tactical Command Post (TAC-CP). The TAC-CP was created to be the mobile command post that would follow the maneuver units in Iraq. I was excited about the move, although I'm sure my parents wouldn't have been excited had they known I was moving closer to the front. I linked up with my senior section sergeant, who was already at the TAC-CP, and immediately realized I was in a different world. The atmosphere in the command post was much different than the TOC. I can recall my initial conversation with my sergeant, explaining to me the importance of communication and integration with all the other sections. He went on to explain that the command post was still learning to work together as a team. I was a bit shocked, excitedly so, as I left an environment that was somewhat disciplined and entered something markedly better. This unit was squared away, highly disciplined, and motivated to stay on point. The difference was the command climate, or simply put, the leadership of the command post.

Colonel White was the commander of the post when I arrived, and he created an atmosphere within his command that would set the example that I would follow for years to come. He was influential in teaching me several noteworthy aspects of leadership that I will carry with me to my dying day.

What I found most profound was how the environment made me feel. I felt and believed that I was an important part of a well-oiled machine because Col. White cared enough to instill a level of confidence and responsibility in each of us. His encouragement motivated us to perform to the best of our abilities. This in turn, elevated each of our capabilities. He did not run the unit dictatorially as the colonel; rather he taught us that the unit was highly functional because of the sum of its parts. We each had an iron in the fire, so to speak. This was the key ingredient that separated him from the vast majority of other commanders I encountered during the second part of the operation, the offensive known as Desert Storm. This helped build on my education from Capt. Sobers.

Later in my career I was able to reflect on Col. White's ability to create an environment of unit success, as opposed to personal success. My experiences in the military taught me that even the most competent leaders will be less effective without complete trust in, and concern for, their subordinates. I have been led by commanders that were successful, mission-focused, and smart. Yet, these same commanders were not able to harness the complete potential of their people because of their narcissism. Everyone understands that there must be balance between the mission and the men. When the scale never shifts in favor of the men...then the leader's intentions speak volumes. The subordinate's perception of their leader is in part related to the leader's priorities. Subordinates will always ask themselves, "Is he looking out for me or himself and his career? Will he back me up, or throw me under the bus when push comes to shove?" Col. White was all about the mission; he incorporated everyone underneath him, down to the lowest level when he trained his people. This balanced the scale between his mission and his men. The end result was a high functioning unit; we believed we could easily accomplish our mission and excel at what he asked us to do.

As the preparation for the ground war progressed, Col. White was replaced by a higher ranking officer. The impact that he left on the organization never diminished, as we all stayed motivated and worked toward a common goal. We packed up and left our staging area and moved to the northern part of Saudi Arabia, anticipating crossing the border and following the ground units north into Iraq. Once we got settled and went operational, the 18th Airborne Corps Commander, Lieutenant General (LTG) Luck, became the ranking officer of the command post. He spent the majority of his time working in the day, so all the higher-ranking officers in all the sections worked day shift in order to respond directly to LTG Luck. Correspondingly, my section sergeant worked the day shift, and therefore, I was the night shift leader for the Air Defense Element. This was highly unusual for someone of my rank; I was a specialist with just three years in the army and I was reporting to field grade officers.

Nevertheless, as the night shift leader for the Air Defense Element, the vast majority of my time was spent working for Colonel Zannie O. Smith, the officer in charge of the night shift for the tactical command post. He was a Vietnam veteran, and one professionally composed individual. My first interaction with Col. Smith was significant for me because of how he dealt with me; not just because I was a young soldier, but because of the responsibility I was assigned as the air defense section night shift leader.

In our first conversation Col. Smith said, "One thing I want you to know is I will always *ask* you to do something for me. If I have to *tell* you to do something, then things have deteriorated, or I feel that more direction is needed." Later this same night I received an urgent report from one of the frontline air defense units that involved injured soldiers. The unit was moving from one staging area to another closer to the border and was involved in a vehicle accident. Initial reports were sketchy, but it was clear that the accident caused several casualties.

I read the report and radioed the unit to get an update on the situation. The leader on the ground was too busy to discuss specifics with me and said he would send a report after the injured were triaged and stable. I took the information and briefed Col. Smith on the situation. When I was finished he looked directly at me and he said, "Would you please keep an eye on this and update me as you get new information?" Obviously, my response was, "Yes, sir."

I was a bit surprised, because he did exactly what he said he would do, and it made a lasting positive impression on me. A true leader keeps his word. I found that succeeding in a trusted responsibility builds confidence. I adopted this method of asking before telling in my early years of leading, primarily because it transferred some of the decision making process onto the subordinate, and facilitated engagement, confidence, and responsibility.

Col. Smith had a knack for making you feel comfortable and important, regardless of your rank. To my knowledge he never spoke down to, or at, any of his subordinates myself included. This was important because I was the most junior person on his staff; the next senior person was a master sergeant. Col. Smith made me feel just as important as the captains and colonels in charge of the other sections. Perhaps he knew I was the only person available, and he needed to work with me or work with nobody. Regardless, he incorporated me into the process by treating me as a member of the team and his staff, and I felt like I mattered.

As the night shift leader, I received and followed, word for word, orders or directives from my section leader. For example, when receiving a directive from my superior it was always...do this, do that...no room for leeway, and definitely no room to problem solve on my own. When I interacted with Col. Smith, he didn't just tell me what to do, he asked me to accomplish something. In this way, he promoted initiative, and wanted me to be exposed to and involved in problem solving. That meant a lot to me as an impressionable soldier.

In the spring of 1991, the United States and our allies successfully pushed Saddam Hussein's army back into the heart of Iraq. The main ground campaign was over, and our military began sending troops home. I was part of a small group shipped backed home to Ft. Bragg early, and a couple of months passed before the rest of the unit would make their way back to the States. That summer I was contacted by the unit's retention NCO who informed me that the army was phasing out my job and I was required to re-classify, or change jobs. I was asked to choose from one of three new assignments: cook, truck driver, or mechanic. They sweetened the deal and offered bonus money if I stayed in the army and selected any of the jobs offered. The other option was to leave the army, with no strings attached.

I was not going to make my decision based on money, and I knew I wasn't done in the military just yet. I had long dreamed of becoming a Ranger. Until that point in my career the military hadn't been what I expected, but I knew what I wanted and it was time to seek a challenge. I shocked the retention NCO when I told him that I wanted to become an infantryman...a grunt. Not only did I want to be an infantryman, but I wanted to be a Ranger, assigned to one of the Ranger Battalions of the 75th Ranger Regiment. He prepared the paperwork, and I signed it without hesitation. I didn't know it at the time, but I was at a pivotal juncture in my military career. I was about to mature...both professionally and personally.

My key leadership lessons learned at this point in my career:

- **As a leader, you must take your position seriously, and remember that you have more influence than you think you do**
- **Genuinely care about your subordinates**

- Be motivating and inspirational by supporting those around you and those you lead
- Be approachable - both professionally and personally
- Instill personal responsibility in your subordinates as you take responsibility for them
- Attempt to give ownership to your subordinates by asking instead of directing when possible
- Treat your people equally and fairly
- Remember, it's not about personal success

3

LEG LAND TO RANGER LAND

September 1991 - Infantry and Ranger training

The celebrations for the troops that served in the first Gulf War were over, and it was time to get back to work. Most Americans were listening to C + C Music Factory's "Gonna Make You Sweat" (Everybody Dance Now), trying to figure out how a human being could run a hundred meters in less than 10 seconds like Carl Lewis (he ran it in 9.86 seconds), and were happy to hear that Nelson Mandela was chosen as president of the African National Congress. I was elated, but it wasn't because of current events; it was because I held my orders in my hand, assigning me to the infantry training unit at the Sand Hill training center on Ft. Benning, Georgia.

I was excited, and a little apprehensive to leave and move on to what I thought would be something new and better. I loaded my personal belongings into the bed of my truck to begin my drive southwest toward Georgia. I wanted nothing more from the military than an opportunity to complete infantry training, and then attend the Ranger Indoctrination

Program, with the prospect of being assigned to a Ranger battalion in the 75th Ranger Regiment. The drive to Ft. Benning was long, but my excitement allowed me to drive the entire trip without stopping. I arrived in Columbus, Georgia, around midnight, and drove directly to the army post, figuring I would be able to find a hotel in the local vicinity. I found an old motel on Victory Drive and tucked in for the night.

The next morning, I woke up excited to start infantry school. It was a sunny and muggy morning as I checked out of the motel and grabbed some fast food on the way to the post. I arrived at the reception station on Sand Hill and I delivered my orders to the sergeant. My orders stated that I was only to attend the infantry portion of the training. He explained that all the units were still attending basic training or already began infantry training a week prior to arriving. Just my luck. I would have to wait another month in the reception station. At times, the army really knows how to suppress your excitement! I had signed out of my old unit and was considered in "transition" status by the army. I thought about leaving and coming back in two weeks, as the last thing I wanted to do was stay in the reception station for a month, but I was stuck.

It was approximately a week before someone realized that I was an E4/Specialist promotable to sergeant waiting to attend infantry training. I had orders to wear the higher ranking corporal stripes, but I elected to wear my specialist rank instead. I guess I didn't want to be seen as bragging about my rank around a bunch of young new soldiers.

A group of us soldiers waiting for assignment were at the chow hall after our morning physical training session. The chow hall felt like a dungeon. For some reason it wasn't well lit, and there were no windows that allowed light in from the outside. It was a typical chow hall, with stacks of trays and a food bar manned by soldiers and cooks, slapping the food on our trays. I grabbed my tray full of wonderful army chow and made my way over to an empty seat for breakfast. After sitting there eating with the other soldiers for a few minutes, I noticed a staff sergeant eyeballing me. A few minutes passed and he approached the table. The trainees around me immediately got uneasy; they weren't sure what was going on.

"Hey, Specialist, what are you doing here?"

"I'm waiting to get assigned to a training battalion, Drill Sergeant."

"Oh, you're a trainee? How long have you been here?"

"I've been here almost a full week Drill Sergeant."

"I'll check and see if we can find a unit for you. It's better if we get you out of here and assigned to a unit, even if you have to attend a little bit of basic training."

"Roger that, Drill Sergeant."

The next day I found myself packing my bags and making my way to my new unit. I was introduced to my senior drill sergeant, and he assigned me to a room by myself on the third floor of our Starship: large, multi-story buildings that were self-contained units which housed all the supporting elements in one location. The Starship not only housed us, it had a chow hall, armory, and administrative support. I was located in the same living area with the rest of the trainees, but I had a small room of my own, which was cool. The unit I was assigned to needed to finish three weeks of basic training before starting infantry training. I didn't care. This was better than rotting away at the reception station. I was required to attend all of the training with the rest of the unit, but sometimes on the weekends I would jump in my truck and drive somewhere, just to get some alone time.

The one thing that made my situation better than I expected was my senior drill sergeant. I was lucky, he treated me with respect and he trusted me. He reviewed my packet and learned that I had orders to wear corporal stripes: I was promotable to sergeant. After this he made me wear my corporal's rank and referred to me as "my corporal." If any of the other drill sergeants tried to push the limits with me he would step in and back them off my tail. Looking back, I was lucky to have had something of a guardian angel.

The training was fundamental and necessary. I don't remember much, as I had already learned most of the information in my first basic training at Ft. Bliss, Texas. I do recall the infantry instructors teaching us basic battle drills, and many times it was difficult for me to understand. Drill instructors do not necessarily teach everything you need to know during basic training. Particular subjects are taught by army personnel with experience or expertise in that specific area. This makes sense most of the time, because it allows those personnel to focus on those particular tasks.

The flip side of that coin is that having experience or being an expert does not directly correlate with being a good instructor. I made a mental note in regards to what I considered a deficiency with this particular training design. If I ever got the opportunity, I was going to make sure that those instructing were not just experienced and "experts," but also possessed the ability to easily and efficiently deliver information. Making sure instructors are actually good at teaching allows each individual trainee the opportunity to reach his or her full potential on the battlefield.

Fortunately for me, one of my drill instructors was a Ranger, and had served with the 3rd Ranger Battalion at Ft. Benning. I asked him if he could assist me in making contact with the Ranger liaison sergeant. After a week or so, he told me he scheduled me an appointment for the following day. I could hardly wait.

Around lunch time the next day I walked into the Ranger liaison's office and told the sergeant that I wanted to attend the Ranger Indoctrination Program (RIP). The Ranger liaison sergeant asked one question as he reviewed my packet.

"What Ranger battalion do you want to go to?"

I stood there and thought for a few seconds and replied, "First or second battalion."

The sergeant finished reading, looked up at me, closed my packet and asked, "Well, which is it, first or second battalion?"

I answered almost immediately with, "Second battalion." He finished his paperwork and explained to me that I would get my orders assigning me to the Ranger regiment's RIP course after graduating infantry training. Apparently it was difficult to keep the Ranger regiment filled at that time, as it was and still is a completely volunteer unit. Luckily for me, I was able to get a slot for the training without any issues.

While completing the infantry training course, my drill sergeants used me to manage the trainees. This didn't bother me one iota. As a matter of fact, I felt that it was my duty and it helped me exercise my fledgling leadership skills. When the graduation ceremony was over, I packed my bags, loaded my truck, and got on the road to the main post, Fort Benning, headed for RIP.

It was a Friday when I arrived at the Ranger Indoctrination

Program, and it was obvious that I was different from the vast majority of the RIP candidates. The candidates that graduated from airborne school the same day that I graduated infantry school were greeted immediately after their graduation and were shuttled away by the RIP instructors. I didn't get the royal treatment by the RIP cadre like my counterparts; I drove my privately owned vehicle to the RIP compound.

I pulled into the parking lot and found an open spot. Before getting out I stopped to think and take in the moment. It was a strange moment for me. This was something that I wanted more than anything at that point in my career. After dealing with the butterflies in my gut, I grabbed my paperwork, jumped out of my truck, and looked for the RIP barracks. After I found the training barracks, my first interaction was at the Charge of Quarter's (CQ) desk, where I presented my orders assigning me to the unit. My orders were reviewed by the CQ sergeant and I was assigned a room, issued some linen, and ordered to be in formation at four thirty in the morning on Monday for a physical fitness test.

I grabbed my linen and packet of papers and made my way to the second floor of the barracks building. I located my room, unpacked my gear, grabbed the bottom bunk and made my bed. This was a standard army-issue facility. The rooms had bare white cinderblock walls that made them somewhat reminiscent of prison cells. The beds were metal framed, and there was one metal wall locker for each bed in the room.

As I settled in I began meeting some of the other RIP candidates in the barracks. I met Michael Vaulx, who became my friend and Ranger buddy. I can't completely recall our first interaction, but I soon discovered that he, too, was an import, as well as a specialist, like me. Mike was, and still is, one of the most energetic and driven guys I know. We became great friends then, and I still carry that level of friendship for him to this day, though we don't see each other often anymore.

On Saturday Mike and I sat around discussing what was in store for us during RIP. We knew the training was hard, and it was weighing on us a little. He said, "Hey, Trivino, you ready to get started? Because I'm ready to start right now. I'm ready to go!"

"I'm ready for whatever they toss at us, and I'm gonna do my best to max the PT test; but I'll be happy to just pass."

Both Mike and I were in great shape; Mike was then and still is an incredible athlete. Then Mike said, "After the physical fitness test we'll have to go to the swimming pool for the swim test." He really caught my attention when he made that statement. I hadn't thought about the swim test in a while. I had put it out of mind for one simple reason: I didn't know how to swim. Growing up poor in rural New Mexico does not lend itself to swimming opportunities (although at least one memorable near drowning opportunity!). I knew a swimming test was part of RIP, I guess I was hoping I'd be able to pass it with a desperate dog-paddle.

A little self-doubt seeped in as I thought about possibly failing RIP because I couldn't swim. I explained my situation to Mike and prepared to head to the pool to practice.

Without hesitation, he said he'd help me. "Give me five minutes to pack a bag and I'll come with you." There was no way in hell I was going to fail RIP because of the swim test, and I was determined to learn enough in the next two days to pass the damned thing.

I knew I wasn't going to learn to swim in just a few hours in the pool. What I wanted to do was boost my confidence a bit to help me be mentally prepared, perhaps develop enough skills to pass the test or at least not to drown! The RIP swim test involved not just swimming, but swimming fully clothed and with gear. It had been a long time since I had tried to swim, much less in my uniform and boots. It can be a challenge for some swimmers, but for those like me who couldn't even dog paddle well, it was literally life or death. If I couldn't improve my skills, I might as well kiss my ass good-bye and fail RIP in the process. I knew I'd rather drown than quit.

Over the next two days, Mike and I spent many hours in the swimming pool. Mike coached me on how to enter the water and perform the side stroke. I practiced in swim trunks initially and then transitioned to my Battle Dress Uniform (BDUs) and boots. Learning to swim was difficult enough, but when I added the BDUs and boots to the equation, the difficulty level grew exponentially. All that weight, dragging me to the bottom.... Not only was I uncomfortable in the water, but the thought of failing RIP was affecting me mentally. To say that I was worried would be an understatement. I simply didn't have enough time to figure it all out.

Monday morning came - test day. It was dark, and we were all in our formation, with equipment ready for all the evaluations. There was one small light on the back side of the barracks building where we all stood in lines, waiting. It was November and cold. A sergeant in BDUs walked out of the door, put his cap on his head, and took control of the group. I can still remember not being able to see his face as he pulled his cap down just before he yelled his first command: "Group! ATTENTION!" But it sounded more like: "Group....Ahhh, ten, HUUH!"

We were marched to the one-mile track where we started the physical fitness test. The senior instructor made equal lines of RIP candidates behind his junior instructors. The physical fitness test consisted of push-ups, sit-ups, pull-ups, and then a two-mile run, in that order. After everyone completed the pull-ups, the instructors provided each of us a vest with an assigned number affixed to the front and back. When the gun sounded for the start of the two-mile run everyone bolted. We needed to run two laps on the one mile course. We also were required to yell our assigned numbers on our vests and name to our instructor when we finished our first lap. The instructors needed to track our distance and time at the one mile point which was one lap. This was most important at the finish, our instructor made it clear to his group that he wanted us to approach him and make sure he annotated our times with us present to see. When I crossed the two-mile mark I yelled, "Trivino, 28!" After this I walked over and to see my instructor write my time down next to my name on his paperwork.

Once we finished the physical fitness test we ran back to our barracks to change clothes for the combat water survival swim test. The swim evaluation consisted of three separate tests to be completed wearing BDUs and boots, while carrying our weapons and load-bearing equipment.

In the first one we were required to jump into the pool backwards, and then swim twenty meters with all our gear, including our weapon. The second phase was a walk off the three-meter diving board blindfolded. We entered the water with all our gear and then swam to the edge of the pool without losing any of our gear. The final test was referred to as the "Ditch and Dawn." Once again, we were blindfolded, and then required to enter the water backwards. When we entered the water we were required to ditch our weapon and load-bearing equipment under water and swim to the edge of the pool. Looking back at the testing requirements, I realize that it is a realistic testing procedure and super simple for many. But for someone who didn't know how to swim…it could really be a bitch!

I was nervous like a drunk criminal at a bar full of cops. I will never forget my first jump into the water. The water in the outdoor pool was frigid. Everyone's muscles tended to seize up as soon as they entered and I was no different. The sun was barely starting to shine over the trees as I splashed into the icy water. I was focused and fueled with adrenaline because I didn't want to fail and be sent home. Also, I didn't want to die. I kicked and clawed with every bit of survival instinct I could muster for what seemed to be an eternity. Wham! I felt my head hit the end of the swimming pool.

I made it! It wasn't pretty, and I took about four times longer than most of the other candidates, but I made it. I was labeled a weak swimmer but I passed, and that was my goal. I knew I wasn't going to set any swim test records, but I was smiling from ear to ear. I would rather have drowned that day than fail any of the tests.

The remainder of the tests went well, and after it was all over, I felt like the weight of the world was off my shoulders. I had proven to myself that when I put my mind and heart into something, nothing could stop me.

The swim tests were some of the hardest obstacles for me during RIP, and in my few short years in the army. I will never forget the day I finished those swim events. As I look back on that, I realize that it was more than merely a phase in a testing process. It was a test of my own fortitude and commitment toward a personal goal. I truly felt as though it was the seamless integration of my mind and heart that drove my physical capabilities and allowed me to pass the swimming tests. This was the beginning of my understanding of what we as humans are capable of, if we believe in what we are doing.

Later in the day, I was pulled out of our map reading class and instructed to meet with the commandant of the course. I followed the instructor down a hallway not visited by many candidates, and we stopped outside an open door. I remember this hallway was filled with pictures and paintings of past and current Rangers. It was inspiring to see the history of past Rangers immortalized in pictures but it was also a little intimidating because I wasn't sure what was going on.

After knocking, the instructor advised the commandant that Ranger Trivino was standing by outside his door. The instructor turned away and disappeared back down the hallway. The commandant, who was a sergeant first class, asked me to enter his office, which I did. He knew I was an "import," a term used to describe someone that didn't initiate his military career or "grow up" in the Ranger regiment. Additionally, he knew that I had nearly three years of service time already under my belt, far more than the other candidates, the vast majority of whom were privates directly out of basic training and airborne school. It was clear to him that my three years of service didn't prepare me for the Ranger way of life, discipline, and military courtesy when he asked his first question.

"Do you want to be a Ranger?" asked the sergeant.

I answered emphatically, "Yes!"

Without hesitation he snapped back at me with, "Yes, what? Yes, motherfucker? Yes, asshole? Yes, shithead? YES WHAT?!!" I was dumbfounded, instantly uneasy. I knew he was upset with me, but I had no idea why, and I was not sure where he was going with his line of questioning.

I believe I managed to say something like, "Yes, I really do want to be a Ranger." I could see he was becoming increasingly upset as he sensed my confusion, and he verbally guided me along by informing me, in as nice a manner as he could muster, that whenever a subordinate addressed a higher ranking soldier, the subordinate was to always answer respectfully by recognizing the soldier's rank. Aha! I immediately responded with, "Yes, Sergeant!" He looked at me witheringly and told me to get lost in not so nice of terms. I'm sure at that point he was convinced that I wouldn't make it one day in the training.

The concept of being respectful wasn't foreign to me, it was just that the manner in which I exercised my respect was completely wrong. My old unit didn't do me any favors. I never had to answer any sergeants in my old unit with their rank, aside from the first sergeant and the command sergeant major. I was never required to stand at parade rest like I failed to do when I reported to the commandant at RIP. He must have thought I was a complete undisciplined loser with no future in the Ranger regiment. I understood his point of view, but when I reflect on that moment from a leadership perspective, it struck me as a bit of a failure on his part. Then again, I needed to remember that I was in RIP, and not talking with the manager at the local country club.

What I am trying to convey is the concept that someone new to an environment is obviously not well-versed in the "way" things are to be done. A true leader would guide first, in a most professional manner. If a mistake was made after being shown the "way," then the individual would have to be confronted or disciplined. Given the manner in which I represented myself, I would have thought the same if I were in his shoes - but I would have approached the situation differently, and from a more positive viewpoint. In the end, I realized that the situation was worth my reflection, and while I understood the sergeant's perspective it made me think about how I would address the same problem as a leader.

As I remember it, at the time there were four requirements all candidates needed to pass in order to graduate from RIP. The requirements consisted of a twelve-mile road march in less than three hours while carrying a forty-pound rucksack, a five-mile run in less than thirty-five minutes, the army physical fitness test, and finally the field training exercise at the end of the course. Each test was a milestone for a candidate, as it meant that you were one step closer to being assigned to a Ranger battalion. There were many other components to RIP, like map reading, land navigation, knot tying, rural tactics, and fast rope training. But the four major events listed were considered "must pass" events. After three weeks of training, I found myself standing in formation, graduating from RIP. We were all elated to finally be assigned to our Ranger battalions.

After graduation, I reported to the commandant again, except this time I was ready. RIP prepared me. He said that he had reviewed my packet, and realized that I was a corporal, promotable to sergeant. He then asked why I wasn't wearing my corporal rank, primarily because I had orders to wear my stripes. I explained to him that I was not in charge of anyone while in training (as a corporal typically would be), so I didn't want to wear the rank. The commandant told me that he could not send me to my assigned Ranger battalion without my Ranger tab - without completing

Ranger school. The Ranger tab is a curved patch with a single word, Ranger, that is worn on the left shoulder (at the time), indicating that you've successfully completed Ranger school. In order to be a sergeant in an infantry platoon in the Ranger Regiment, one needed to have graduated from Ranger school. No exceptions. My only option was to attend Pre-Ranger, which was scheduled to start in three days. If I passed Pre-Ranger, I would immediately attend Ranger school.

As a young RIP graduate, I wanted nothing more than to attend Ranger school as soon as possible, especially understanding my position as an import. My friend Mike was in the same boat. This allowed us to stick together all the way through the process as Ranger buddies.

Mike and I finished Pre-Ranger and then Ranger school together, graduating from Ranger school in April of 1992. Mike and I were ecstatic to be Ranger qualified, and couldn't wait to get to 2nd Battalion. That said, our first priority was the Four Winds, a restaurant that served the largest hamburgers I had ever seen. During Ranger school our squad made a promise to each other that if we earned our tabs, we would go immediately after graduation and eat the classic "Ranger Burger." Soldiers are hungry a lot in Ranger school, working hard and living on limited Meals Ready to Eat (MREs), the military's pre-packaged food. This was a special treat and something we all looked forward to.

Two hours after the graduation ceremony, those of us who earned our Ranger tabs met at the Four Winds for an early dinner. We drove up and parked outside of a little building that looked more like a house than a restaurant. When we entered the front door, we could smell charred meat, a smell that so impressed my hungry brain I would not forget it. I couldn't wait to get my hands on a burger. It's hard to explain to people who have not experienced being in the woods, living in the outdoors for long periods of time. Your senses truly come alive.

As an example, when in Ranger school, someone could open a packet of food from an MRE and almost instantly I could smell that food from fifty to one hundred feet away if the wind was right. The hamburgers at the Four Winds were monstrous, and I was barely able to eat a portion of one. Mike completely demolished two! Unbelievable. Then again, I remember seeing him drink five cups of steaming hot coffee in under a minute during Pre-Ranger.

While in Ranger school, one of the hardest things for me to comprehend was the process of planning and briefing the operations order. The operations order is a format that is used for planning and briefing a mission. I didn't have the experience to fully understand all the steps. I knew all the paragraphs of the mission order, but initially I had a problem figuring out what composed each paragraph. Specifically, where the information belonged in the format, and how to get the information to create a mission order. Once I figured that out, I realized all I had to do was follow the briefing format and I would be good to go.

This seems simple enough, but the harsh field conditions and the mental and physical conditions of each individual Ranger in the field made for a challenge. The lack of sleep was the hardest thing for me to deal with. Many Rangers will tell you it was the lack of food, or lack of direction from the Ranger instructors; but the lack of sleep really took a toll on me and many others. I remember falling asleep standing up. In a couple of instances I hallucinated, seeing shiny objects and people that weren't there. I remember seeing people face-plant...dead asleep, and being completely incoherent. Luckily the lack of sleep didn't affect me to that level, at least I don't remember if it did.

The lion's share of the course was conducted in a field environment where we lived out of our rucksacks for weeks. Each day, the Ranger instructor (RI) selected leaders for the platoon. The senior student leaders were the platoon leader and platoon sergeant. The instructors also chose the squad leaders which were graded (evaluated) positions just like the platoon leader and platoon sergeant. The squad leaders were allowed to pick their subordinate leaders. The subordinate leaders or team leaders were not graded positions, meaning that they were not evaluated by the RIs but they could make or break a mission. Therefore, it was imperative that each squad leader pick the best sub-element leader available if they wanted to be successful.

You didn't want to pick someone who had questionable land navigation skills to be the navigator for the entire element. As a result, the guys that proved to be reliable tended to get used a lot. In one particular case I was a team leader and navigator for my squad back to back to back, and it was having an effect on me - I was getting really tired.

When I was a team leader for a third time, our platoon's mission took longer than expected and we walked all night - and I was the navigator. The following morning I was selected *again* to be a team leader by the newly appointed squad leader. I was told to meet with the platoon leadership to find out the new mission location so I could create routes for the squad and platoon. I was beat, a zombie walking, barely awake. I moved to the center of our security perimeter where the instructors and student leadership were located and took a knee, pulling out my notebook and pen, waiting for the information.

Next thing I knew, I woke up to, "What's your problem, RANGER!?" I had fallen asleep right in front of the Ranger Instructor, who was fifteen feet in front of me. I opened my eyes, put my pen to my notebook acting like I was going to write something, and within ten seconds I was asleep again. When I opened my eyes this time I could see the Ranger Instructor angrily crawling towards me - I mean, he was upset! "Ranger, if you fall asleep again I will fire you from your leadership position! Do you understand me?"

This was the first time an RI got in my face in the field, so I struggled to wake up and I said, "Roger, Sergeant, but I'm only a team leader, and I've been the team leader for the last three missions and I'm smoked."

Normally I wouldn't have given the RI an excuse, but I was just being honest. I really was smoked! Maybe my truthfulness was all I needed to get a little break because once he heard that I was just a lowly team leader he backed off...a little bit.

After sitting in the initial briefing from the RIs and listening to the guidance from our platoon leadership, we split up to get to work on our tasks. After getting back to my team, I briefed them quickly on what I was doing, and then I got to work. My task was to create the routes to the next mission location and to assist with building the terrain model for the mission brief. The first thing I did was grab a giant pinch of chewing tobacco and put it in my lip. Then I grabbed some Tabasco hot sauce from my MRE and put some on both my eyeballs, trying to keep myself awake. After this, I sat against my rucksack, pulled my map out and got to work on the routes.

The next thing I knew, I was drooling chewing tobacco down my chin and all over my uniform. I fell asleep....again. Luckily for me, the RIs didn't catch me. I'm not sure how much sleep I got, but it was sufficient for me to stay awake long enough to do a good map reconnaissance and develop a good route. After briefing the route to the student platoon leader I got caught up in the squad's sleep rotation, which is something that I badly needed before I started with the terrain model and everything else I needed to do.

One great thing about my experience in Ranger school is that I was part of a great squad. In one instance, two Ranger Instructors followed us during one of our squad's dismounted patrols in the jungle phase in Florida. At the end of our foot patrol, both instructors said that our squad performed better than any other they had instructed. The senior RI said it was the first time he followed a squad in training and didn't have to give guidance or make corrections. I was really lucky to be a member of this squad, because squad assignments are pure chance. Two members of our squad earned awards at the end of the course. Ranger Warburg was awarded the William O. Darby Award as the Distinguished Honor graduate. I was awarded the Merrill's Marauders Award for having exceptional land navigation skills and for attaining some of the highest peer ratings in the class.

Ranger school's core curriculum was geared toward task-oriented leadership, or dare I say, managerial leadership. I don't think this was done intentionally, but that is what I felt from my experiences. At the time, the army considered Ranger school a leadership skill building course. While I did learn some leadership skills, I didn't learn how to inspire or mentor anyone - I didn't learn to truly lead. I was in charge of people, but not a leader. In Ranger school I learned the tasks I needed to accomplish in order to conduct and be successful in small unit combat operations in a rural environment. I was taught to follow the troop leading procedures, issue an operations order, enforce timelines, spot-check using my junior leaders, and NOT get lost while moving to the objective. You can be a horrible leader while understanding small unit tactics, tasking your people, and ensuring they follow what you ask of them - and you can graduate from Ranger school.

The focus of the course was plural in nature. Leadership as it affected the whole. For me, I believe that leadership initially needs to be singular in nature. Learn to become the best soldier you can be, and then prepare yourself to lead others. One needs to learn what makes a good leader before one can become a good leader.

A leader has to be able to influence people and be the facilitator for problem solving within a group. The leader must be an individual who inspires a group to follow. Not because they have to due to rank or position, but because they want to as a result of trust and respect. That was something I was never exposed to or trained to do in Ranger school. At the end of the course I was confident in my abilities to function as a Ranger, or what I thought a Ranger was based on my short exposure to the Ranger world.

Next stop…approximately twenty six hundred miles away…the 2nd Ranger Battalion at Fort Lewis, Washington. Once again, I loaded all of my worldly goods into my trusty old truck and headed out.

***

My first stop when I arrived at Ft. Lewis, Washington, was the replacement detachment reception unit that is responsible for processing newly assigned soldiers onto the post. Most soldiers typically stayed anywhere from two to five days in the replacement detachment, depending on the number of soldiers arriving each day for processing. This was my first visit to the Pacific Northwest, and it was summertime and beautiful. The smell of the evergreen trees was in the air, all earthy and piney. Whenever I encounter that smell it sends me straight back to Washington.

Mike and I were both assigned to the 2nd Ranger battalion but we didn't make the trip to Washington together. After I was processed onto the post, Mike and I found ourselves making the trip to the 2nd battalion compound with two other Rangers; a young private who had just graduated

RIP, and another Ranger-qualified specialist. We met a member of the Ranger Battalion Personnel Support Section just after lunch. After quick introductions we headed to the battalion area. It was a large, fenced-in area with four separate barracks buildings surrounding a large grass field. I took a moment to take everything in and thought to myself, *This is it. This is what I've wanted since joining the military…so don't screw it up dude!*

We were taken into the Battalion Headquarters Personnel Support Section office, and our packets were submitted and reviewed by the personnel section staff. Once the paperwork was completed, we were told that we would all be assigned to Alpha Company. I drove my truck to the opposite side of the quad area and parked in the Alpha Company parking lot. The four of us walked into the company area together and were met by the Charge of Quarters (CQ) runner around two o'clock in the afternoon. The situation for the leaders in the company was odd, to say the least. Out of the four newly assigned Rangers to Alpha Company, three of us were specialists, or E-4s, and were Ranger-qualified - had already completed Ranger school. I heard stories about how difficult life was for new arrivals to a battalion. I was a bit wary, especially since I'd be taking a leadership role immediately.

As we stood there at the CQ desk waiting for the next step in the process, several members of the company came to see the newbies. Most of them were E-4s, like me, and I could see the confusion on their faces when they saw my rank, and the fact that I was Ranger-qualified. It was even worse when they realized that two of the other newbies were also Ranger-qualified specialists. The vast majority of the E-4s/specialists that came to see us were recent graduates of Ranger school and were looking to express some newly earned authority. In the Rangers at that time, having a Ranger tab was everything and meant that you were a potential leader. This led to some power trips with some higher-ranking soldiers with Ranger tabs targeting privates without one. No E-4s that came to the CQ desk that day forced their newly acquired authority onto any of us…not even the private who arrived with us.

We were taken to the first sergeant's office where we received our assignments. I was assigned to 2nd platoon, which is known as the Blacksheep Platoon. All the platoon sergeants were in the first sergeant's office waiting for the new guys. My new platoon sergeant approached and said to come with him. I remember walking up the stairwell to the second floor where the platoon area was located. At the top of the landing at the center of the platoon hallway was the stuffed head of a bighorn sheep. Once fully inside the common area I saw a large display case, a memorial for fallen soldier PFC John Mark Price. PFC Price made the ultimate sacrifice during Operation Just Cause in Panama in 1989.

I was led down the hallway towards the platoon sergeant's office. Just prior to entering, we paused for a minute. The platoon sergeant needed to jump on the phone before dealing with me. I took a moment to try and calm my nerves a bit and looked at the squad picture boards and the Ranger scrolls painted on the walls. The scrolls looked like they had been there for a long time, and each scroll bore the name of one of the four squads of the platoon.

"Specialist Trivino, come inside."

"Yes, Sergeant," was my response, as I entered and stood at parade rest for my new platoon sergeant.

"I have you assigned to take a team leader position in 3rd squad, so one of the squad members will be here in a few minutes to take you down to your squad room."

"Roger, sergeant."

"The current team leader has less time in rank and service than you, so you'll be taking his team."

"Roger that, Sergeant."

Within a few minutes one of the team leaders from 3rd squad showed up. I was escorted around by Specialist Redley, who was formerly in command of the team that I was now responsible for commanding. Taking a leadership position away from someone who grew up in the Ranger battalion didn't make me the most welcome soldier in the platoon. To say that there was hatred and contempt in the air directed at me would be an understatement. Most Rangers start their army careers as privates in a Ranger battalion, and then are sent to the pre Ranger course and Ranger school. Since I hadn't started my army career in the Rangers and put my time in at this unit like the others, some felt slighted, and blamed me for taking a position they felt should have been for one of them.

Let me make a military clarification for those that don't know about infantry platoons. A platoon is formed by four squads of typically ten soldiers each. Three of the squads are rifle squads and the forth is an automatic machine gun squad. Each rifle squad has one squad leader, a staff sergeant, and underneath him are two rifle fire team leaders that lead three or four soldiers each. The rifle fire team rank is filled with privates and specialists that serve as automatic riflemen, grenadiers, and riflemen. I was assigned to be a team leader in a rifle squad.

Specialist Redley did not say a word to me and just casually motioned me to follow him. After reading his body language, I could tell he wasn't a fan of what was going on and was going to be as disrespectful to me as possible. He took me into 3rd squad's common room, which was to be our squad room, and introduced me to the squad members by saying, "Hey, guys, here's your new team leader." He immediately walked out of the door and left me standing there in front of my new squad members, feeling like an idiot. I felt awkward, not knowing what to do, and eventually decided to introduce myself to the guys in the room. There was minimal response, and I could read from their expressions that they wanted nothing to do with me.

Several minutes later, the platoon sergeant made his way into the room and instructed me to follow him. As I followed him into the hallway, I could see all the squad leaders huddled together, waiting to approach the platoon sergeant. I knew something was amiss, and that it definitely was about me. They explained that they figured out a solution for the "new guy"; they wanted me assigned to 1st squad instead of 3rd, working as a team leader for a different squad leader. I got the feeling that the 3rd squad leader wanted nothing to do with me. My opinion of him was low and I didn't have much respect for him from the beginning. It was my personal feeling that since he didn't have the balls to meet me face to face, and at least, let me know how he felt, then he wasn't worth my time or thought. I wondered why these guys wouldn't give me a chance in the position assigned to me, and then I thought, *Hey, maybe Redley is a phenomenal leader and his subordinates don't want to lose him.* My initial thoughts of, and feelings toward Redley were not favorable, but I would come to find out that he was (and is) in fact a great individual, and we eventually became very close friends. The squad leaders' recommendation was accepted by our platoon sergeant and I was moved to 1st squad.

The next introduction was much better and a lot smoother. I met my new squad leader, Staff Sergeant (SSG) Michael Villot from 1st squad, which is known as the Deerhunters. Come to think of it, any introduction aside from a straight slap in the face would have been better than what I experienced with 3rd squad. This second introduction was totally professional, and the way I should have been introduced to my new leaders.

SSG Villot took me to one of the squad's rooms for a private one-on-one conversation. He asked me to sit down so he could begin his squad in-briefing. He talked with me for nearly an hour. He completed the platoon in-briefing checklist and paperwork, which consisted of personal and professional information along with some questions that I needed to answer. One question that caught me by surprise was, "Why do you want to be a Ranger?" I gave this some thought. At that point in my career, I had been in the army for several years, and during that time I'd come to the realization that I wanted to be in the best unit in the world. I promised myself that I would do exactly that. I wanted to be in an organization that does the right things for the right reasons, where all the members work hard and are good soldiers, not because they're made to do so but because that is who they want to be.

Once he finished his in-brief he introduced me to my peer, the other team leader in the squad, Sergeant Victor Valdez. Sergeant Valdez didn't say a word to me as he walked me back to the platoon sergeant's office. The platoon sergeant was in the process of trying to figure out a place for me to live. He assigned me to a room with a sergeant from another squad. Sergeant Valdez showed me where my new room was, and then he disappeared.

I made my way over to my assigned room and entered. My new roommate was sitting at his desk.

"Are you a fucking thief?" he asked me as he stood up to talk with me. It was a hell of a greeting.

"Negative, Sergeant." At the position of parade rest I replied, rather taken aback. I was met with a look of utter disgust.

He walked towards the door and pointed to a wall locker indicating it was mine, and his final words to me before leaving the room were, "Don't touch any of my fucking shit."

I felt like I just got jabbed and then received a right cross! First off, I didn't understand the attitude or the need for the accusation of being a thief, and secondly, the room was full of his shit. It was all over the room, as well as on my assigned bunk. Luckily for me he moved all of his gear out of my wall locker, but left a bunch of trash, dirt, and rags in there for me. Since complaining was not my style, I got to work cleaning my new wall locker.

Shortly thereafter I made my way to the latrine to get some cleaning supplies. On my way I was approached by a team-leading sergeant from another squad, whose expression of disdain was obvious. As I walked past him he asked, "Do you think you can come into this platoon from another unit and just take a team leader position...just like that?"

I wasn't sure how to respond so I said, "Sergeant, I believe I have the ball, and I'm going to run with it."

He looked at me with complete disgust and replied, "Really? Get the fuck out of here. Just get the fuck out of here." *Great, another guy who doesn't like me.* I thought to myself, *The line just keeps growing and growing.*

After retrieving the cleaning supplies, I went back to my room and cleaned out some space for myself, taking care not to touch any of my roommate's "shit." When I finished, I moved my gear into the room and placed it all in my wall locker. My squad leader came in to inspect my gear to make sure everything was correct before placing me in front of my guys as their leader for the first time. At the end of the day he left me with some work to accomplish before the next morning. So, I spent my first night assigned to my Ranger battalion alone in my room, working on my gear.

When I finished I was exhausted and emotionally drained, not from working on my gear, but rather from the environment I was subjected to all day. I needed to get some sleep, but realized my roommate's gear was not only all over his bed, but mine as well! My roommate lived off post with his girlfriend, but was required to keep a room in the barracks because he wasn't married. I recalled his order not to touch any of his gear, so I decided to leave it be, grabbed my wool blanket and slept on the floor. If he wanted to be an ass that was fine with me. I wasn't sure if this was a test, some strange way of making me want to quit, or if they just really hated me that much. Regardless, I was on the floor and I was good with it, as I had slept in much worse places before. These guys seriously underestimated my commitment to becoming a Ranger.

SSG Villot was my first squad leader in the Ranger battalion. He spent most of his time in the 82nd Airborne Division and deployed for Operation Just Cause in 1989. From the beginning, SSG Villot was a good leader to me, and I was glad that I was assigned to his squad. He did not treat me like a dirt-bag subordinate or talk "at" or "down" to me most of the time. He knew my background and realized that I didn't have any infantry experience. So he took it upon himself to teach me what I needed to know, even on his time off. He explained how a squad functioned, and taught me tactics on the weekends. He constantly showed me how to be a successful team leader. His dedication for teaching may have been from his understanding that if I failed, he would also fail; or perhaps he just wanted to help me for some other reason. I never knew what drove him to do what he did for me, but the process inspired my desire to learn from him, because he wasn't afraid to give me a chance.

He knew that since I was an import, my peers and subordinates would make it difficult for me, hoping and wishing for me to fail. The military had a specific job for him, but his personal job was to make sure I would cut the mustard. The first physical training session for me, now a team leader, was a fifteen-mile rucksack march in full gear and at a blistering pace. We averaged twelve-minute miles for the entire march. The squad was feeling the pain, and I knew SSG Villot was doing this to test my will and physical abilities as well as the rest of the squad members.

I also realize now that he needed to be sure that in my position as his new team leader that I was physically capable of accomplishing the march. He needed the rest of the squad to see this, too. At the time I felt he was testing me, unable to grasp my determination to be a leader in the Rangers. But there was nothing short of amputating my legs that would have made me not finish that march. Looking back at my first few weeks, I believe SSG Villot was killing two birds with one stone. By pushing me he would find out if I was capable, and it would also show my team that I was capable, thus earning their respect.

For the most part, life in my new squad was difficult but bearable, which is pretty much what I expected. The other team leader in my squad didn't care for me, but he dealt with me because operating procedures required him to. Regardless, while he was there we managed to get along well enough. The lower-ranking squad members were adjusting to me, and I must say that they did their best to help me. There were a lot of questions that I wanted to ask my squad members but didn't because I was supposed to be their leader with the answers to *their* questions.

This was a transitional period in my understanding of leadership. I always thought, and was taught, that a leader knew the answers and would not depend on, or ask subordinates for assistance or input. That was considered a show of leadership weakness in the military. I learned through experience how wrong that perspective truly is. I suspect many have paid with their lives due to that kind of thinking. A leader looking for information should never dismiss or discount the input of their subordinates. When you do not know or understand something, your ability to ask questions and value the opinions of others is critical. They may well know something better than you, and you will gain their respect by showing you are not too arrogant to learn.

While I was getting my feet under me with my squad, outside of the squad things were different. For the first month or so I felt like a leper, as no one outside of my squad other than my platoon sergeant uttered a word to me. The majority of the young Rangers that grow up and live the life of a brand-new member within the Rangers have the support of other new members in the platoon. They entered the Rangers as privates, then attend Pre-Ranger when their leader believes they are ready, then Ranger school, then come back to the battalion.

The life of a brand-new Ranger private is hard, and this was something that I didn't experience. I felt like these guys who didn't even know me were passing judgment on me just because I didn't go through that experience. I knew I didn't completely understand the culture and norms of the infantry world (much less a Ranger infantry platoon) to that point, but the aura of being an outsider made things extremely difficult. No one wanted me around. I had no experience leading people in the infantry, and I began to internally question my confidence in my abilities.

I made a personal decision. Regardless of what I experienced, or what was intentionally thrown at me, I was not going to quit. Why? First off, my heritage would not allow such an act. I would never discredit my family name by quitting anything. Most importantly, I am just not a quitter, period. I worked hard to understand everything around me and my responsibilities as a team leader. I also observed that this unit favored those individuals who were physically fit and knew their jobs inside and out. My work was cut out for me.

Unfortunately, my environment was not very conducive to learning my job or the traits of being a leader...or at least that is what I thought at the time. Life sucked in many ways. I was sleeping on the floor with a single blanket although there were two beds in my assigned room. I thought my roommate was a total asshole, which he was. I was marginalized in front of my team by other team leaders, and I was treated like shit. The worst part for me was that I felt alone and I didn't have anyone to turn to for companionship or to answer my questions. Unfortunately, my Ranger buddy Mike was assigned to a different platoon and we rarely saw each other. I don't want to sound like a sissy, but at times, we all need a shoulder to lean on for advice and support. I don't care what any "tough guy" tells you...there is a point where every soldier, warrior, stud, etc., needs a helping hand. It was hammered into me that Rangers are all about each other, regardless of the situation. At that juncture in my military career, I wasn't feeling it.

Regardless of my situation, competence in leadership was my goal, and I wasn't going to let my lack of integration within the platoon stop me from learning. I was there to be the best soldier I could be, to learn the ins and outs of good leadership and the Ranger way of life. To hell with everyone else! I decided on a new philosophy: if they weren't going to help me, then I wanted them out of my way. So I spent most of my time alone, trying to figure things out, and during my off time I would read the platoon's Standard Operating Procedures (SOPs) while sipping on a beer and listening to the new grunge rock coming out of Seattle.

Failure was not going to be an option for me. Non-infantry folks may think that being an infantryman is easy, and only the uneducated or dumb soldiers become grunts. For the majority of entry-level army positions, you succeed by doing what you're told, being a good soldier, and being motivated. As you progress in the infantry things get harder - a lot harder, especially if you want to be good at your job. I knew there was a tough road ahead of me, but as one of my favorite role models, Theodore Roosevelt, once said, "Do what you can, with what you have, where you are."

Nearly two months after I joined the platoon the entire battalion deployed for a month long training operation at Ft. Benning, Georgia, or as it is commonly known by most infantry soldiers, "Fort Beginning." I found myself back in the Sand Hill Infantry Training Area. The temperature was Georgia - summer - hot, and with the high humidity the environment was a stark difference from summertime in the Pacific Northwest. Our schedule was tight, and there were numerous preparations for the training events over the next month.

The day after our arrival we had a small amount of downtime, and I was approached by the squad's senior rifle team leader, SGT Valdez, who stated that he needed to speak with me in private. My first thought was, *Alrighty then…let's get it on!* I was mentally and physically preparing myself for some mano-a-mano battle time. I couldn't have been more wrong.

We walked outside the building and found a quiet place to talk. When SGT Valdez spoke, I could tell by the tone in his voice that this conversation had meaning. There was not going to be any physical confrontation. SGT Valdez knew my character and understood my will to succeed, regardless of the challenges I faced. He spoke about the "focused look in my eyes," and he wanted to temper that with some positive advice on how to lead my team.

He started by explaining to me that I must ensure that my guys were always on time, preferably early, and ready with their required equipment. He advised me to always be on my game, as I would always be judged, and the guys would look for any faults in me and my abilities. In conclusion, he stressed that I needed to lead by example. No excuses. If I wanted my guys to follow me, I had to make sure I was capable of doing whatever it was I was asking them to do. At the conclusion of the conversation, I knew his focus was on leadership guidance and his compassion for me. I truly believe that he wanted me to succeed just as much as I wanted myself to succeed.

I learned a lot during that training deployment, mainly by observing, primarily because no one talked to me. We trained on a variety of different tasks, and having this experience helped me sprout as a new leader in the squad. I would observe my peers and their actions and make note of any new information, without saying a word to them. This did a lot for my self-confidence. I found I was able to operate well on my own, without assistance from other team leaders who weren't inclined to assist me in the first place.

The most important thing I learned during this deployment was that my guys could see that I was a capable leader. One of my young privates approached me and told me that he liked the fact that I would look to help them instead of just barking commands at them. This developed out of my own experiences of being treated like a piece of shit for no other reason than an individual having rank and the wrong attitude. I was treating my guys the way I wanted to be treated. This was an important leadership lesson for me. It may be a cliché, but it's an important truth: always treat your people and everyone around you the way you want to be treated.

***

I was covered in sweat and dirt as our platoon moved back to our rest area. It was mid-morning, clear, and about eighty five degrees at Fort Lewis, which is hot for the Pacific Northwest. We just finished our first live-fire run of the day on a trench and bunker complex. This was a platoon-level training event, and it was a critical event for us. We were shooting live ammunition at paper targets while moving through a fortified trench and bunker complex. This was a coordinated effort by my platoon in which the squads worked together, as one, to overtake the enemy trench complex.

While I had been in the platoon now for some time and things were better, I was still trying to earn my place with my fellow Rangers. After the first training event we made our way back to the platoon rest area to conduct our after-action talk. We knew there were some issues we had to discuss and correct regarding our last training evolution. The biggest issue was the untimely response to what is known as the shift-fire signal given by the lead squad moving and fighting in the trenches to the machine guns at the support-by-fire position. The shift-fire signal is given to the support-by-fire line (in this case the machine gunners and their squad leader) to ensure that the fire on a specific area is moved to its secondary targeted area. This clears the initial area for the maneuver squads to move forward without the risk of being engaged by friendly fire.

Ideally, the machine gun squad would occupy key terrain on a flank position from the advancing rifle squads. Best case, the machine gun squads would occupy elevated terrain that allowed them exceptional visibility of their target area and us, the rifle squads moving to overtake the complex. At a set time, they would initiate machine gun fire onto a predetermined area on the bunker complex. The goal is to suppress enemy fighters from engaging the maneuver squads as we made our way to the trench and fought our way to secure it. The machine gunners had to shift their fire from certain locations to others so as to not shoot those of us in the trench as we moved forward. We had to signal them, and they in turn responded, informing us that they received our signal and they shifted their fire. We could not safely move forward without this signal. During our training iteration, the visual shift-fire signal given by my squad was not acknowledged, which caused a long delay in our assault. We didn't want to move forward until we were positive that the machine gun squad shifted their fire.

Back at the rest area we removed our gear and the squad leaders gathered with the platoon sergeant and the platoon leader to discuss the issues. I was standing with my team when one of the team leaders from 2nd squad, Sergeant Richard Knoth, pulled me into the team leader group huddle and asked if I observed the shift-fire response from the support-by-fire position.

"Hey Trivino, did you guys see the shift-fire response from the maggots (the machine gun squad nickname)?"

I was caught a bit off guard, as this was the first time another team leader asked my input. I answered, "We tossed the shift-fire signal twice, but the maggots never responded. I think Sergeant Villot confirmed on the radio but it took forever, there was a lot of traffic and comms were broken; it was a shit sandwich."

Sergeant Thompson followed up, "We waited a long time before we got moving again. We gotta figure out what the fuck went wrong."

"Yeah, you're right," I responded, "We were there for a long time, but we couldn't move without confirmation from the maggots. We did the right thing, even though it took a while to get rolling again."

This was the first time I was acknowledged as a leader, and the first time I felt like my peers recognized that I was capable and competent. As inconsequential as that simple inclusion into the informal discussion may have seemed, it was a turning point for me within the platoon.

I believe sometimes we must earn our way. For me, at that time, I felt I earned the right from my peers to be a Ranger fire team leader, and I was happy. Like the first stanza of the Ranger Creed states, "Recognizing that I volunteered as a Ranger, fully knowing the hazards of my chosen profession, I will always endeavor to uphold the prestige, honor, and high esprit de corps of my Ranger Regiment." I fully knew the hazards of my chosen profession and understood that my road would not be an easy one. Nothing worth having comes easily in this life.

Ranger culture includes unwritten norms and a written code, specifically the Ranger Creed, which can be distilled to guidance for going to combat and winning with integrity. This desire to be the best soldier, or Ranger, encompasses every part of the Ranger existence, including being extremely physically fit, knowing your job to the best of your ability, and being mentally and physically tough. Rangers know they must be prepared to fight next to each other in combat at some point in time. My peers had to know they could trust me.

In the end, I learned that my peers were testing my character to see if I would quit. They all knew each other, and understood that they would not fail one another; but they didn't know that about me. I had to prove to them that I was worthy, capable, reliable, and just like them: not a quitter. I learned as fast as I could. I learned how to operate in the culture I was living in. I learned my job and I learned a lot about myself and my character. This experience became one of the largest bricks in the foundation of my character.

As I spent more time in the Rangers, my relationships with my team and squad mates improved greatly. I suppose as people got to know me, they grew to respect and even like me. After sleeping on the floor for some time, I got a bed, and eventually moved to a room designated for sergeants with a roommate - SGT Redley! I worked hard to develop trust on my fire team, not only between me and my guys, but also amongst the team members. As I gained experience, I became confident in my abilities to do the job, which fueled my desire to become the best leader possible for my guys. I worked hard professionally, grew as a leader, and was eventually promoted to squad leader.

At the same time, I grew personally. I developed many lasting friendships. During block leaves - a military version of vacation - I went home to visit my family in New Mexico. I usually spent these breaks tanking up on my mom's New Mexican cooking, fixing up my parents' house, and doing whatever I could to help them. I could never be myself unless I was helping others whenever possible. Everyone at some point in their life will need help from someone.

***

As the C-130's troop jump door opened I could feel the cold, damp air flow past me and circulate through the aircraft. It was almost midnight on a dark, moonless night, and my unit was making a static-line parachute jump over Rogers Drop Zone on Ft. Lewis, Washington. My team was in line behind me, preparing to jump out of a perfectly good airplane. Along with the rest of our company, we connected our static lines to the anchor line cable, which would open our parachutes as we exited the door.

We finished our personal safety checks. The final safety check was ongoing, conducted by a jumpmaster called the "safety". This inspection was critical in ensuring that each jumper's static line was routed correctly, to minimize static line injuries and parachute malfunctions. We were positioned near the rear of the aircraft, in close proximity to the exit door, allowing me to see the glow of the jump indicator lights above the doorway - they were still glowing red, not time to go yet.

"Thirty seconds!" The jumpmaster yelled near the exit door as he extended his right hand to the first jumper and held his thumb and index finger about an inch apart, indicating they'd just passed the thirty-second mark. The signal was passed up the line. As the jumpmaster moved the first soldier into the doorway with the command, "Stand in the door!" I knew that the conditions were safe to jump. As we tightened the line toward the door, the pain on my shoulders caused by the weight of my rucksack pulling down on my parachute harness disappeared. Adrenaline was surging through my body and I was excited as hell! The indicator light above the door changed to green. The first jumper disappeared out the door, and the rest of us lemmings moved toward the door to make our own exit.

The powerful blare of the aircraft engines, the rustling of my teammates, and the cold rush of the wind propelled me forward in the chaos. The guy in front of me disappeared through the door into the dark night. My turn! My left foot was on a physical platform that I could actually feel, and my right foot stepped out into nothing; crazy, dark, windy, swirling, nothing. As I initiated my jump, I started counting to myself, *one thousand, two thousand, three thousand.* The few seconds of near freefall was exhilarating, but it was even better to feel my parachute open. The jerk of it opening took my breath away, and suddenly the plummeting slowed way down. As I descended under the canopy of my chute, I could see the glow of lights on the horizon, but I could not see the ground. It was beautiful, but I didn't have time to think about that shit; I was busy worrying about where the ground was in the darkness! Determining my elevation from impact was difficult, at best. At that point I kept saying to myself, *Feet and knees together...feet and knees together.* Smack! I impacted the ground hard because I couldn't accurately judge my elevation in the darkness. Once I hit, I attempted to do a parachute landing fall. This is a military term used to describe the proper way to fall or land while descending under the canopy of a parachute. I suspect the instructors at airborne school might have failed me had they witnessed my landing. But, in my favor, my feet and knees were together, and that's all that mattered.

After hitting the ground, I released one of my risers to my canopy to dump the air and keep from being dragged on the ground by the wind. This was followed by a brief self-exam, checking for severe pain or injuries, moving my legs to make sure they were working properly. The smell of wet evergreen trees was in the air. After my check, I got out of my parachute harness and got my weapon into action by removing it from the carrying case and loading a fresh magazine.

On my way to the consolidation point I linked up with the members of my team and performed a head count. All my guys were accounted for intact. We were all wet from the waist down; only in the Pacific Northwest do you get wet like that even when it's not raining. We moved in a dismounted fighting movement formation all the way to the platoon link-up location. Once we arrived, I placed my guys in our part of the security formation to protect ourselves and the area. Shortly thereafter, I was approached by my squad leader - my boss - who asked, "Sergeant Trivino, do you have all your people?"

I replied, "Yes, Sergeant."

I was presented with what most people would consider a simple question. But his phrasing contained a critical distinction that helped me realize the importance of my responsibility. He didn't ask about "the" people...he asked about "my" people.

It didn't hit me during the training mission preparation, during pre-jump training, or during the long flight in the aircraft before we jumped. The reality smacked me in the face in the middle of night, while I was kneeling on a wet knee talking with my squad leader. He acknowledged the fact that I was the leader of my team. This was the first time I felt the responsibility of leadership. My decisions didn't just affect me, but also the lives of the soldiers under my direction. That night I set my goals on becoming the best leader possible.

In life, many of us progress through different phases, with each phase we change and most of us acquire more responsibilities. This was true for me and my first four years as a junior leader. Reflecting on my progression from a team leader to a squad leader, I saw some serious flaws in my behavior as a team leader. For example, most, not all team leaders in my platoon at the time were over-aggressive screamers. Sometimes they would be so demeaning that it could have been disastrous for a weak-minded soldier…although the same team leaders would probably tell you that there were no weak-minded soldiers in the Rangers, and that their style built character and toughness for combat. I would agree with that to a point; if you can't handle someone screaming at you, then you might have some trouble in real combat.

My problem was, I modeled my behavior after others because it was socially acceptable within my environment and not because I believed it was proper. Unfortunately, I rationalized this behavior and accepted it thinking that I was doing the right thing, even though it felt wrong. It wasn't right treating my guys in that manner, and it had nothing to do with being a good team leader. Demoralizing is hurtful and impedes positive growth.

***

It was the middle of the night, pitch-black and kind of cold in Ft Bliss, Texas. The ground was soft from a recent rain, making it too easy to stumble with a heavy pack. My Ranger fire team and I were making our way to our platoon's objective rally point as part of a battalion-size training operation. For this training operation, enemy soldiers were role players from another unit, and we used non-lethal simmunitions for bullets and simulated mortars and air supporting fires. We inserted via a mass tactical static line parachute jump, and once we landed, I searched for members of my team as I made my way to the link-up site. Luckily for me I found my team members rather quickly and we moved in a fighting formation to meet up with everyone else.

We could hear machine gun fire in the distance, near one of the other companies' main objectives on the opposite side of the airfield. Our platoon was responsible for securing a barracks building that housed a number of enemy security forces. The intelligence portion of the mission brief stated that the barracks housed the forces that would respond as a reactionary element for the enemy. These reaction forces would move to support their mates once called upon by elements that needed reinforcements.

When we arrived at the rally point, I realized that my squad leader wasn't there yet. As the senior fire team leader in my squad, which is the lowest leadership position in an infantry platoon, I immediately moved to the platoon leader huddle. I was surprised to learn that the entire platoon leadership was absent, and another team leader from the 3rd squad and I were the senior leaders. Initially, we decided to wait for our squad and platoon leadership. As we waited, I evaluated the totality of the circumstances. How long do we wait? Do we have enough people to accomplish our mission? Do we have a medic? I could hear more gunfire in the distance. Time was of the essence. We needed to move. The enemy located at our objective were on high alert and waiting for us, I was sure of it. After a period of waiting, all the fire team leaders met and we unanimously decided to move to the objective without the platoon leadership.

The other senior fire team leader and I hustled over to the company rally point, located approximately five hundred meters away, to have a face-to-face meeting with the company commander. Captain "Combat" Carlson was the company commander at the time, and we informed him of the situation and our intentions. Without hesitation he looked me directly in the eye and stated, "Continue with the mission and drive on Ranger." Knowing we were junior leaders, I was surprised at what appeared to be a confident response from him.

Just as we were departing, he asked us to keep him updated with the progress of our mission. We ran as fast as we could back to our platoon rally point. When we arrived, I grabbed the other team leader in our squad and explained the plan, and then advised him that he would be in charge of our squad, as I would be acting as the platoon leader. The other senior team leaders and I met and agreed that continuing with the same plan was the best course of action with one amendment. I made the suggestion to isolate the structure rather than move in to clear the building. I explained to the others that the size of our assault force translated into less combat effectiveness, which would ultimately limit our ability to engage a larger enemy force. The rest of the fire team leaders agreed.

We moved to our release point with the junior fire team leaders inserting their squads in an L-shaped formation around the building. Once all the squads were situated, I radioed the company commander and informed him that 2nd platoon, "Blacksheep", was in position. It was dark and there was only one light on inside the large, two-story structure in front of our platoon. While watching for any enemy movement, we took sporadic small arms fire from an area about three hundred meters south of our location. I radioed the commander and provided him with a situation update as I mentally processed my platoon's next move. Capt. Carlson advised me that aerial fire support was available, if needed. Unfortunately, I didn't have a Fire Support Non-Commissioned Officer (FSNCO) with me to call in aerial support strikes. The FSNCOs are masters of using all manner of fire support, including indirect fire like artillery and aerial platforms. Since I didn't feel completely confident in my ability to call in aerial fire support, but was comfortable in relaying grid coordinates for the mortar personnel, I chose to utilize the company mortar section instead.

I immediately sent an estimated grid coordinate of the enemy's location, and within a few minutes simulated 60mm mortar rounds began impacting near the enemy, but not exactly on their position. I adjusted the grid coordinate and requested that the mortars fire for effect, meaning that they would launch a set amount of rounds on the enemy position. The rest of the platoon held their positions as the mortar rounds hit the enemy location.

While observing the effectiveness of the mortar strike, I received a call from one of the squads reporting movement in the target building. As I turned toward the targeted building, I could see lights turning on, both on the first and second floor. A few seconds later, all of the outside security lights came on. I informed the platoon leadership to hold their positions and wait for the enemy to exit the structure. Because of the limited size of our platoon, I didn't want to enter the building and engage the enemy, primarily because we couldn't afford to take any casualties.

As the enemy exited the building, we controlled them from a

distance and managed to secure them without firing a single shot. The platoon leadership arrived just as we finished cuffing and containing the enemy soldiers, and they took control of the situation after a briefing from the fire team leaders.

The platoon leadership realized what we accomplished, and they were pleased with our performance. My squad leader, Staff Sergeant Villot, mustered up a "Good job" for me as he resumed control of the squad. I took comfort in the success I achieved during this training evolution - I saw an opportunity to assume responsibility, took it, and we successfully completed our mission. This helped me realize that I had the ability, both mentally and physically, to be a good leader. I would continue to work hard to become one.

$$***$$

It was midday on a Thursday when we jumped off the back of our two-and-a-half-ton trucks commonly known in the military at that time as deuce-and-a-halfs. We'd finished up another training event and returned to our company area and barracks to take care of our gear and equipment. We were transitioning from being out in the field and walking around in the woods to cleaning and inspecting weapons and equipment. This sometimes took a couple of hours, but other times as long as six to eight hours, depending on how long we were out and what we were doing. We were never allowed to leave our barracks until all of our gear was accounted for, cleaned, and stowed. In this particular case, we finished up and were dismissed by our company first sergeant after a few hours. We immediately switched gears and a group of us decided to head out to one of our favorite watering holes.

Jimmy Hendrix blared on the jukebox at the Shamrock Tavern as my friends and I played a game of pool. I was 23 years old and easily frustrated - I swung and unintentionally broke my pool cue after missing a simple shot on the pool table. The Shamrock was famous for serving large mugs of draft beer called "mega-mugs", they must have been 30 ounces at least, and after a few mega-mugs of liquid courage I was feeling seven feet tall and bulletproof!

I immediately looked at the bar to see if the bartender was watching. Uh-oh, Karen saw me break the pool cue. She looked extremely pissed, and she had already moved around the bar and was walking my way. Feeling like a bad-ass Ranger initially, my demeanor changed and I was a little uneasy, but more embarrassed than anything else. We spent a lot of time at this bar, and she knew all of us by name. We knew her well enough to be friendly, but I was still preparing for some tough love.

As Karen walked up I immediately jumped on the apology wagon, but she wasn't having any of it, and immediately read all of us Rangers the riot act and promised to boot us out if things got too wild. After that verbal circumcision I felt like an asshole, and elected to sit down and watch the next pool game for a while. I down-shifted my beer intake into first gear.

As I sat there watching the balls bounce off the rails, I saw another Ranger walk through the breezeway accompanied by a really good-looking woman. Rangers were easy to spot back in the early nineties; we all sported a cue ball for a head. High and tight haircuts, which were shaved skin-tight on the sides, with very short hair on top. Everyone called the new guy coming into the bar "Dirty Shawn," but I had yet to formally meet him, as he was recently assigned to the company.

He casually walked up and slapped down a twenty on the felt. We never played for money, but it was obvious that he wanted to have some fun and wasn't afraid of a friendly wager. Shawn had a presence about him which exuded an aspect of coolness, and a guy with "game." During my first conversation with him I realized that he was definitely a smooth and self-confident character...and the gal he was with helped solidify that notion!

While my early days and months in Ranger battalion were difficult, as I paid my dues, I found I earned the respect and trust of my fellow Rangers and developed many close friendships. Shawn and I and the other Rangers we hung out with, all became good, close friends. Many of us would continue our careers together in other units. Our tight-knit relationship included fun after work and on the weekends, an occasional bar brawl, when necessary, and plenty of beer as a rule. Those were good times that I will always treasure.

***

A year and a half later I was the squad leader of the same squad I started out in as a team leader, 1st squad, the Deerhunters. During my time as a squad leader, I wanted to fix some of the flaws that I felt I possessed while serving as a team leader. One of the most important flaws I wanted to correct was how I treated subordinates. As a senior team leader, and now a squad leader, I realized that I wanted to treat everyone the same way that I wanted to be treated, with respect and trust. That said, I still wanted to create a strong mind to go along with the strong Ranger body. I still stressed my guys mentally, but it was with purpose now; I had a goal. I have found that people may treat you with respect, but that doesn't necessarily mean they trust you. Showing a subordinate that I not only respected him, but I actually trusted him went a long way in increasing what I got out of my guys, as opposed to demeaning them at every opportunity.

Don't get me wrong. I didn't turn soft-hearted and begin each morning with hugs and flowers for my guys. When they screwed up I made sure they knew I was upset. Sometimes I raised my voice to get my point across to them, but the big difference was, my default behavior was different. It was no longer the behavior that was modeled for me. I became my own person, based on who I wanted to be: my character, not someone else's. I focused on leading my guys based on what I knew to be right, and what I believed was proper to create fighting Rangers.

When I served in the capacity of rifle team leader and eventually squad leader, I wanted to give guidance to my squad based on what I had experienced in my life thus far. I created my three general rules that all members in my squad, including myself, would follow.

First general rule: do the hard right over the easy wrong. It's easy to follow the wrong path in life. Wrong often feels good, is easier, quicker, and more fun. I wanted to make sure that my guys knew they would succeed by doing the right thing, regardless of how difficult the circumstances. That philosophy helped me tremendously in my life, and I wanted to share that with them.

Second general rule: seek responsibility and take responsibility for your actions. I never would have succeeded at being a leader in the Rangers had I not looked to be a better leader from within. I knew as a leader I was expected to take responsibility for my actions, regardless of whether I was successful or a complete failure. You must be overtly accountable for your actions. There is no honor or grace in hiding in the shadows of an unclear situation that you developed or assisted in developing. By always taking responsibility for your actions, you immediately create a foundation for your character to build upon. I wanted my guys to have a solid foundation held together with good morals, values, and honor.

Third general rule: hope for the best and expect the worst. Hope lets us believe in the possibility of a positive outcome. Hope is something that no one can take away from you because it is internally driven. If you lose hope, you lose your internal will, and that takes you down the path of the easy wrong. Anticipating possible negative outcomes or potential problems and preparing for them keeps you ready to roll with the punches, and gives you the best chance of dealing with them. By hoping for the best, you have the will to succeed, but by expecting the worst, you are prepared for whatever comes your way. This was something important to me, as I knew that at some point, we could get the call to go to war. I had to prepare myself and my squad for possibly the worst thing the future had in store for us. For me, at the time, it wasn't the next training mission, it was the potential for us to go to war.

I loved to train the men within my squad - I mean, I *really* enjoyed it. I found that as I developed my confidence in my ability to do a certain task, it gave me a lot of assurance in what I was teaching. Competence is critically important, and I worked hard at it. It was satisfying to see the men underneath me learn and grow based on what I was teaching them. I believe this gave them confidence in my ability to not only train them, but to lead them. Another key ingredient in my love for and success in training was my ability to identify achievable goals for those that I led, and establishing a plan to accomplish the goals. This is a critical aspect of building confidence.

We have all seen "leaders" responsible for training that have difficulty with not just teaching the task, but actually knowing and understanding the task itself. This does two things to destroy a leader's credibility: one, it shows that this person, as a leader, has not made it a priority to understand the task at hand, and two, it displays a huge fault in character. Looking like a fool in front of your people costs you 50 million cool-guy points. You should never try to teach something you don't know.

An important aspect of a Ranger's life is the fact that one is expected to be physically and mentally tough. As a junior leader within the organization, I understood that my men, and everyone else within the unit, looked at each individual and judged them based on their physical abilities as well as their mental capacity to do their job. I understood this, and tried to prepare my guys for the environment they lived in and would become leaders in.

One of the most important things I learned - again, as a brand-new squad leader - was to lead by example, regardless of the task at hand, just like SGT Valdez told me. As a young squad leader we would conduct weekly ruck marches which were no less than 10 miles in distance with at least a 40-pound pack. The majority of the physical training was driven by the squad leaders who were responsible for training their squads. Each squad leader developed their own month-long physical training schedule, and would incorporate the weekly ruck march into their schedules.

During the majority of my weekly marches, I would offer to trade rucksacks with any of my squad members, and anyone who wanted to trade could come forward and pick up my pack to check its weight. I never traded my ruck, although initially I did have some squad members come forward to check the weight. Probably just to make sure I wasn't bullshitting them. Once they realized I was carrying more than they were, I earned their respect, and more importantly, their trust.

I tried to take what I had learned from my experiences with leaders and apply it to my leadership style. I poured my heart and soul into what I was doing, and tried to make my guys feel like we as a squad were capable of accomplishing anything. This aspect is key - I really gave a shit, which would prove to be crucial in becoming a great leader later in life. I worked hard to master the skills that I felt my guys should have. I also did my best to learn and to understand not only my job, but also the job of my superior. I developed a systematic approach for leading: first, have genuine concern for your people; second, lead by example; third, follow my general rules.

Military leaders, like other leaders outside of the military, can lead through fear. The fear of losing one's job or money is a huge motivator for someone to excel in their profession. Fears of losing the prestige of their current position, or failing to attain the next higher position are also motivators. I wanted my guys to follow me because they believed in me and my ability to lead them. I believed if I earned their trust, my guys would follow me with heart instead of out of fear. I tried to pass this concept on to my men. I wanted them to learn, as I did, to be a better person, a better soldier, and a better leader.

***

It was another late night and another training mission. My squad and I were waiting to load our tactical vehicle onto a fixed wing cargo aircraft for movement back to our base, and back behind "friendly lines." It was dark and I was sitting in the passenger seat of our vehicle, reviewing the night's events in my head and writing them down in my notebook. *Where did I screw up? What do we have to work on?*

The airfield we occupied was considered secure. All of the structures were cleared of bad guys, and we could see for hundreds of meters in all directions. We were in a relaxed security posture as we waited. My guys established a loose perimeter around our vehicle, and we spent most of our time talking and solving the world's problems.

I approached one of my team leaders and asked him to do something for me. I said, "Hey, Jake, what do you think about our security posture here?" I could see his brain kick into overdrive as he analyzed my question. I helped him along and said, "This is what I want you to do for me. I want you to walk about fifteen feet in front of your team and take a knee and wait there for a few minutes, and then come back to talk with me." He went and took a knee in front of his team without saying a word. Once his team saw what he was doing, they all assumed their formation behind him and took a knee, just like Jake. A few minutes later he came back and we talked some more. "Do you see what just happened? Once you went out in front of your guys and they saw what you were doing, they did exactly what you did. Now what I want you to do is go back to your formation and lie down in the prone position, wait there a few minutes, then come back to talk with me." He moved back to his position and moved from the kneeling to the prone position. Everyone on his team did exactly what he did. In its simplest form, he was leading by example.

Jake came back to talk with me and this is what I said: "Your team members are always looking to do the right thing. Your guys will always look to you to lead them in the right direction. Remember, it's your job to know what is right, and to take them in that direction."

Jake simply replied, "Roger, Sergeant."

I continued to explain my point, "Remember, *you* have to be the one to do the right thing first, for your guys will do whatever you're doing. If you're not proactive, they won't be either. And if you fail to see and do the right thing, you and your guys may also fail, just because you decided not to act."

***

During the latter part of my squad leader time, I was approached by my platoon sergeant. He asked if I wanted to compete in the Non-Commissioned Officer (NCO) of the Quarter competition, which was to take place in three weeks. I immediately turned down his offer, and this started a week-long struggle between him and me, where he would try to convince me to volunteer, and I would tell him that I didn't want to compete.

Preparing for this competition meant that I would have to fill my off time reviewing study manuals and practicing answering questions in a formal interview manner. This was the last thing I wanted to do, primarily because my off time was for having fun with friends. If successful, the NCO of the Quarter event would lead to a Soldier of the Year competition, and even more studying and practicing. I knew that my platoon sergeant could order me to compete, but he wanted me to volunteer.

At the end of the week I told my platoon sergeant that I didn't want to compete because I didn't think that I would do well, and I might make a fool of myself. My platoon sergeant, SFC Calpena, replied with a single question: "Do you actually think that the other squad leaders in this battalion are that much better than you?" That single question changed my mind. Standing there at parade rest in front of him, I decided to compete. After that meeting I spent much of my time off studying. Over the course of two weeks I reviewed several military promotion board study guides. I felt I obtained a base of knowledge to work from. I then switched gears and studied on certain aspects of my job where I knew I lacked an in-depth knowledge.

The competition consisted of a military board, a formal interview filled with questions about my job, policies, and Ranger standards. After the competition, the battalion command sergeant major (CSM) summoned the participants into his office and informed us all that I won the competition. This meant that I would compete against three other NCOs for the Battalion NCO of the Year. The competition was to take place in two weeks, and would be a similar type of event consisting of a PT Test and a formal question and answer session.

Two weeks flashed by, and before I knew it, I found myself in the CSM's office again, where he informed us that I won and would serve as the 2nd Ranger Battalion NCO of the Year. This was great, but it also meant that I would represent the 2nd Ranger Battalion in the 75th Ranger Regimental NCO of the Year competition.

The 75th Ranger Regiment NCO of the Year competition was somewhat of a condensed version of the "Best Ranger Competition", with many of the same events. It took place at the regimental headquarters at Fort Benning, Georgia. It was led by the regimental sergeant major and supported by the regimental training cadre.

The day of the competition began around 4:00 a.m. with a standard army PT test, immediately followed by the combat water survival swim test - the same swim test I took in RIP. This was followed by several other events, including a timed static line spot jump, advance rifle marksmanship, and orienteering with full gear and rucksack. During the orienteering event we had evaluation components at each land navigation point that tested our Ranger skills. After a full day of physical events it was about 10:00 p.m. and we were more than ready to finish up the day, but we had one final event - the mystery event.

All of the competing Rangers were shuttled to a classroom in the regimental headquarters; we were exhausted. We knew there was one final event, but no one had the faintest idea what it could be. As we sat there, trying to stay awake, several cadre members from the RIP and Pre-Ranger courses came in. We were told to stand, and we were blindfolded. Each cadre member guided us into another room. I was guided through several doorways and finally into a large room; during this time, my blindfold moved and I was able to see slightly underneath it. I thought for a split-second about the situation I found myself in. This gave me an advantage, and I could potentially win the event if I decided to keep my mouth shut. As I stood there at a table, my three general rules echoed in my head. There was no way in hell I could continue and possibly win by violating my first general rule: do the hard right over the easy wrong.

I told the cadre member that I was able to see and he needed to fix my blindfold. After he fixed my blindfold we began the event. A box was placed in front of each competitor filled with parts to several weapons and we had to put them all together, blindfolded. After the mystery event the competitors were told to be ready at 0800 the next morning for the start of the formal board, which would be similar to the boards I participated in for the other competitions.

After the board, we gathered in the regimental conference room for the results of the competition. The Ranger regiment command sergeant major told everyone that I won the competition. He said the final event was what put me over the rest of the competitors; I'd won the mystery event. It felt great to hear that I won, but more important to me was the fact that I won without violating my integrity and my first general rule. This was the first experience that I can recall where my character truly guided me. I didn't realize at the time how significant character would become in my leadership style in the future. But leading people was not in my near future; I was to become a follower, again, and this would eventually make me a better leader.

During my time serving in the Ranger regiment, I thought it was important to pass on what I believed to those I led. I wanted my guys in my squad to learn, but I also knew someday my team leaders would become squad leaders and assume more responsibility. In a sense I wanted to prepare them as best as I could. I didn't want them to just wallow in a world where they didn't look into the future. I learned the importance of not only identifying potential, future leaders, but also taking an active role in developing them, just like many of my leaders helped me. Leadership isn't just about leading, it's also about helping people. When I decided to leave the Rangers, I learned several important aspects of leadership that I would never forget, and would apply in the future.

First, was an understanding and deep appreciation of what hard work, perseverance, and having a never-quit attitude can do. By working hard and not quitting, I *earned* my way into the platoon, and by doing so, I created some of my best friendships.

Second, the importance of leading by example. Coupled with that were my three general rules that guided me then, and continue to be a cornerstone in the foundation of my character.

Finally was the understanding of the importance of being competent, not only at your job, but also as a leader. It was this realization that helped me understand that I needed to work at my leadership skills in order to improve on them. I believed that if I accomplished competence as a leader, I would develop mutual trust and respect with those I led, which would be the pathway for leading without fear. My guys would follow with heart. This notion was most important for me.

Outside of the leadership aspect, I gained a wealth of knowledge on squad and platoon-level tactics, and a great understanding of maneuver. These became the foundation for my tactics and are still in place today. I developed these skills through the tough, realistic training we conducted. The knowledge and training, coupled with the Ranger culture, creates some of the best soldiers in the world. I learned to be physically tough, which made me mentally tough. The mind controls the body, and only a tough mind can wield a Ranger body to its maximum potential. There is no better large military organization than a Ranger unit to bring the wrath of war to its enemy.

***

Life is one long roller coaster ride, with highs and lows. At a low point as a squad leader, or what I thought was a low point, I decided that I wanted to look for reassignment, and try to move up to the next level. The leadership and command climate in the platoon and company supported my decision fully. I realized that I wanted and needed a challenge. I attended a recruiting brief for participation in a selection course for training and assignment to a US Army Special Operations Special Missions Unit - the most elite unit in the army.

After attending the information and recruiting briefing, I volunteered to take the physical fitness test, which I passed. All of the volunteers that passed the physical fitness test moved to a classroom where we took a series of psychological tests. This took a full afternoon to complete. At the end of the day, the recruiter explained to us that we would be notified in writing if we were invited to attend the selection course.

A month later, I received a letter in the mail saying that my packet was reviewed and I was invited to attend the selection course. I was excited, and ready for a new chapter in my life. I worked hard to be the best Ranger I could be, and now it was time to try something new. Little did I know how much harder I would have to work in the upcoming months, or what was in store for me.

Quick notes for aspiring leaders or those already in leadership positions...

- Work hard and earn your way into your leadership position - never quit!
- Treat your subordinates the same way you want to be treated
- Lead by example - no exceptions
- Choose the hard right over the easy wrong
- Seek responsibility and take responsibility for your actions - both good and bad
- Hope for the best and prepare for the worst
- Be a leader with character

4

IN THE UNIT NOW...THE FIRST FOUR YEARS

Fall 1995 - Special Missions Unit selection course

The lyrics to my favorite song was on repeat in my head over the past few hours (Soundgarden's "Birth Ritual", if you want to know), but now my mind was focused on my footing as I walked. My legs were dead-tired, as I rested a little too long during my last break, and my muscles cooled off and stiffened up a bit. This made my thigh and calf muscles extremely tight as I made my way to my next land navigation point. My stride shortened considerably, and I felt like I wasn't moving as fast as I should. My rucksack was on my back and it was heavy; I carried my weapon in my right hand, and a map in my left. As I approached my next location, I observed an individual coming out from behind a vehicle. I recognized the sergeant major as he addressed me and informed me that I had successfully completed the physical portion of the selection course. I was relieved, but I knew this was only the first step of a long process.

This selection course was the first step in the process of attempting to earn the right to attend the training course for potential assignment to the premier counter-terrorist unit in the world. The selection course placed candidates in an extremely ambiguous environment with little direction, encouragement, or correction. We were assigned tasks and placed in situations that forced us to make decisions on our own. We operated alone, and we were always expected to do what we thought was right. This environment was difficult for some people, especially those individuals who felt they needed clear, concise guidance or positive reinforcement, and considered anything less unprofessional. At one point during the course I overheard another candidate saying that he hated the lack of communication in the selection course. He didn't last long.

The course itself was humbling. During the first few days, I realized I was in the company of some of the best physical studs not only in the Ranger community but throughout the army. Some of these guys were known for competing in the Best Ranger Competition and winning. Some other candidates were simply physical beasts - I mean, they were in *great* shape. Not only was it an extremely tough physical challenge for me, it was also a mental challenge. During the course I would say to myself, *This course is looking for the person with a very strong mind, not just a strong body.*

At the end of the selection course, I didn't see many of the physical studs standing with me and the few others who made it through. I firmly believe that my heart, which fueled me physically, empowered me with the will to succeed. I was in decent physical shape prior to attending the course, but not a 7 foot tall beast. My point is this: you must not take anything at face value. You must look deeper to find the true person. If you saw me walking on a sidewalk, you would never guess that I was an operational member of the Army's premier special missions unit, much less a leader in the unit.

This course was designed to allow those running it to see what we were made of, what drove us internally. It's easy to make mistakes during the course, which affects the overall outcome. A small, seemingly little mistake can snowball into a situation that ends really badly.

The next step for me was the training course which, at the time, was approximately eight months in duration. I didn't know anyone in the unit, but most everyone knew the building housed some bad-ass counter-terrorism experts. At near the midway point in the training course, I noticed a significant change in my thinking. I realized that I was entrusted to do what I thought was correct. It was liberating. Until that point in my military career, I'd always had a feeling of limitation over my head, because I always felt I needed to ask permission to do anything. Somehow, an environment where you always need permission makes you feel a little bit incompetent or incapable of doing your job.

During the training course, we were constantly reminded of the fact that selection was an ongoing process. Just because we were chosen to attend the training course after completing the selection course didn't mean that we were good to go. Every day was a new test, with new challenges that we were to meet and overcome. Yesterday's events didn't matter…today's actions were the focus. This concept was explained to us on day one. We were expected to perform each day, regardless of the situation. During those eight months of training, I learned more about myself than the entire time I'd spent in my first unit. It was like the initial army blinders issued to me were now removed and I could see everything.

After successfully completing the training course, I was assigned to an operational team within the organization. I had mixed feelings as I walked into the common area of my new unit. My entire element was out training, so the common area was empty. But the plaques on the walls showed some of the history. I felt excitement and happiness in knowing that I successfully completed the training phase for assignment. It was a tremendous honor to be assigned to this unit.

I also felt some self-doubt, somewhat intimidated by the company of heroes. I questioned my individual skills and abilities as compared to those who operated within this environment. Perhaps most soldiers initially feel like they're not worthy to be assigned to that unit; it was a bit difficult for me to process at first. I expected my team leader to be the smartest and sharpest soldier I would ever meet. I was not surprised by what I encountered when I joined my first team. It was everything I expected, and more. The experience was both awesome and humbling. I couldn't believe I was there.

When I joined my team, I was reminded of the "selection is ongoing" philosophy. Being operational did not mean I was "in". I was required to perform to the standards expected of all operators. This culture and working atmosphere encompassed everyone at the unit, not just the operators on the teams.

The desire to perform to the best of your abilities was driven from the operators at the bottom, and ascended up through the leadership at the top of the organization. This was a contagious feeling, and every member caught this virus soon after becoming a member of the unit. I believe the majority of all small tactical teams have the ability to create this environment at the team level. The challenge lies in being able to disseminate it to all levels within an organization. The small tactical team cannot do it without the support of leadership, and vice versa. It doesn't work well when leadership tries to unilaterally force it on subordinates. This can easily result in subordinates revolting against the mental pressure.

As the new guy on the team, I did not want to be the weakest link. The only areas I could excel in were physical fitness and individual skills. The other members of my team had more experience, as they had been members of the unit much longer. It also meant that, at a minimum, they did not have fault enough to be asked to leave. I felt that the best way to be valuable to my team was to ensure that my individual skills and physical fitness were never in question. I trained extra on my own time and spent the majority of my weekends on the shooting range, honing my skills. Late nights were spent in the gym working out. There was an immense amount of "me" time.

I was single at the time. No girlfriend. No wife. It allowed me to really focus on my career. It never occurred to me that other members of the unit were doing the same thing that I was, yet they had families waiting for them at home each night. I didn't realize the sacrifices family members made in support of their significant others until later in my career. People tend to see everything from their own perspective.

After about a month on my first team, it was obvious to me that there was some distance between the team members and the team sergeant. It took me some time to figure out what was going on, and who created the issue. I realized that my first team sergeant micromanaged at times, and it was affecting the team. I was assigned to a team with an operational focus on climbing, from rural rock climbing to urban building climbing, and everything in between. If something needed to be scaled, my team was responsible for making that happen. It was my team's responsibility to be subject matter experts, and also to familiarize the other teams on the basics of climbing.

My team was preparing for a rural rock climbing training event. We were planning on leaving in two days, so we were checking and preparing all of our gear. I was partnered with a teammate who had tons of experience, not only in the unit, but also in climbing. We were checking the rope logs on each rope to see which would work best for this particular training event. We would be transporting equipment as well as people on the climbs, so we wanted to use the older ropes for the equipment. As we checked the rope logs, I learned that many of the ropes were on the verge of being unsafe for people to use. Most of the ropes I checked had sustained too many falls and appeared to be in poor shape. I asked my teammate what he thought about the ropes.

"Hey, Al, most of these ropes are really chewed up. What did you guys do to them on the last training trip, climb with your teeth?"

Al, the second in charge of the team, said, "We tore the crap out of these ropes on our last climbing trip bro, not sure exactly how it happened either. All these ropes need to be marked and used for equipment only." It was crystal clear to me that we needed to cut new lengths of rope and put the current ropes in the general purpose box for other uses. I immediately started moving boxes and equipment so that we could lay out the new rope to be cut.

"Hold tight Rat, I'm gonna run down and tell the team sergeant what's going on before we get busy." My call sign, Rat, was bestowed on me at the start of the training course. Not for my love of cheese, although I do love cheese. It was given to me because of my initials. I must say that I am lucky, because most unit members get their call signs when they mess something up, or names that describe their personality, or worse. Who wants to have the call sign Stinky, for example? (Although Stinky is a really good dude.)

At the time, I didn't think much about what was happening. But later in the day I said to myself, *what the hell was that all about?* It was clear to both of us what the right thing to do was, but my teammate knew that the team leader wanted to make all the decisions. Even as a new guy, I could see the problem with this. There certainly are some occasions where you must, in a way, micromanage your people; for example, when there is a time constraint. If you only have five minutes to accomplish something that typically takes you an hour then you, as the leader, will have to just give direction with no input from your people. Additionally, you might have people on your team who for a variety of reasons (personality, experience level, etc.) may need a bit more direction than others.

If you have a super star on your team, you can give him or her simple guidance and let the reins go. The same task given to a different but capable individual on the team may require more detailed guidance, and perhaps some periodic checks to ensure that things are proceeding in the proper direction. If you have someone that you must follow around every second of the day in order to ensure that the task gets done correctly, then you should probably question your hiring or training practices or possibly, your counseling methods. In the end, you must understand that no one likes to be micromanaged.

This particular incident was not a major issue because my teammate was just trying to keep our team sergeant informed, which is always important. I didn't know this at the time but figured the team sergeant was somewhat of a micromanager. It turned out that I was wrong, but it gave me an opportunity to consider the impact of the issue. As a leader, you must inspire and encourage initiative. Micromanagement stifles initiative and team cohesion. The best way to help eliminate any tendency for micromanagement is to provide clear guidance, and then try to separate yourself from the situation and let your subordinates execute what you've requested. Micromanagement will negatively influence people in any organization, especially an organization full of free thinkers.

***

"Rob, you're the man for tonight's mission. You're going to be the acting team leader." I knew my team sergeant was going to select me to fill his position during this training mission. My heart was pounding, a strange combination of excitement and fear of failure. I knew failure was not an option with this crew. I had been assigned to the unit for just over a year and was getting fairly acclimated to how the unit conducted business. Now I was being thrown into the fire.

"Roger that," I replied. I found myself thinking, *I may not be ready to fill his shoes, but I am up for the challenge and the experience. This will definitely be a leadership test for me.* Our commander, a lieutenant colonel, and our command sergeant major decided that the junior team members of each team were going to be responsible for planning, briefing, and executing the upcoming training mission.

"Hey, Dan, do you know what this mission is all about?" I asked my team sergeant.

"I'm not sure. You'll find out at the intelligence update. It starts at 0900. I recommend you get your gear laid out 'cause you're gonna be busy, my brother."

"Sounds good to me. Anything else?"

"The only sure thing I know is that this training will not be a live fire event. We'll be using simmunitions." Dan continued to talk as I moved over to my gear bags and started pulling out my equipment. "I recommend passing off your breaching stuff to D, since you're gonna be the team leader."

"Roger that," I said.

I pulled my body armor and helmet out and placed them on top of my kit bag. Grabbing my team radio and survival radio, I put them in the appropriate pouches on my armor. Three non-lethal flash-bang diversionary hand grenades went into some pouches on the back of my armor. I pulled all of the live ammunition from my vest and replaced it with full simmunitions magazines. I was preparing for what I suspected would be a direct-action hostage rescue mission. After laying out all of my tactical gear, I grabbed my notebook and pen and placed them next to my gear. I thought about what else I needed to get done, but I was drawing a blank. I decided to grab my note taking material and head to the planning room.

I was the first one to enter the empty planning room so I grabbed a seat. This allowed me to see all the junior members entering with their team sergeants. I slowly came to the realization that I was the senior guy of the junior team members and, therefore, was going to take charge of the mission. Then it hit me…I knew this entire training mission would be my baby, and I was a little excited and a bit nervous. Not nervous in the traditional sense, rather, primarily because I didn't want to fail my team.

Dan assisted me in the first stages of the planning process, and then he directed me based on the information provided to us. At that point, he let me exercise my leadership skills and knowledge, and execute what I thought was appropriate. We worked for hours on the plan, gathering intelligence on the targeted area and then determining what should be done, along with assigning teams to execute each specific task. All aspects of the mission were discussed, including contingency plans for any problems that we might encounter. The vast majority of our planning time was spent war-gaming the overall mission.

At the end of the planning session, everyone agreed that I would lead the entire assault element. That put me in a unique position, as I had to make sure the overall logistics of the mission were conducted properly, not just the assault piece. After a couple hours of planning, I made my way down to my team room, I needed some input from my mates.

As I entered my team room, I observed several of my teammates preparing equipment, ensuring the team's responsibilities for mission preparation were being accomplished. I gathered the other team members and verbally briefed the overall plan in general terms, as well as our team's responsibilities. Our mission was a hostage rescue. This was to be a stealth mission, which meant that we would not be utilizing explosives to breach the entry points. My team was to be lead in the movement, on foot, to the target area. Upon arrival at the structure, we would be responsible for breaching, or opening the front door by manual and mechanical means, as quietly as possible.

After the breach and during the entry, our primary responsibility was clearing the first floor in order to find the hostage. When our clearing was complete, we would then shift gears and assist any other element, if there was still work that needed to be done. Once I felt that the basic structure of the plan was understood, I decided to head back up to the planning area.

As I was exiting the room, one of my teammates, Eric asked me a question. "Did you make a packing list of equipment for all of us to carry? It would be nice to have a list of stuff that you want the team to take as a whole, then we can have all that ready before the briefing".

I thought about it for a second and responded, "Bring what you want." Little did I realize that this was not the response my experienced teammate anticipated, and, even more importantly, that he was actually trying to help me out by suggesting a task that was considered my responsibility, one which I failed to complete. The mission and our tasks were crystal-clear in my mind, since I was the guy constructing the plan. I knew what we needed, and in the rush of my planning I just assumed it was equally clear to my teammates.

When I arrived at the planning area, two of the other junior team leaders approached me and inquired about the rehearsal site for the mission. Crap! I had to make some time to build a rehearsal site, then complete a rehearsal. Then, if necessary, we needed time to implement any changes to the plan based on the outcome of the rehearsal. Shit! I had forgotten to manage the time and task a teammate with making sure we were adhering to the time schedule. I was really starting to feel the pressure. I had to make sure my personal gear was straight, I needed to coordinate the rehearsal, and I had to get to work on my notes for my briefing after the rehearsal. God only knew what I forgot or failed to do up until that point.

I grabbed several of the junior team leaders and told them what I needed. "Bill, hey bro, I need you to build a rehearsal site outside for me. I know it's late in the game but we have to do a rehearsal. Oh, by the way, you have twenty minutes, dude."

Immediately after, I tasked one of the other junior team leaders to get the word out to all team members about the schedule change. "John, I need you to make these changes on the chalkboard for me and make sure to send a message over the intercom system as well. Our rehearsal starts in 30 minutes, so make sure everyone knows the deal." After this I headed upstairs to the planning area to check on the progress of the mission brief. Everything was in the works and one of the junior team leaders was building the PowerPoint presentation for me.

Fifteen minutes passed, but it felt more like fifteen seconds as I made my way out to the rehearsal site. I was given a one minute orientation onsite, and had about three minutes to prepare for the rehearsal before the entire assault force was to be on scene. This particular rehearsal was a scaled-down version of a full mission profile rehearsal. The most important aspect that I needed dialed in was the coordination between the sniper elements on the ground and the assault force. I wanted to make sure we were all on the same sheet of music, and that there would be open lines of communication between the snipers and the assault force. Communication was essential for any updates by the snipers or if the assault force needed any assistance in the target area.

The next responsibility was to make sure that our contingency plans were rehearsed and on point. The importance of the contingency plans cannot be overstated, because shit happens. During rehearsals, if we identified any coordination issues, then it was my job to get them corrected before the mission. I felt the assault teams would function effectively and would execute their mission flawlessly. I was beginning to think I was the weak link as the overall leader.

Thirty minutes after the rehearsal, I was standing in front of the entire assault element, waiting to begin my brief for the night's training mission. There I was, a special missions unit operator and scared shitless. I did my best to appear composed, calm, and cool to my mates. As I introduced myself to begin the mission brief, I was concerned about my voice stuttering and sounding like a leader without confidence. I referenced the introductory PowerPoint slide for the mission brief and realized that the computer and projection system weren't working correctly. The first slide was cut in half horizontally; there seemed to be a glitch in the system. There was a several minute wait while the system was fixed.

I felt a wave of relief, as this would provide me with a few minutes to compose myself. I was no longer thinking about the drops of sweat I could feel sliding down my spine, but began to focus on speaking confidently and professionally in front of the best fighting force in the world. The delay provided me with enough time for a short reflection to find inspiration in myself and my capabilities, and a calm and steely resolve prevailed.

When the PowerPoint was back online, I continued my brief. I was confident in my knowledge and ability to relay the information to the team members present, and it showed as the briefing progressed. At the completion of the briefing, we all departed the room and made our way to gather our equipment and load up in our assigned vehicles. Departure was in fifteen minutes.

As I walked towards my team room, two team sergeants and several senior team members from other teams approached me. I mentally braced myself for their constructive criticism. To a man, they stated that I briefed the mission well. I was somewhat confident before this, but their verbal pat on the back really bolstered my confidence and desire to impress them with the end result. Not to impress them from an individual perspective, but rather from a team-mentality perspective. Little did I realize that the briefing would prove to be the easy part of the operation.

When I entered my team room, my team was waiting for me. Brian was the first to chime in, "Rob, you did a good job, dude."

Followed by Al, the team joker, "That's what I'm talking about, brotha. My man can brief!" That was somewhat of a relief, as I did not want to reflect negatively on my team by performing poorly.

I focused on the mission. "Hey, guys, do you have any questions?"

Eric spoke up first. "Hey, dude, you still haven't made a packing list for us. What should we bring?" Shit! What did I do? My teammate wanted to make sure he was taking all the necessary equipment for the mission, and needed more guidance from me. Clearly but, unintentionally, I took the "do what you think is right" concept too far. As a leader, it was my responsibility to give direction. At that point in my special operations career, I didn't fully realize the importance of appropriate leadership direction.

The unit encouraged the idea that each member, as a true operator, was allowed to do what he felt was correct. That was extremely liberating to me. It opened my mind and allowed me to grow intellectually as a soldier. It inspired me to think through problems in order to solve them, out of the proverbial box, instead of a typical army step-by-step approach that was taught at the time. Traditional army training involved a sequential training methodology that required automatic responses by soldiers with stock answers to set questions. In my experience, the "if A happens do B and C" method worked well some of the time in rural environments, but was difficult to apply in a counterinsurgency war. As an example, during my time in the Rangers, we were tested on our ability to react to enemy fire. We were graded by a lock-step set of standards that we executed, in order, to be considered trained on a task. The first thing we were told to do when fired upon by the enemy was to get down, seek cover, and return fire. But in actual combat, sometimes it is better to run as fast as possible to cover instead of getting down. Independent thinking and problem solving are crucial skills, but I was learning that guidance from leadership was still just as important.

My team sergeant stepped in and stopped me from wandering off the cliff by feeding me some information, which allowed me to make better decisions. He began with, "OK, here's the deal. We need some night vision. Our approach to the target will be in the dark. Aside from some additional key pieces of gear, Rat, you have to talk about our team actions once we get off the truck and discuss our order of movement so we can rehearse our actions."

"OK," I said. "We need to make sure at least half of us takes some night vision goggles. I will leave mine here. D, you're the breacher, so you need to determine who will help with the manual breach." I continued to answer their questions and help our plan of actions flow.

At this juncture, I realized I had been so focused on the overall mission planning that I had neglected my own team. I quickly went over the team's actions with them on our chalkboard, which gave them a snapshot of what we were doing. Once the team felt comfortable with their mission responsibilities, we moved to load our vehicles. The entire assault force loaded onto several disguised moving trucks, as this was to be a surreptitious approach to the target. The plan was to dismount from the trucks at a specific location and then move by foot to conduct the mission. The contingency plan was to drive straight to the target based on target indicators. Either way, it would ultimately be my decision based on the enemy's actions.

While the assault force was en route by vehicle, there was a sniper team already on scene set up in their hide, with eyes on the target location. I had direct communication with the team so that they could advise if they felt the vehicle approach compromised the mission. If so, I would have to make a decision; do I immediately institute the contingency plan and have our vehicles drive straight to the target or not? The assault force would then attempt to isolate the enemy and move rapidly to rescue the hostages. Obviously, we wanted to keep the element of surprise on our side, and moving by foot would have been the best way to execute the mission in this particular situation. In some strange way, I hoped that our approach was going to be compromised so as to institute the contingency plan. I felt that being compromised would allow me to really test my leadership abilities, because decisions would have to be made immediately, in real time.

As we approached our final check point, I contacted the sniper team so that I could make a decision on our final approach. "Sniper 01, this is Bulldog 05. Request update. Over."

"Bulldog 05 this is Sniper 01, all is calm. No Tangos external. Activity internal on the second floor. One light on, ground floor, appears to be the living room. Break."

The sniper team leader continued after his pause on the radio. "All elements this is Sniper 01, be advised, the activity on the target indicates a green light for option one. They did not hear the vehicle during your approach. This is Sniper 01 out."

Based on the sniper's update, I decided to go ahead with a foot approach. I passed that information via radio to the rest of the assault force. After passing the info, I contacted headquarters, requesting permission to continue with movement to the target and execute the mission. The commander gave me the authority I needed and I immediately gave the command to dismount the vehicles. "All teams, this is Bulldog 05, we are cleared to move, all teams move to the target, over."

As we began our movement I understood the sideways look my team sergeant gave me earlier when I said only some guys needed to bring night vision goggles. What a fool he must have thought I was, and what a fool I was feeling like as we proceeded to the target location on foot. In the dark. Trying to be stealthy. With only a few of us with night vision goggles! During the planning stage, I didn't think it was too important for the rest of us to have night vision, and I didn't even think about the possibility of perhaps someone else on the team needing to see in the dark other than the guys in the lead. What was I thinking? I realized this was a failure on my part, and cursed myself as we walked toward the target location in the pitch blackness. Wouldn't you know it, there happened to be zero illumination because of the cloud coverage, just like the weatherman briefed.

This was mistake number one of the night...one of many more mistakes to come. Once my team and the rest of the assault force were postured for entry, it was my responsibility to coordinate the entry for all of the teams. Prior to activating my radio, I realized that I was too close to the front door and would have to move away if I wanted to talk covertly on the radio, otherwise I would risk compromising the team and perhaps the mission. Yes, that was mistake number two; I failed to determine where I needed to physically be as the mission leader in order to command and control the assault force. I elected to fall back on contingency planning and coordinated the entry on a time hack, which was not ideal. At that point in my leadership trial exercise, I realized that I had focused on the main 'meaty' parameters of the mission. I failed to sweat the small stuff, and mistakes were starting to compound themselves.

As we stood motionless outside the target's front door, I couldn't help but feel like my leadership for this mission was substandard, at best. I crushed those thoughts, as I had to focus my attention on what was to come. At the predetermined time, which was discussed in the mission's planning session, I gave my team breacher the signal to make entry into the target. He grabbed the manual entry tool, affectionately known as the "enforcer," signaled to the assistant breacher to take the slack out of the door, and went to work.

Looking back at this mission now, with all my years of experience, I've come to realize that leaders at all levels in the unit provide much more than guidance; they provide something that I can only explain as a calm confluence to the force: a convergence of strengths. The extremely high level of training of each and every operator, coupled with the leadership, procedures, planning, mindset, and most importantly, the love for what we are doing, produces an almost out of body experience for all of us on the ground; we are in the zone. Our individual and collective skills are honed to the point that we operate with no mental pressure, adrenaline, or stress, which allows the group to function as one without working to do so. Our minds are clear, our senses are alive, and we operate without fear and with minimal or no communication. Many people have experienced this, but there are few people in the world who have experienced this in the form that we have. It is truly an amazing feeling.

Mike Durant referred to this when he spoke to us after publishing his book, *In The Company Of Heroes*. He described his interaction with the two snipers that came to rescue him, saying, "they were calm, moved with purpose, and were acting like it was just another day at work. They really made me feel like everything was going to be okay."

Unfortunately for me, this training mission wasn't flowing perfectly smoothly. As our team breacher made his initial movement backward with his entire body to gain momentum for the enforcer, I jumped on the radio and called, "Enter, Enter, Enter," our code words to start the mission. The team breacher made easy work of the door, and we made entry quickly into the building. As we moved through the doorway and each cleared our sectors of fire, one of the first things we observed was the staircase that led to the second floor. Without speaking, we all formed up to move up the stairs. We moved quickly and with purpose. After marking the bottom with a predetermined signal for the other teams indicating that a friendly team was upstairs, we moved up.

Wouldn't you know it, as we reached the top of the staircase we were greeted with a short hallway. There were no lights on and it was totally dark! I was really missing my night vision goggles, and could only imagine what nice words the rest of my teammates without night vision goggles would have for me. Regardless, we pushed on and unfortunately, I was going to have to utilize the flashlight mounted to my gun to see. But before I was able to press the button to activate my light, another team member with night vision goggles grabbed me by the shoulder and moved in front of me.

I followed rapidly behind as the lead element made entry into the first room. The team then split in order to cover more ground, and I moved to the next room with another team member and made entry. We moved like water: smoothly and seamlessly. As I entered to clear my corner, I activated my flashlight so I could see. My teammate, on the other hand, was operating with night vision goggles and observed an adversary with a gun pointed at me, drawn to the illumination of my flashlight in the dark. I heard the unmistakable sound of my teammate's rifle firing the simulated training ammunition as he was engaging someone in the room. I still hadn't seen anyone, so I continued to collapse my sector in the room and saw that the bad guy was already down and no longer a threat.

After processing the room, we continued to move to help the rest of the team. Another element of our team located the hostage, who was unharmed. I quickly shifted gears and began preparing to move the hostage. I could hear the teams downstairs continuing to work, so I radioed for an update from the team leaders. "Stand by," was the reply from all of the team sergeants. While we waited, my team spoke with the hostage, trying to garner any information regarding the target and the hostage takers. Approximately one minute later a team leader on the first floor radioed me that the first floor was clear, and they were ready to initiate the "exfil" (exfiltration) plan.

We finished searching the second floor, processed the bad guys we killed, and moved the hostage downstairs to the first floor, where we linked up with the rest of the teams at the bottom of the stairs. I called for a quick huddle with the junior team leaders for an update. They informed me that they had accounted for all their people and equipment, and were ready to move. I jumped on the radio, "Bulldog 06 this is Bulldog 05. We are secure and have located the hostage unharmed, over."

"This is Bulldog 06. Roger, let's get that hostage out of there. You're cleared to exfil, over."

"Roger, Bulldog 06, I copy, proceed to exfil."

I switched frequencies and talked to my team leaders. "All elements, this is Bulldog 05. Prepare to exfil, over." At this point the vehicles moved forward to the target structure based on our plan. Once the security teams were in place, the hostage was loaded with a team for security, and we quickly loaded the remaining teams onto vehicles and prepared to move back to base.

I called my boss. "Bulldog 06 this is Bulldog 05, exfilling off the target area, over."

"This is Bulldog 06, roger exfil, continue back to base where we will conduct handover of the hostage to the proper authorities, over."

"This is Bulldog 05, roger, out."

We all gathered in the briefing room for the After Action Review (AAR) for the entire training event. The unit understood the importance of not just conducting an AAR, but carrying forward the valuable lessons learned from them. Mistakes were noted, solutions were identified, and those solutions tested in the next training sessions. Whenever possible, all participants of the mission attended the AAR, and leaders went to great lengths to ensure everyone was able to attend. Rightfully so, those involved should attend to have the opportunity to learn and grow from the mistakes that were made during the training.

During the AAR I got hammered pretty good. Although, I must admit that I thought I'd leave with a fork in my back indicating that I was done! As the leader, it was my responsibility to start the AAR with a quick briefing covering the time schedule, how the day progressed, and where the major decision points were for me and the rest of the leaders. Once all those present gained an appreciation for what we leaders did, I began the formal process.

The first thing I did was inquire about any issues with the planning session, starting at the moment that I received the mission and ending with the mission brief. I started by asking the team leader of Team One if his team identified any issues. He stated that the information from the leaders needed to be more forthcoming and timely during the planning session to help direct the team's actions for preparation. He was correct in his statement, and I should have allowed time for breaks in planning so the team leaders could update their teams regularly as major decisions were made, solidifying each aspect of the plan. Then I continued to the next team leader and sequentially progressed until all had provided their input.

After the team leaders, I inquired if anyone else involved in the exercise had issues with the planning session. Luckily for me, only one person spoke up. He was the lead driver for the convoy, and stated that once we determined that the means of infiltration was to be by vehicle, he should have been informed sooner with a list of drivers so they could prepare the vehicles for the mission. As it was, he didn't get the information until midday, which caused him to hunt down the other drivers, locate the vehicles, and perform pre-mission checks in an abbreviated time period. He needed and wanted more time. I agreed. The next phase of the AAR was to be conducted in the same manner, but focused primarily on infiltration of the assault force, our actions on the target, and finally our exfiltration.

After the AAR, my team and I retired to our team room for what I consider one of the most important and coolest aspects of the culture…team bullshit time over a few beers! There's nothing like working hard and then chilling out with your mates over a few tall, cool frosty ones, as a friend of mine likes to say. During this informal time, I talked with my team sergeant and voiced my concern regarding my performance, and how I wished I had performed up to expectations for the unit. He looked right into my eyes and said, "Hey, dude, you're human, and you're gonna make mistakes. I'll start worrying about you when you begin making the same mistakes over and over again." He continued his discussion with me and said, "Remember, just about everything you've seen in the unit so far was learned by making mistakes. You're allowed to make a mistake. This is how we learn."

Here was a true leader. He had no intention of breaking me down and criticizing me. Quite the opposite. His goal was to build me up from a positive perspective, and to help me to learn. I thought to myself how lucky I was to be in this incredibly awesome environment for growth and true leadership. Not leadership based on rank, but leadership based on your individual skills and abilities. There was no better test of leadership in my mind. I quickly surmised that obviously no one ever wants to make a mistake, but if you have a zero-tolerance culture within your command as it relates to training, then you are placing your people in a position to fail. You must allow your subordinates to make decisions and to make mistakes and learn from them. That is how people grow and develop into great leaders.

No one has the correct answers all of the time. If you train in an environment where individual decisions are frowned upon, or you hesitate to act because of a fear of repercussions or looking like a fool in front of colleagues, then prepare yourself for failure. This type of environment is detrimental to any organization.

***

Periodically, team sergeants would test their guys by creating challenges at the individual and team levels. Dan, my team sergeant, scheduled a team training day that tested our physical abilities, judgment, medical, and weapons handling skills. The day started out in the swimming pool with a two-hundred-meter swim in our combat uniform and boots. Dan swam it in record time. I swear the guy is part fish. I had a tough time with the swim. While I've worked on my skills and have improved, I'll never be a great swimmer. I was the last person out of the water, and my teammates had a significant lead on me.

The next event was a short three-mile run to an array of shooting and fitness tests, and then on to scenario-based events that tested our judgment, medical, and radio communications skills. The last event was an accuracy shoot with our M4 carbines. The shoot entailed each member hitting and breaking ten clay pigeons before running back to the team room, which completed the event.

After my horrendous display in the pool, I fought my way back into the competition, and we were all hustling to finish first. As I approached the firing line for the final shoot, I saw Dan jump up from the prone shooting position with all his gear and start running back to the team room. There was no doubt in my mind that the he was going to finish first. Regardless, I dropped into the prone position and prepared to shoot. As I did so, I noticed that my heart rate was through the roof. Before I could send any accurate rounds downrange, I needed to control my breathing and focus on the fundamentals of marksmanship. I was about three and a half hours into the challenge, and I knew, if I was lucky, I was competing for second place.

From one hundred seventy-five yards away I took aim at the first clay pigeon and fired. Miss. Shit. I fired again, and a piece of the pigeon fell off. Hit. I continued, but because of the distance I wasn't sure if I was hitting my targets, so I stopped shooting and ran up to the fifty-meter line to inspect my targets. As I approached, I looked at the bank of targets and realized that Dan failed to hit two of his clay pigeons. I finished the drill and ran back to the team room.

When I arrived, two team members were already there, still in full kit, waiting for the rest of the team to get back. After I caught my breath I explained to Dan that he missed two clay pigeons. He looked at me with complete surprise. Within a second, and without hesitation, he turned and ran out the door and back to the range.

Approximately twenty-five minutes later Dan returned to the team room after completing the shoot and sprinting back. When he caught his breath, he apologized to the entire team and explained that he did not realize he had missed those clay pigeons. He proclaimed himself the loser of the weekly team competition. As the loser, he was responsible for buying the team a round of libations of our choice.

Some people might think that Dan was a great person for owning up to his mistake, and I will wholeheartedly agree; but this was and is a common trait for all unit members. We were all expected to do what is right, to own up to our mistakes, and to do this without oversight or correction because it's the right thing to do. If we all, as individuals, did anything less than this, it would be considered questionable at best. Anyone in the unit would've done the same thing in this situation. Good morals, acting ethically and with integrity are fundamental components of the unit's culture.

As a young team member, I quickly realized that Dan was not only a good person and great leader, but he was also a family man with a good moral compass and great values. One of the most critical leadership skills I learned from him was how to be performance-oriented. As a young operator, I knew performance was key, but as a leader, I had to ensure performance would be my primary measuring stick. Not only for myself, but also for those I led.

In practice, it is hard to measure people by performance alone, although Dan did it flawlessly. When you work closely with a tight-knit crew, a leader may tend to be drawn to an individual, or individuals, who exhibit a similar personality and drive. The tendency is to consider a person with whom one shares such camaraderie as a "good guy".

Developing this degree of camaraderie with subordinates can make it difficult to objectively assess performance. It places a leader at risk of engaging in favoritism. If other subordinates perceive that their leader is engaging in favoritism this can quickly erode their trust. Additionally, this can place a leader in an awkward emotional position. Just because someone doesn't meet performance standards doesn't mean he or she is no longer a good person.

A good performance-oriented leader must strike a proper balance by having a strong relationship with subordinates without developing a degree of camaraderie that would compromise objectivity. Conducting robust training is critical in assessing performance. One must then support subordinates by informing them of their strengths and weaknesses, and advising on how to improve upon their weaknesses as well as how to continue to progress in their strengths. It is intolerable for a leader to allow substandard performers to wallow in inadequacy while letting them think they are performing at an acceptable level.

***

After spending nearly two years on my first team, Dan, my team sergeant, informed me that I was going to be the senior breacher within our platoon-sized element. Part of my responsibility as the senior breacher was to take and maintain control of a series of books pertaining to explosive breaching. These books held key information regarding breaching all manner of things including doors, windows, walls, and the like. If we wanted to build an explosive charge to gain entry into something, chances were the explosive charge was listed somewhere in those books. The information was a compilation of the unit's work towards developing, testing, and certifying explosive breaching charges. Although not classified, the information contained in the books never left the halls of the unit. The books were precious, and as senior breacher they were my responsibility.

Two months later we were on the tail end of a training trip. We arrived around midnight by airplane at an airport near our home base and unloaded our equipment onto a large box truck for transport back to our compound. We had spent the last month on a whirlwind trip during which we trained on desert survival, mobility, and urban warfare. While we were unloading the aircraft I was unable to track the breaching books to ensure they off-loaded from the aircraft and were placed on the truck for transport. It was the middle of the night, and as I checked the entire back of the aircraft and found it empty, I concluded that the books were loaded onto the truck.

Once we arrived on base, the teams began gathering and segregating the equipment based on the tags on each bag and box. We could tell who owned each piece of equipment by the tag or label. The process was quick, and the teams immediately took control of their items. Once the teams accounted for all their equipment, the team leaders started issuing reports to the leadership stating that their team was "up" on all equipment and sensitive items. When my team leader approached me and asked if I had all my stuff accounted for I told him I did, but for some reason, I forgot about the books. Later that night after arriving home I remembered about the books. I decided to go into work the following day to find them.

Early the next morning, I drove into work and searched the entire area for the books. I looked for five hours through every nook and cranny and never found them. At that point I realized they could be anywhere between the airplane and Ft. Bragg. I called my team sergeant and told him the deal, and he told me that he would inform the chain of command. The next work day came, and the first order of business was to look for the books. My team was given two hours to find them, and after that, the rest of the unit would begin searching for the books as well.

Two hours flew by with no luck in locating the books, and my team was joined by the rest of the unit in the search. I was on center stage, as everyone knew I was responsible for taking them away from the shooting range, team training, and everything else they'd rather be doing to look for books which were my responsibility.

After another hour of searching, I went to my team sergeant and explained that perhaps the books were left on the aircraft. He jumped on the phone and contacted the air shop and explained the situation and asked them to contact the air unit that flew us home. About thirty minutes later we got word that the books were left on the aircraft. What a load off my back! I was extremely happy that the books were located, but with my happiness came concern, because I knew I'd get reprimanded sooner rather than later. The documents were sensitive in nature, which made the offense worse than just losing something that cost a lot of money.

I was initially counseled by my team sergeant, and I felt like a little kid being counseled by my dad. I knew that I let him and the team down. The first thing he told me was that I did the right thing by coming forward and admitting that I lost control of the books. He continued and said that I needed to have a system for keeping track of the books, and he laid an example out for me. This advice was passed to me based on his years of experience. In the end he finished by saying that we all make mistakes, the one thing we have to do is learn from them.

I was later counseled by my sergeant major, who counseled me in much the same manner. The difference between these counseling sessions and others in previous units was the fact that I was treated as a person of value. They held nothing back, which was important to me. There was not a single bit of "could haves" or "should haves" in the sessions, and there was definitely no bullshit. They were honest, direct, and firm, and they laid out a plan for me that included the potential for being asked to leave the unit if I continued to display poor judgment.

After this incident, my teammates and I were in our team room discussing the importance of counseling, and what each of us did while in a counseling session. One of my teammates spoke up and said, "I always ask my leaders how I'm doing so that I can make any corrections before potential issues become major problems."

This seemed like a great idea to me, but I felt it was probably more important to ask my subordinates that question. I decided to start doing both, adding both questions to my personal counseling sessions as I became a leader. I wanted to have sessions where I would counsel team members, and sessions for the team to tell me how I was doing. I felt this was important due to the fact that they were going to be following me in combat...not a leader two steps above me. I tried to incorporate many of my leaders' counseling techniques into my own style of counseling. I'm not saying that I became a master counselor as the junior guy on my team, but I learned I wanted to counsel my people in the future the way I was counseled by my leaders that day. This was the most serious counseling session I received and I wanted it to be my last.

As I matured on my team, I decided I wanted to be a sniper. I asked Dan what he thought. He was supportive of my decision, and a few months later I was assigned to a sniper team. Dan was a great team sergeant to me and all his guys, so I felt happy that he supported my decision to try something new. He truly supported my ambitions and desire to better myself. Little did I know that our paths would cross again nearly a decade later under extreme circumstances, which would prove to be a pivotal moment for both of us as leaders.

I was assigned to my first sniper team in January of 1998. My sniper team sergeant was a unique soldier. He was super talented, and had a natural ability to direct his training based on his team members' personalities and weaknesses. He trained us for war. He was a focused individual with the ability to back up his words with action. I learned a lot from him, aside from the obvious sniper-specific stuff, and he solidified my notion that hard work yielded results. Because of his talents, he was mentally ahead of the rest of the team. While most of us were still focusing on the basics of whatever task or training event we were engaged in, he was ahead of the curve, looking at problems that might arise.

Sometimes my team sergeant had problems working with others. It wasn't that he was disrespectful or malicious...sometimes he was just grumpy. We've all been around grumpy co-workers at some point or another, and we all know how a person like that can make situations difficult. As a result, in addition to learning numerous ways to train my people, I also learned about the attitude I wanted to project as a leader.

This situation taught me how a workplace could be disrupted or negatively affected by someone's personality. I remember reminding myself to focus on being a positive person, even when I didn't feel like it. It takes some self control to keep a good attitude, regardless of what is going on internally, and it ultimately improves the work environment for all.

As I gained experience as a soldier, I learned that we all become products of our environment. Everyone is affected differently by their environment, some more than others. My belief is, most people learn to live within set standards and rules that guide them based on their environment. This can best be described as a culture, a set of socially accepted norms and behaviors, usually with members who share similar values. All organizations have a culture, some stronger than others. Within the unit, the culture would not only allow me to grow as a person and a leader, but it would force me to develop as both. A former unit sergeant major coined a phrase that really hit home with me. We had just finished a war gaming session, and were feeling good about the plan we developed. The group discussed how unique and great the plan was because we used some truly outside-the-box thinking. Our command sergeant major chimed in and said, "We do not think outside of the box. We think inside of our *own* box."

This resonates with me every time I talk with someone outside of my normal group of friends, when I talk with someone who follows a completely different path in life. I love speaking with people like this, primarily because I believe it opens my mind. I don't go overboard with this. When people start badmouthing our country, with nothing concrete to back their views, it really gets my blood boiling. And, I don't spend lots of time hanging out with the local crack dealer trying to get his spin on politics. However, sometimes it's good to get perspective on issues from someone who has a completely different view on life in general. It helps me grow. If nothing else, it allows me to see something from a different point of view.

One of the neatest aspects of this unit was the fact that everyone's vote counted. Even the brand-new guy assigned to the unit yesterday was given a vote. I can't begin to explain what an incredible feeling of acceptance that vote carried for the new guy. While everybody was allowed to ask questions or have input, it was understood that there were certain ways that the message was to be delivered, especially when it was coming from the newbie. Typically, his message would get passed through the team sergeant. Even more awesome was the fact that most of the team sergeants would credit the newbie as he presented the message.

One of the most significant events that I experienced as a young team member was an occasion known as the Annual Information Exchange. Once a year, throughout the organization, information was unselfishly and widely shared, covering all areas of training and operations. Sometimes we had the opportunity to learn from other units or entities separate from our own. As our guests, they would share their information and experiences with us, which allowed us to stay current on various operational aspects, and gain invaluable insight into how other units conducted business and their missions.

On one occasion we received a briefing from an outside organization about a mission in which they trapped a group of known terrorists inside a two-story residence. As the operation evolved, the assaulting element attempted to call out the terrorists barricaded in the home. The structure was isolated and secured, so no one inside the structure was able to escape. All attempts to persuade the terrorists to surrender failed. The assaulting element then escalated to the next level of force, and they tossed hand grenades outside of the structure to get the attention of the occupiers within the structure. Still...no response. After that they fired rockets into the front door, without the intent of harming anyone inside. Still...no response. Once it was obvious that the terrorists were committed to their cause and were not in any mood to surrender, the assault force determined it was time to end the siege.

The decision was made to destroy the structure with the terrorists trapped inside. Boom! Sling the M4s, boys, and get the brooms! Our guests continued to brief us on their post-assault procedures and the intelligence they'd gathered, along with several other aspects of their mission. I wasn't paying much attention to the rest of the brief, as my mind was stuck on the fact that they never assaulted the house. Why didn't they move to a breach point, make entry, and clear the structure? I needed to find out why they hadn't done what they'd trained to do...and do well! I couldn't take it anymore, so I stood up, raised my hand and asked the question.

During this information exchange, I was still somewhat of a new guy in the unit and, typically, I would have funneled the question through my team sergeant. But I felt the need to ask this question personally. The commander of the unit turned around and simply responded, "We've lost too many guys assaulting structures like this when targeting low-level bad guys, and we don't feel it's worth the risk."

I felt stunned. How fucking smart their actions were, and how fucking dumb my question must have sounded to them. I should have thought about asking about their assault philosophy here, as opposed to generating a question based on how we might have approached it. My perspective was based on what I perceived as our unit's strength, physical assaulting. The whole incident was less about physically assaulting the terrorists and more about mentally assaulting the terrorists, without providing them with any good-guy targets. What a powerful message the commander delivered to me.

After the briefing, I thought about their unit and my unit, and what I perceived as the differences between each. Their crew was a lot more dialed-in than I initially gave them credit for. On my way back to my team room I asked myself, *I wonder how many guys we as a unit are going to have to lose before we learn this valuable lesson?* This was a difficult position for me. I wanted to go back to my team room and talk about the briefing and their approach to this incident. Perhaps we might consider incorporating some aspects of their assault philosophy into ours.

When I walked into my team room, however, I kept my mouth shut. I felt that culturally, as the new guy, it was not my place to voice my concerns, not just yet. We were taught to move to the designated breach point, make entry, clear, fight through the problem, and deal with the end results. The end results were the price of doing business. I wasn't sure we were ready to learn or accept something different. Perhaps I was wrong. Maybe I was afraid my teammates would have thought I was a coward for not wanting to make entry on a structure with known terrorists that wanted to do me and my team harm. Who knows? The fact of the matter is that I never brought the subject up and, to this day, I consider that decision one of the biggest failures in my career. It's not what we do that wears us down, but what we fail to do.

I learned a lot during my first few years in the unit. Most importantly, I learned how the organization's culture governed its people. It guided us in all that we did, whether it was mission planning or simply setting up a shooting drill. The culture permeated the entire ranks and existed at all levels. It was a culture defined by selflessness, service, hard work, integrity, and independence. The culture within the organization supported the self-determined and drove out the unreliable and undisciplined. Unethical individuals stood very little chance there. It was the beating heart of the organization that drove each individual to go the extra mile, or work later than closing time, all the while working toward a single goal under clearly established morals and values. This culture was fundamental to the organization, and was sustained by leaders and the men and women who served under its banner.

During my transition from the regular army to the special operations world, my initial years in the unit solidified my belief that the heart is the strongest muscle in the human body. But there is also a mental heart - a spirit or soul. It provides strength beyond the physical. When you look at my stature, you would never guess that I was a member of the greatest anti-terrorist military organization in the world. Most people picture a six-foot-six-inch tall, barrel-chested freedom fighter. There are plenty of unit operators like that, but not me. My heart and determination gave me the will and the ability to succeed. My physical heart kept me moving when I thought I couldn't. My mental heart made me strong and drove me when I felt weak. The selection process for the unit brings the best of all the services together for a chance to meet the challenge for assignment. Many people were physically strong, but in the end they lacked the heart needed to be successful.

Quick notes for aspiring leaders or those already in leadership positions...

- Leaders create and support the culture within their organization - be aggressive in doing this
- Don't micromanage. Micromanagement destroys individual creativity and initiative
- Provide clear, concise guidance and allow your people to make you successful
- It's okay to make a mistake, but learn from it and try not to make the same mistake again
- Counsel your people often and well - have a plan for this
- Good leaders work well with everyone - try to have a good attitude regardless of circumstances
- Learn from others as best you can
- A strong heart is critical to true success

5

TEAM SERGEANT TIME

January, 1999 team Military Free Fall (MFF) training

The impeachment trial of former President Bill Clinton was underway, and those of us in my unit found the events a little wild, to say the least. We formed our own opinions on former President Clinton's issues. I for one believed, and still believe, he was guilty of the accusations. Outside of politics was a more significant event: The Racak Massacre, a tragedy in which 45 Albanians in the Kosovo village of Racak were killed by Yugoslav security forces. This occurred days before I became a team leader in my unit. I was becoming a military leader during a trying time, not just for me, but for most Americans and people around the world, and things would soon get a whole lot worse.

***

The jumpmaster gave our team the command to stand up by placing his right arm extended and pointed down next to his leg, and then raising his arm parallel to the ground with his palm facing upward for everyone in the aircraft to see. As I stood, I moved to my teammate in front of me and opened the protective flap that covered and protected the pins which kept the parachute container from opening. I did a visual check to ensure the pins were fully seated. After checking, I gave my teammate a tap on the shoulder and passed him a thumbs up.

We all did this for each other, and then passed the information to Chumley, the jumpmaster and fellow teammate, that pin checks were complete. We also made checks on our own gear. We were preparing to make a freefall parachute jump from twelve thousand five hundred feet above the ground with full combat equipment. Our rucksacks hung low on the back of our thighs, just below our parachutes, or on the front, depending on personal preference. Our sniper weapons were strapped to our sides, and we wore our ballistic helmets and personal equipment vests with ammunition, team equipment, and personal gear. We had rehearsed our freefall actions on the ground. The plan was to "launch two pieces," meaning we were going to jump from the aircraft in two separate groups, each group hanging onto each other. The first to exit would be me, with two other teammates, followed by the next three-man group, which was to exit approximately five seconds after us.

"Move to the rear!" commanded Chumley. He was now able to see the drop zone, and we needed to move near the rear of the aircraft and be ready to move into our exit positions. Chumley was on the ramp of the aircraft on his knees, watching the ground. I walked over to him to peek over his shoulder. I could see what I thought was the drop zone, and then I moved back to my team.

"Stand by!" was his next command. Chumley gave us the stand by signal by placing his fist with a thumbs up on the floor of the ramp of the aircraft, and then raising it straight up above his shoulder. We were about fifteen seconds from being cleared to jump. My teammates and I moved to the edge of the ramp and assumed our three-man position. I grabbed my teammates' chest harnesses, one in each hand. My two teammates faced me with their backs to the open ramp, and we moved until the heels of their boots hung just over the edge of the ramp. My teammates then each grabbed one of my arms with one hand and placed their outside arms down at an angle to help stabilize our formation as we exited the aircraft. Once we were ready, I looked at each one of them and we each nodded to one another, waiting for Chumley to release us. I looked down past my teammates' boots and saw the 15-second mark on the ground which was determined by map reconnaissance; a dirt road that was two cars wide, and I knew we'd be off any second.

Chumley stood up, looked at the jump caution light to ensure it was still green, and then looked at me and pointed out the aircraft ramp with his index finger, clearing us to exit. We all looked at each other and prepared to exit. I leaned forward to my teammates and yelled, "Okay, ready, set, go!" As I yelled "go!" my teammates and I jumped, hanging on to each other.

The initial wind blast coming off the aircraft was a rush. All the weight of my gear was gone from my shoulders and I felt weightless as we fell from the aircraft. I hung on tight to my teammates' chest straps, trying to keep our formation together. One teammate was having a difficult time as we cleared the "hump," a term used to indicate the transition from horizontal wind caused by the forward movement of the aircraft to the wind caused by falling straight down towards earth. We were traveling approximately one hundred knots when we exited the aircraft, and when we transitioned to falling straight down we would reach nearly one hundred twenty miles per hour.

The free fall was exhilarating. We held our piece, and once we were falling flat and stable towards the ground, I shook my teammates' chest harnesses to let them know to transition to upper arm grabs. I released their chest harnesses and grabbed their uniforms near the triceps on each of their arms. Our formation was spinning slightly, caused by a teammate's rucksack; he was wearing his rucksack front-mounted and it wasn't flying well. It was tossing him around, causing instability in our formation. He looked at me and shook his head as I checked my altimeter; we were reaching pull altitude. After falling roughly thirty seconds we all eyed our altimeters. At the appropriate time we shook one another's arms, which told us it was time to break apart, turn away from each other, gain separation, and go into our pull sequences to activate our main parachutes.

We broke apart. I spun one hundred eighty degrees and moved my arms back towards my waist, trying to make an arrow out of my body in order to move forward or horizontally away from my teammates. I traveled a few seconds and stopped the horizontal movement by placing my hands in front of me. I looked up and waved my arms over my head, indicating to anyone that might be above me that I was getting ready to pull. After waving off, I pulled my main parachute rip cord and I could feel the parachute bag break free from the container and open. The shock of the parachute opening was incredible - it happened so fast and stopped me from falling so hard that my throat hit my chest harness. Son of a bitch...that hurt! It felt like somebody karate-chopped my throat.

Our assignment was to hit the intended drop zone and land together, as a team. This was a training jump to keep our skills up to speed, but we were always looking to sharpen them. By steering our parachutes, the team linked up and created a landing formation. I was closest to the ground and would land first, followed by the next heavier person, all the way up to the lightest team member. Typically, military skydivers in a group who jumps together will land in order of weight, heaviest to lightest. However, as the team leader I felt it was my responsibility to be the "low man" and land first to guide the rest of the team to the ground. Unfortunately, I was the smallest and lightest team member. My idea of being the "low man" wasn't working as well as I thought it would, and I found myself struggling to maintain my position. I made my parachute canopy dump air and drastically lose altitude several times, which caused a domino effect up the stack of parachutes above me. In the end, I managed to guide the team to the ground, and we all landed together at the correct location. Everyone performed well. Even me, the brand-new team sergeant.

While we were repacking our parachutes in the hot southwestern morning sun we noticed the wind was starting to pick up. This meant we'd only be able to get one or two more jumps in before the wind got too strong for jump operations. So we quickly cleared lines, folded canopies, and packed them in their containers as we talked casually about the jump.

One of my teammates questioned the split-team concept as

opposed to our usual jump procedures. "Hey, Rat, what's up with the split-team groups? I mean, what are the pros and cons to this?"

I responded. "I'll explain it all in the AAR, but it's something that we tried a few times on my old sniper team and I figured we'd give it shot to see how it works for us." I shifted our conversation to where we intended to dine and drink after the day's training, which took the focus off me. "Where do you guys want to grab chow this evening? I know I'm gonna need a beer for sure."

As simple as that request for further explanation or justification may seem, it taught me an important lesson about leadership. I needed to see how the training progressed and weigh the information myself before I was ready to present it to my team. There are times when a leader, in a professional and truthful manner, needs to shut things down and address them at a later time. This allows the leader time to gather his or her thoughts, ideas, or direct commentary in a way that is more applicable and effective than slinging an off-the-cuff reply to answer a valid question by a subordinate.

This was my first major training event as a new team sergeant, team Military Free Fall (MFF) training. It only took me about half a day to realize that my team members continually looked to me for guidance. I hadn't really thought through the training well enough to give clear and concise guidance. So my first training event wasn't running as smoothly as I had hoped. There was some work to be done if I wanted the rest of the training to flow well and improve.

I started the AAR with a brief overview of the task, and discussed the operation in phases. At each phase it was important to me, as a new leader, to get each of my subordinates' input. Each shared their insights with the rest of the team without hesitation. At the end of the AAR, I discussed the concept for the training jump. I explained my thought process, and why I wanted to try something different from our traditional jumping procedures. The purpose for this stemmed from the varied experience levels of guys on my team. I had some really great military freefall parachutists, and then I had a couple of guys with minimal experience. I thought if I partnered each inexperienced jumper with more experienced jumpers we could mitigate one of the most dangerous factors associated with MFF operations: jumpers colliding with one another either in midair, during the parachute opening sequence, or under canopy. It's easy to avoid your teammates in daylight because you are able to see well; but what happens at night? I was trying to have my team think about this, and designed the training to transition from daytime jumps to night jumps, all using the split-team formation. The verdict was still out on my idea. We needed to execute my concept at night in order to see if the formation was viable and useful.

At this point, the team was split on my idea. The more experienced jumpers wanted to keep things the way they'd always done it, where we all got in a line and exited the aircraft, leading off with the heaviest jumper. I decided to try something different. I was using this particular method for my team only. If we were to have twice as many jumpers, then I would shit-can my idea and go with what has been proven to work for a large number of jumpers. My newest team member really liked what we were doing. He knew where everybody was during freefall, and he really liked the fact that he was able to keep stable when his rucksack wanted to take him for a ride away from us. We, as a team, needed to see how this approach worked in order to determine if it could become a viable option for us.

By the end of the AAR I saw that I needed to share my whole concept and ideas with the rest of the team sooner rather than later. As it was, I told them what we were doing, the standards for our task and how I planned to get us there, but I failed to inform them of the purpose for the new exit technique. Understanding the purpose for trying the new jump formation in advance would have allowed opportunity for potential helpful feedback. At the least the team would've been better prepared.

This training exercise was also an important opportunity for me to establish relationships with the guys on my new team. My assistant team sergeant was already a team member on this team when I was moved from another team and took the team leader position above him. I hadn't worked directly with him before, although I knew he was a good guy. Our personalities were a bit different, but the training helped us develop good working relationships. After our five days of training, we managed to accomplish all of our training objectives, which was a priority for me as the leader. But I knew I had a lot to work on as a new team sergeant.

Being a leader calls for the courage to face down tradition at times. Even though an organization is successful, a leader must always strive to better the team; be looking for ways to innovate and improve. This is best initiated in a limited and controlled environment, and then tested and further developed through reality-based training applications

A leader must also keep in mind that though traditions may be challenged, one must be prepared to face those challenges with well articulated justification for his or her concepts and thoughts. Preparation includes doing your homework before going against tradition. Never fear trying something new for the right reasons. Good leaders always understand the merit in trying something new.

At the conclusion of the training we traveled back to Ft Bragg, North Carolina, to spend some time at home with our families. I took this time at home as an opportunity to review my first training event as a team sergeant, and to evaluate my performance. I quickly realized one very important thing. I was no longer one of the guys. I was viewed differently, and most impactful to me was how the team members treated me. They looked to me for guidance and direction, more than I was expecting. This was a situation that I had not found myself in for quite some time. This was important for me to understand, and I was happy to learn it early in my stint as a team sergeant.

Team dynamics at the time helped me realize my new role primarily because I, as the leader, was considered the new guy on the team. Had I been working closely with those on the team, I think it might have been harder to understand the importance of the, "I'm no longer one of the guys" notion. When you occupy a leadership position you will be viewed differently. If you become a leader of a team in which you are friends with many, it is imperative that you ensure the guys on the team realize you are the leader. I really wanted my guys to see me as just another team member who was the voice of the team, but that wasn't happening. Especially since these members were elite thinkers and fighters. The guys on the team were professional enough to understand my position, and they respected me enough to treat me as their leader.

A leader can and should interact on a social level with his or her crew, but should also understand where the point of no return is. It doesn't mean you have to be anti-social. But you should never get so involved that you find yourself in a position where you might be tempted to compromise your integrity. You cannot be "one of the guys" and be a great leader because at some point in time you will find yourself in a compromising position. I believe a true leader should strive to maintain his or her integrity, and attempt to keep those they lead from ever having to question it.

It's normal for people to be afraid of failure, but I've seen some people take this to the extreme. Sometimes some people will defend their position to the detriment of the organization, just to avoid the perception of being labeled as wrong. Others will reason their way out of a situation, mortgaging their integrity as they do so. A good leader has to be able to admit when he or she is wrong, fix the problem, and learn from the experience.

Becoming a team sergeant in the best military unit in the world was not really an achievement that I anticipated, and the opportunity to become a leader came to me sooner than I wanted. It came in response to senior members in the unit retiring from active service. When my leadership approached and asked me to accept the position, I was floored. Quite frankly, I held my leaders in such high regard that I somewhat feared the opportunity. I felt I didn't have the experience necessary to fill the position, and I was struggling with the fear that I might not be good enough.

I truly believe that the best unit with the best people deserves the best leaders. Was I the type of soldier who warranted such an honor? Initially, I questioned my abilities to live up to the standards that I held my past leaders. Then I said to myself, *What the fuck are you thinking? This is your time to show yourself, and others, what you can do.* It was at that point that I sat down and wrote some thoughts about what I expected from leaders and how I wanted to lead. The following is what I wrote (some of which was based on earlier lessons) and what I believed was and is important for me to be and do at the time.

Rob's Things to Remember

ALWAYS DO THE HARD RIGHT OVER THE EASY

WRONG. Focus on the operation, personnel, and maintenance for future operations, and then think about me.

NEVER BECOME THE LEADER OR THE PERSON YOU DO NOT WANT TO BE.

SEEK RESPONSIBILITY AND TAKE RESPONSIBILITY FOR YOUR ACTIONS - GOOD AND BAD.

REMEMBER YOU ARE JUST PART OF THE MASTER PLAN. Do not be so arrogant as to think that the world revolves around you. Look outside of your world to see what everyone else is doing, and make sure to do your part for the unit and your team. You can learn something from everyone (right or wrong, good or bad). Greater men before you have done a lot more with a lot less. Never think that you deserve more because of where you work or what you've done. The only thing you deserve is the opportunity to work with people around you.

BASICS. The one thing that makes us great men and a great organization is that we are masters of the basics. Always go back to the basics.

CONDUCT REALISTIC TRAINING. Train to a standard that is realistic and combat focused. It cannot be overstated that training where the only thing missing is enemy fire is of the utmost importance. Never "finger drill" anything. If you wouldn't do it during combat, then don't do it in training (within reason). NEVER train to time. ALWAYS train to do the task till it is done right, regardless of what "they" say or think. The end result is confidence in yourself and your team. Expect the worst and prepare for it.

RESPECT AND TRUST. Trust your people and earn their trust in return. If you can't do this, don't work with them. Give them the ability to tell you where you are wrong, and have the self-respect and intelligence to listen and change if needed. True friends will tell you when you are wrong. Saboteurs and people who want to see you fail will talk behind your back.

PLAN TO THE HIGHEST STANDARD. Don't just plan for a mission, develop the BEST plan you can for the mission.

TIME IS AN IMPORTANT RESOURCE. Keep the BS down at work and let your people go home. Always schedule family time. If you are doing nothing - DON'T DO IT HERE.

BONDING. You must have a close team to work well together. The tightest bond between fighting men is when they bleed, suffer, and drink together.

Don't just read these, live by them.

These were the fundamental guiding principles that I was determined to live by. At this point, I felt the worst thing I could do was to be a bad leader to my people. I gave copies of these principles to all of my subordinates. I didn't expect them to live by them like I did, but felt it was important for them to know where I was coming from and what they could expect from me.

***

Basic training graduation with my mom and little brother, Eddie, August 1988.

The most influential leader for me in my first unit, Captain Arthur A. Sobers Jr., 1990.

ROBERT A. TRIVINO

DEPARTMENT OF THE ARMY
HEADQUARTERS, XVIII AIRBORNE CORPS AND FORT BRAGG
FORT BRAGG, NORTH CAROLINA 28307-5000

REPLY TO
ATTENTION OF: 7 May 1990

SPC ROBERT TRIVINO
HHC XVIII Abn Corps
Fort Bragg, NC 28307

1. RANGER! Thank you for support during my tenure with the Air Defense
Element. You were very patient, respectful, and professional. Your
selection as driver of the month and the impressions you made on the
colonels who run the G3 also reflected favorably on me. Thanks.

2. I am very confident that you will do well in this Army. Just remember
to get plenty of rest, eat well, and keep your feet and knees together.
When you get to RANGER school remember these lines:

    WHEN YOU'RE UP AGAINST A TROUBLE MEET IT SQUARELY FACE TO FACE
    LIFT YOUR CHIN, SET YOUR SHOULDERS, PLANT YOUR FEET AND TAKE A
    BRACE.
    WHEN IT'S VAIN TO TRY TO DODGE IT DO THE BEST THAT YOU CAN DO
    YOU MAY FAIL BUT YOU MAY CONQUER...SEE IT THROUGH!

3. Good Luck and again thanks.

———————— ARTHUR A. SOBERS JR.
         CPT(P) AD

Here is the letter that Captain Sobers wrote for me when he left the section.
His words gained significance for me as I matured as a soldier.

Ranger School graduation, Spring 1992. I'm at the far left, with a few of my classmates.

1st Squad (Deerhunters), 2nd Platoon, A Company, 2nd Ranger Battalion. This photo was taken after about a month as a new team leader. I'm at the far left.

My squad, our platoon leader, and a machine gun team in Haiti, Operation
Uphold Democracy, 1994. I'm standing, second from the right.

Training for a U.S. Army Special Missions Unit selection course at the base
of Mount Rainier, Washington, 1995.

My first operational team in a Special Missions Unit, summer 1996.

Trying to keep my pistol reloads close to one second.

Brand new team sergeant, Military Free Fall Training, 1999.

My sniper team in the spring of 2001.

Visiting Ground Zero in New York City, November 2001.

My first deployment to Afghanistan, January, 2002.

My team moving to an observation point in support of Operation Anaconda, March 2002.

Finishing a two week mounted patrol, summer 2002 Afghanistan. Members of our unit wore NYPD and NY City Fire Department patches into battle in honor of those who served their fellow Americans on September 11th.

Three former Blacksheep Rangers. L to R, Brian Stover, me, and Eric
Bohannon. Iraq, Thanksgiving day, 2005.

My boss and I departing for another mission, Iraq, 2006.

My sister and I on Pueblo De Cochiti feast day.

Teaching a rifle course at the Indiana SWAT Officers Association Conference. I also taught urban tactics and gave a leadership seminar.

September 11, 2001, Fort Bragg, NC

I met with my team at approximately 8 am on September 11, 2001, and we discussed the day's schedule. Our morning was slow. We all needed to catch up on paperwork and return equipment used for training earlier in the week. I had to return a freefall parachute that I'd signed out for weekend freefall training and I also needed to reply to a number of e-mails that I'd prioritized lower than team training.

I entered the common area of my unit after dropping off my parachute at the rigger's shed. There was a small crowd of operators sitting and standing around the television. I looked at the television and saw one of the twin towers smoking. I asked the guys what was going on. One of the communications specialists looked at me and said, "An airplane crashed into one of the World Trade Center towers in New York City. No one knows if it was an accident or what." I thought to myself, *how could an airplane accidentally crash into one of the tallest buildings in the United States?*

After a few minutes of news watching I continued on with my daily duties. Later that morning I was in another section of the unit, trying to track down some personal equipment that I left in the parachute bag that I turned in earlier that morning. I went to my friend Jason's team room and asked if he found any gear in the parachute bag that he signed out after I turned it in. I looked in the bag and found my gear, and we talked briefly about the situation in New York City. That's when I found out about the second airplane striking the second tower.

We speculated over what was happening, and then Jason said in somewhat of a joking manner, "Things are crazy, and I think we'd be safer outside of this building." I thought about it for a few seconds and that's when it hit me - the seriousness and magnitude of the events. I said good bye to Jason and went back to my team room to catch up on some email.

A few hours later we got tidbits of information about potential deployments, clearly leaders at all levels of the government and military were reacting to what was going on, and no one was sure what would happen next. After a few days the potential deployment warnings stopped and on September 14 Operation Noble Eagle began. Operation Noble Eagle was the mobilization of National Guard and military reserve units to assist with homeland security. They provided security on military installations, airports, and at other locations considered potential terrorist targets. I realized we were in for a long road ahead.

It was one thing to see the images on TV, but the true impact of 9/11 was hard to realize until we got to ground zero a couple months later for a training event. We coordinated this training event in Manhattan shortly after the attacks and worked together with the New York City Police Department, who hosted us and supported the training. The seriousness of the situation and the terrorist threat were made more real, and definitely more personal. In fact, we later wore the NYPD and FDNY patches into battle in their honor.

Our final segment of training culminated a couple of blocks away from ground zero, and after we finished, we visited ground zero itself. We were given a short, ten minute brief by some of the officers that responded to the incident, and they shared some of their experiences with us. It was all still fresh and raw in their minds and hearts, and it was clear that they did a lot to try and help. I had never visited NYC before, so the magnitude and scale of the buildings coupled with the understanding of what happened here were almost too much to comprehend.

At the time of our visit workers had already removed all of the fallen debris, but there was still a smell of wet concrete and dust in the air. Spotlights shone on what was left of the fallen buildings, and we all stood for several minutes just trying to take it all in. Damage on adjacent buildings showed how high the rubble had been piled up. Even higher were scars left by falling debris from the two towers during their collapse. The destruction was astounding, the sadness and loss nearly palpable in the air.

I tried to imagine how the people and first responders must have felt during the time of the attack... the chaos, the enormity of the destruction, the attack on the second tower while they were trying to save people from the first. I tried to put myself in their shoes - *what would I have done?* What would you have done?

After that visit I knew that life for me, as an American soldier, would change. And the lives of all Americans as well. The following month I deployed to Afghanistan in support of the Global War on Terrorism.

November 2001, Fort Bragg, NC

"Bulldog 06, this is Greyhound 71, infiltration of the assault force complete...over." The helicopter infiltration commander radioed to the overall commander.

"Roger Greyhound 71, I copy infil of the assault force complete...over."

"Bulldog 06 this is Silver 45, building one secure, moving to building two, over." The ground force leader radioed the overall commander.

There were a handful of us clustered around the satellite radio's speaker, listening to the radio traffic from the operation going down on other side of the world. It was a standard, large-scale, direct-action assault. The mission was to find a high value target (HVT). Shortly after the September 11th attacks part of our unit deployed to Afghanistan to initiate the War on Terror, but I was still state-side, listening to it all go down.

At that point it was common knowledge that Al Qaeda was behind the 9/11 attacks, and the entire organization was in everybody's crosshairs, especially Osama bin Laden. We could hardly wait for our turn to head into the action, to exact some revenge on the terrorists who assaulted our country. Unfortunately, we were in a holding pattern, and all we could do was train and follow the action from afar as our colleagues in Afghanistan were in the moment. So, we sat around the speaker, listening, like Americans did during World War II before mass production of the television set. It was early in the evening at Ft. Bragg, North Carolina, and with a nine-hour time differential that meant that it was early in the morning in Afghanistan and the operation had already started.

We monitored the radio traffic as the aircraft inserted the assault force on the target. Something was wrong. We couldn't tell exactly what happened, but it was clear to us based on the radio traffic that one of the inserting helicopters experienced a rough landing. We surmised that the helicopter was damaged, but the extent of the damage was unknown. You could hear a pin drop as we listened, and I couldn't help but feel a little strange about the entire situation. Here I was, back home, listening to an operation taking place far away, and learning that perhaps some of my fellow unit members might be hurt, or worse, as a result of the helicopter landing. I couldn't help but feel a bit ashamed for not being there and being able to bear the burden with them. We continued to listen and wait for any news on the condition of our teammates.

As the mission progressed, we followed the status of the assault based on the reports from the leadership on the ground. We could tell when they made entry into buildings, once each building was secure, and when the entire target area was secure. We were on the edge of our seats, waiting to hear a radio transmission that the HVT was either captured or killed.

"Bulldog 06, this is Silver 45. Location secure. Target not on scene. Repeat. Target not on scene. Out." No one said a word as the radio transmission was given stating that the HVT was not found. We continued to listen to the radio traffic and followed the progression of the assault all the way through the exfiltration of the assault force. Once we heard the pilots radio that they were clear of the objective area with all their people onboard, we all left the room. I walked back to my team room, anxiously awaiting the opportunity to get over there and get into the fight.

The team room door closed behind me, and I found myself alone with the pungent smell of weapons cleaning solvent still present from our weapons maintenance earlier in the day. I sat down and began thinking about the war, the overall situation, and the future difficulties we would be facing, both professionally as well as personally. During my time in the unit we hadn't experienced any extremely long deployments, and we hadn't suffered any casualties. I knew the future was going to hold situations where serious injuries and death were going to become a harsh reality. As a leader, I would be one of the ones bearing the burden of telling family members that their father, husband, brother, or son was killed in action. I wasn't sure if I was well prepared to do that, but I don't think anybody ever really is.

As I selfishly reflected on myself and my own teammates, I felt a twang of guilt as I realized that a tremendous amount of people were already suffering. My people...fellow Americans. On September 11, 2001, there were a lot of innocent lives affected; those who were killed or injured during the attacks, and the many more who would carry the losses and pain in their everyday lives. Now I wanted to get into this war more than ever. As I left my team room and headed home, I found a calming comfort in knowing that I had made the right decisions in life so far. Decisions that got me exactly where I wanted to be: ready to go to war for my country. It couldn't happen quickly enough for me.

The next two months were filled with continued reports from the front as the fight wore on. We continually trained for what we thought the conflict was going to be, but reports from the guys in the mix told of a fight we did not envision. The current battlefield in Afghanistan was nothing like the unit had encountered in the past, and definitely not something that we trained for on a regular basis. Some of the teams, especially the climbing, sniper, and reconnaissance teams, which had spent time training in mountainous and rural environments, still were not fully prepared for what was being encountered. Just a year before, my team and I spent two weeks in the Teton National Forest in Wyoming, training primarily on winter skills like skiing, winter survival, and cold-weather operations. Although Wyoming has similar terrain, our focus was more on operating in snowy and extremely cold environments which we hoped would prepare us for Afghanistan. Time would tell.

As the team sergeant of a sniper element, I knew that some of the most important capabilities would be in sniper and reconnaissance roles. One of my responsibilities was to master all of the team equipment, which included special sniper weapons systems and all manner of special and tactical communications equipment, such as the tactical satellite radio system. This made me one of a handful of operators in my small element that were completely proficient on the radio systems, aside from the designated communication specialists. I wish I could say that I foresaw the potential importance of the communication devices and therefore, that was why I decided to focus on them, but that was not the case. Rather, as a team leader, I felt it was important for me to master all assigned equipment, specifically the most efficient and effective operation and deployment of each item, before I would ask my teammates to do the same. I was responsible for teaching new team members the caveats of all the items, including most of the specialized weapons and all other team equipment. The radio system is the lifeline for all sniper and reconnaissance teams. Without being able to call for support, a small team could possibly find themselves in deep shit really fast.

December 2001 arrived, and the guys in my group were getting antsy. They couldn't believe we were not deployed yet, and felt like we were going to miss the war. I can remember walking by the common area, stopping by the bulletin board to check on any updates and seeing an extra large Snickers bar thumb-tacked up with a note stating, *"Not going anywhere?"* Obviously, this was a play on the Snickers commercials at the time, where an actor would pull out a Snickers bar and eat it while waiting for something. The joker made sure he got the largest Snickers bar he could find, meaning that we weren't going anywhere for a while. At the time, it was appropriately funny, in an odd sort of way. Once I finished reviewing the board I made my way up to the chow hall for some lunch.

My team and I had spent the morning on the range with our sniper rifles and definitely needed to refuel. I loaded my plate with veggies plus extra jalapenos from the salad bar (I grew up eating New Mexican chile at most meals and have yet to find a food too spicy for me). I sat down with my team for lunch, and overheard the conversation at the table, which focused on a possible deployment. One of my team members was immediately interested because he was next to the guy with the "intel." As was the norm, speculation flew like airplane traffic out of Atlanta's Hartsfield Airport; massive and continuous. I tried to eat my food in silence, but my curiosity got the best of me and I inquired. "So what's the deal, dude?"

"I'm not sure, Rat, but it sounds like they're getting ready to send some people out. They've not said anything about the size or numbers, but it looks like it might happen."

"Wow, that'd be fucking awesome it if pans out. All we can do is wait and see," I said.

I speculated that the chow-hall-net caught wind that the command might be looking at deploying additional forces to assist with advance force battlefield preparation. Basically, teams would deploy and assist with finding the enemy and establishing the conditions to either kill or capture any enemy personnel that were located. I continued to listen and figured, like most chow hall info, that there was about a fifty percent chance that the information was solid. Still, this was more hope for deployment than I had before I sat down to eat, and I couldn't help but feel a little bit of excitement.

As I made my way to my team room after lunch, I was approached by my sergeant major. He spoke briefly about identifying and training a select group of folks for deployment, and he wanted me to assist with training. These lucky few would need training on communications and gear specific to reconnaissance missions. Even though the deployment was not solid, leadership wanted to be ready when the call arrived. Finally, this was it, what we all wanted, a chance to deploy! Without hesitation I agreed, and began mentally developing a training schedule and prioritizing the tasks to my team. Later that same day, each troop named six individuals to begin the training process for potential deployment: a pool from which the final small group would be chosen. Those selected were from assault elements. Therefore, the majority of the training would focus on sniper and reconnaissance capabilities, as well as utilizing tactical satellite communications.

Over the years I had acquired a distinct skill set that was tailor-made for this assignment, due in large part to my tenure as a sniper. This is what set me apart from the rest of the group, nothing else, as everyone in my unit was extremely capable. In most deployments or missions, snipers are the first ones on location, usually arriving days before the assault element. They are always the last ones to leave the target, covering their assaulting teammates' exit. When the command to go is given, the assault teams approach quickly, get the job done efficiently, and then exchange high fives as they are leaving the target location with all the glory. The snipers are left behind to surreptitiously make their way back. If they are lucky they will catch a ride home with the assault force, but other times they may find themselves walking out.

In most training missions, the snipers come back late to find the assault teams already cleaned up, relaxing, waiting for the snipers' return for the After Action Review. As inglorious as that may sound, I loved being a sniper. It was standard procedure for snipers to routinely operate alone, with their team leader somewhere in tow. As a sniper team leader for my unit, I was armed with the autonomy to make immediate decisions without necessarily consulting the leadership. The trust my leadership had in me made me more confident in my leadership and decision making .

It was mid-December, and we were just over a week into training on the satellite communications systems, working on set up, break down and troubleshooting. The training was progressing smoothly. During one of the training sessions I was approached by my command sergeant major, and it was obvious that he had some information for me. He advised me that the leadership decided to deploy a single team to Afghanistan in the near future, and that he wanted me to lead it. The team's task was going to be battlefield preparation, a military term meaning that the team's primary mission would be locating terrorists and establishing the conditions to capture or kill them. This team would be working independently from the other unit members already deployed. I stood outside in the rain as he explained the situation to me, and I almost couldn't believe what he was telling me. He ended his conversation with, "Rat, you can request anyone you want for the deployment, but the team is limited to two people including yourself. You have to be ready in 48 hours."

"Roger that, Sergeant Major. I've got a lot to think about before I make my decision if that's okay."

"Sure thing, just let me know who you want so we can get the ball rolling."

"Yes, Sergeant Major."

After arriving at my team room, I gathered my teammates and explained the situation to them. It was obvious to me that they all were eager to go, but unfortunately that was not the directive. "Hey, guys, here's the deal. The sergeant major just dropped a bomb on me. He said he wants me to be the team leader for the team that's deploying. Right now it looks like they want just a two-man team, so some of you will not be able to go. Sorry, fellas, that's all the news I have right now. Once I get additional information I'll update you guys."

Later that day, I asked if I could see my commander, command sergeant major, and my direct leadership to discuss the deployment. We met shortly thereafter in the commander's office. I entered the meeting with every intention of selling the advantages and necessities for deploying my entire team to my superiors. After a short time I learned there was more to the deployment than I initially thought, and the commander informed me that the restriction was placed on them by the Joint Special Operations Command (JSOC) Headquarters. My commander could sense my disappointment, and then informed me that he received approval to increase the team size to three. Although not perfect, this was better than two. He stated that the third member of the team would be a Combat Control Team (CCT) member provided by the Air Force 24th Special Tactics Squadron (STS).

My unit worked well with the members of the 24th STS in the past, and I hoped that our assigned combat controller was an individual that I worked with before. Regardless, a combat controller would be a great addition to the team because of their unique skill set, one of many being their ability to call on any aircraft for fire support. The command was doing its best to help me out. But the bottom line was, while they knew what I was asking for was correct, their hands were tied. At the end of the meeting, my direct leadership and sergeant major asked to speak with me. "Hey, Rat, here's the deal. We need you to pick someone that was identified to deploy earlier in the month, and not necessarily someone from your team." This took me by surprise, as I wanted to take someone from my team, but now it was suggested I could pick someone else.

After some reflection, I felt there were positives and negatives to both options. Obviously, I wanted to take a team member, but I could see why perhaps the sergeant major might want me to select someone outside the team. Perhaps he didn't want me to deplete the team of experience, thus limiting the unit's combat capabilities. Or perhaps he knew if I selected someone that wasn't identified in the initial selection process for deployment that it might cause concerns of favoritism. The fact was that several of my new team members didn't have the experience yet to operate the tactical radios on their own. Ultimately, I never asked for his reasoning and toed the line, ending our conversation by replying, "Roger that."

I needed to make my choice quickly, because we needed to pack our equipment and be ready to deploy within forty-eight hours. I took a look at the names on the list and decided to select my best friend Raymond Redley. Ray joined the unit a few years after I did. I didn't choose him because of our friendship, I chose him because I had worked closely with him for many years and I trusted him completely. He was and is a great operator.

I was growing concerned with our task once we hit Afghan soil. We needed to prepare and pack for this mission, and as the team leader, I felt like I should give some guidance to the team regarding what we might be asked to do. The hunt for Osama Bin Laden was on, and the teams currently on the ground were using a lot of close air support, primarily delivering two-thousand-pound joint direct attack munitions (JDAMs), which were something I personally had never utilized. I had called in supporting fire from a number of aerial assets, but I never even thought of using JDAMs. These bombs have an internal guidance system linked with a global positioning system (GPS), which makes them somewhat of a "smart bomb." They were the munitions of choice in the mountainous terrain. On our end, all we had to do was send the pilots a grid coordinate of the enemy's location, and the pilots would program the guidance system to strike the location indicated. Obviously, the hard part for us would be finding the enemy and determining their exact location. We made sure we obtained the correct equipment for these tasks, and we also made sure we packed the appropriate equipment and clothing for the weather.

I tried to think about preparing the team based on what I thought we would be doing. Unfortunately for me, at this point, the only thing I knew was that we could be asked to do anything - there are many ways to go about finding the enemy. The mission was ambiguous and we needed to be ready for a wide variety of tasks. I wanted to be prepared for everything but I clearly couldn't bring all of my equipment. As you can imagine, being in the best special missions unit in the world provided me with the opportunity to use and have on hand the best equipment available, but we couldn't bring all of it, and what we did bring had to be fairly portable.

I thought to myself, *How do I provide guidance to my people when I don't know what the team will be tasked with doing?* I decided to focus on the basics, which were being able to shoot, move, communicate, and survive the elements. I learned early on in the unit: the most significant thing that separated us from everyone one else was the near-flawless execution of basic skills at the individual and team levels and above. This allowed us to focus all of our attention on the problem without having to worry about basic issues or tasks that tend to hinder other entities. Obviously, it didn't hurt that the unit's ranks are filled with some of the most intelligent and talented people in the business of conflict.

It was my responsibility to prioritize what to bring to enhance our capabilities, and I relied on my experience to guide me. As I thought about our potential tasks, I knew we would need the capabilities to shoot long distances. I'd bring my sniper rifle, along with my M4, with an M203 grenade launcher attached to the underside of the rail system. Reports from the front told us that our guys were locating targets at long distances and then using fire support to eliminate them. Optics would be key, and most definitely a big force-multiplier, as I needed to see the enemy from afar.

Operations would be conducted during the day, as well as at night, so I made sure I brought the proper equipment for both environments. Staying warm and maintaining that warmth even when relatively immobile meant that proper clothing selection was of the utmost importance. The winters in the mountains of Afghanistan are vicious, making operations difficult, at best. We knew we would probably be hiking a lot and carrying a lot of our gear on our backs, so we brought along several different packs. It was important to establish some team standard operating procedures (SOPs) that outlined our actions for enemy contact and other contingencies. Communications would be critical, so we brought satellite radios, amongst others. In between packing and working on the radios, we spent time refining our SOPs.

As we prepared for war, everyone in our unit was excited for us. Members of other teams asked if we needed help, and offered to assist us with anything we needed. The support made us proud to be a part of this elite unit, and it made Raymond and I feel like we weren't heading out against the enemy by ourselves. We were the initial small force that would soon be joined by the rest of our mates. As the team leader, I felt a little overwhelmed at times. The act of preparing for war wasn't new, but it was a bit difficult to prepare when the mission was so broad and nonspecific. I dealt with this by understanding my position, and what would be expected of me by virtue of my position. I was a leader and member in what I considered to be the best military organization in the world. Greater men before had done much more than I with a lot less support and guidance. I kept my mind in the proper perspective.

At the end of the day, I knew I lacked true combat experience, and recognized that this was affecting my confidence. I never doubted my level of commitment to do what was needed to become the best combat leader possible. I knew I had the individual skills to get the job done. As I look back at my situation, abilities, and state of mind, I realize that I needed to grow personally and professionally. This would be the first of many war time experiences that would profoundly mold and shape me as a person and leader.

It was a brisk morning on December 20, 2001, the day we deployed. After long good-byes with our loved ones at home, we boarded a C-17 cargo aircraft bound for Doha, Qatar. From Qatar we would travel to Afghanistan. Joining Raymond and me was Bruce, a combat controller from the 24th STS. We hadn't worked together before, but he was definitely a welcome addition to the team.

After we loaded our gear onto the aircraft, we were advised that the aircraft was having mechanical problems and the flight could possibly be delayed twenty-four hours, depending on the severity of the problem. So, we left our gear onboard, walked off the ramp, sat on the asphalt and tried to relax with some fresh, cool air.

As we waited on the airfield for news on the aircraft, Raymond, Bruce, and I sat discussing the situation. Raymond said straight out that he hoped that we wouldn't have a lengthy delay. He didn't want to have to say good-bye to his family again. I'm sure leaving his wife and daughter was extremely hard. I, on the other hand, didn't want to get delayed because I wanted to be in the fight already. We eventually departed, and fortunately another round of good-byes was averted.

After a lengthy flight we arrived at Doha, Qatar, at approximately four o'clock in the morning local time. We drove our Toyota truck, which was loaded with our gear and weapons, off the aircraft and looked for someone we knew. We were greeted by a unit logistician, he was there to help us get settled in and to coordinate our travel into Afghanistan. We were excited. Unfortunately, the next available flight didn't have enough room for our vehicle. We discussed taking the first flight and leaving the bulk of our equipment behind to ride on another flight in a few days. Raymond was the only voice of reason when he said, "We probably shouldn't separate ourselves from our equipment, what if we get on the ground and we have get to work straight away?" I knew that he was right but I let my excitement overtake my better judgment. Eventually, I convinced Raymond that our equipment would be left in the capable hands of unit members, and we would survive without all of our gear for a few days. We quickly rummaged through our bags and boxes of gear and found what we needed. We took take our weapons, radios, a rucksack with the bare essentials, and a small camera.

Later that evening, after getting some chow, we made our way back to the airfield to wait for our flight into Afghanistan. We were told that it would take a few hours to get to Bagram Airfield, our link up point with JSOC colleagues who would command our team. We initially flew into a secure forward operating base, dropped off some equipment and picked up a couple of resupply pallets for airdrop to some troops on the ground. Thirty minutes into the next leg of the flight the ramp opened up, and we saw the moon shining on the snow-capped mountaintops of northern Afghanistan as the loadmaster pushed the pallets out of the aircraft. Once the pallets cleared ramp the mountains peaks were in full view, and it seemed as though we could touch them, they looked so close.

After all the supplies were delivered, we were finally on our way to Bagram. The loadmaster announced over the intercom that we were making our descent to the airfield. After we started our initial descent, the pilot began an aggressive corkscrew dive, which surprised everyone onboard. The pilots were not taking any chances, there was a significant threat of surface-to-air-missiles. After our aggressive descent, we landed in the middle of the night.

We put our helmets on with night vision goggles mounted so we were able to see what was happening on the airfield, which was very little.

First impressions last forever, and the impression I got was that we arrived at an abandoned airfield. There were just a few dim lights on in the distance, and the two-story guard tower that I saw was riddled with bullet holes. The night was dark, with no illumination, which required the continued use of night vision gear. I could hear a forklift, but wasn't able to see it until I turned my head; the operator was using night vision goggles as well. I could see a small pickup truck approaching. When it stopped, two people exited, and then walked towards the aircraft's ramp. It was Major Smith, a JSOC commander, and one of his assistants. We greeted each other and began loading our equipment into their truck.

We were driven to the unit's living area, which was a very small tent city. We were given an area in one of the tents and we moved our gear inside and accounted for all our equipment. After a short while we made our way to the headquarters and operations building, which was manned twenty-four hours a day. I linked up with the commander and tried to figure out what our mission might entail. The commander said that he was looking at several options for our team. Our mission depended on how soon one of the options would come to fruition. After a short information dump from the operations officer we determined that we should probably call it a night and have a team meeting in the morning.

The next morning, we knew there was nothing solid for us yet, so we used our extra time to refine our team tasks. One of the most important things we needed to get straight was our team's call-for-fire procedures. The mission to kill Osama Bin Laden in the mountains of Tora Bora was over and unfortunately, he managed to escape and leave the area apparently unharmed. The most significant asset that assisted our forces in killing many Al-Qaeda fighters was the use of air dropped munitions. Members of the unit had dropped a lot of bombs and killed a lot of terrorists. We also knew this to be a dangerous task. Earlier in the war, a Special Forces team sent the wrong grid coordinates to a bomber aircraft, mistakenly passing the grid coordinates to their own location instead of the terrorists' location. A JDAM landed directly on the team, killing and wounding a number of the team members. We wanted to establish a call-for-fire procedure that would make this type of mistake less likely.

About mid-morning I was standing outside the operations building when I was approached by Command Sergeant Major "Ironhead," who was tasked with the mission to hunt down Osama Bin Laden. He and his crew recently returned from the mountains of Tora Bora where they located, chased, and killed many Al-Qaeda fighters. Unfortunately, they were not able to capture or kill the elusive terrorist leader, which weighed heavily on his guys so shortly after the fight. We shook hands, and he explained to me some of the difficulties with the terrain and the cultural issues with the Afghan people. He summed it up by saying, "You know, I never thought we would be hiking in the mountains of Afghanistan with beards, blankets, and pizza hats. Then again, I didn't expect two airplanes to hit the World Trade Center either, so I guess we'd better open our minds or get used to being surprised." (Pizza hat was a term used to describe how his guys looked in the traditional Afghan headgear.) His statement stuck with me during my entire initial deployment.

What real effect would a surprise have if we conditioned ourselves to always expect something, so as not to be surprised? This concept has a deeper connotation. Over time, his statement affected my thought processes as a leader - it taught me to keep my thoughts flexible. I learned to view every situation from different perspectives, including the terrorist's perspective. Basically, we needed to mentally prepare ourselves for situations that we hadn't trained for or possibly envisioned.

For years I trained and prepared for what I thought war would be like for me. Now I was experiencing war, and it was not what I anticipated. It is strange how situations affect you. Standing there in the mud, looking at the snow-packed mountain peaks surrounding Bagram Airfield, I felt myself growing mentally as a leader and soldier. I am grateful that Ironhead's hand was one of the first I got to shake in Afghanistan.

A week after arriving at the Bagram air base, Raymond, Bruce, and I jumped on a fixed wing aircraft that would eventually take us into Jacobabad, Pakistan. We were scheduled to participate in a coordination meeting with a Special Forces team that was planning to come into Afghanistan. We arrived in the middle of the night, and took up bunk space in the hangar where the aircraft parked.

Early the next morning, Raymond and I searched out the meeting location and found the Special Forces team we were to link up with. After talking with the team commander, to our surprise we learned that the meeting was cancelled, and the team commander didn't know when his team would be allowed into Afghanistan.

We realized that there was nothing more we could do, so we needed to get a ride home. We went to the air operations center at the airfield and tried to hitch a ride back to Bagram. We were told that there were no flights scheduled into Afghanistan that day, so we would have to wait for the next day's flight schedule. Well, again, nothing we could do, so we called the hangar home for another night. We returned the following morning and got the same response, "Sorry guys, no flights into Afghanistan, check with us tomorrow." I was trying to figure out what the hell was going on. I could hear multiple aircraft landing and departing throughout the night; you couldn't tell me none of them wouldn't eventually find their way to Afghanistan. The airbase at Jacobabad was one of the main airbases supporting fixed wing aircraft support flights into Afghanistan.

On day three we got the same story at noon, so we went back to our hangar and waited. At approximately 3:00 p.m. I told the guys to pack their gear because we were leaving that night on something, anything, that would take us off the base. We took our equipment to the air operations center and got the same answer, "Sorry, no flights into Afghanistan."

I said, "No problem. You don't mind if we stay the night here and wait for a flight, do you?"

The air operations officer was a little shocked to hear me say this, then he replied, "Sure, put your gear over there." We waited a few hours and after checking with the ops desk I got the same song and dance, "Sorry, no flights for the remainder of the night". *What the hell*, I thought. I walked back to the guys and told them deal and we decided we should spend the night at the air-ops center.

About 30 minutes after we were told there would be no more flights out of the air base, I could hear the unmistakable sound of C-130s landing on the runway just outside the back door. I told the guys to grab their gear, and we walked out the door toward the flight line. There was no one out there to stop us except for a single ground controller that was parking the aircraft as they taxied in. We were wearing our night vision goggles and we surprised the ground controller when we approached; he didn't have night vision. There were three C-130 cargo aircraft sitting on the tarmac with their blades spinning.

The engine noise was so loud, I yelled at the ground controller to ask him where the aircraft were headed. He hollered back, "All over, where do you want to go?"

"We need to get to Bagram, Afghanistan. Any of these going there?"

He jumped on his communications headset and talked with the pilots, and after a minute or two he pointed and said, "Number two is going to Bagram after a stop at K2 (another support airbase in Pakistan); you want to get on?"

"Hell yes!" I said. "Tell the crew to add three to their manifest. We'll give our names and numbers once we're on board." He talked to the crew and we waited for the aircraft to taxi over to our position.

While we waited to board, the old-timer ground controller told us he did this job in Vietnam, and he volunteered to come out and do it in support of the current fight. *Wow*, I thought, *this dude is awesome.* We boarded through the front cargo door with the blades spinning, and five minutes later were on our way home to Bagram.

This single event helped me burst out of my shell as a young leader on the ground. I realized that I, as the leader, am expected to make things happen for the team. I had to be aggressive and smart. I still don't know why the air operations leadership didn't want us to get on one of their aircraft into Afghanistan. The air force at that point in time was still living in a pre-9/11 culture and was extremely risk averse. Who knows why they gave us the run around? What I did know was we were on our way to Bagram airbase without their help.

***

Christmas day was just another day for us in Afghanistan, and we spent the day training and gathering information from the guys that fought in Tora Bora. Two days after Christmas our boss said he had a mission for us. He wanted us to integrate with a Special Forces team in order to establish an outpost in Khowst. We moved lock, stock, and barrel to Kabul to meet the team and start planning.

Khowst is located in a remote area near Afghanistan's eastern border with Pakistan, and is nestled in a large valley, almost completely surrounded by mountains. As we began planning, it was apparent that we lacked a lot of information on the area, and most of the information we did have was provided by the local populace. Khowst had had little, if any contact with the Western world since the Taliban seized control. We needed up-close imagery but there was none in our database. Our maps of the area were restricted in ratio, which made them of limited use, especially if we wanted to read the terrain. Satellite data wasn't available to us until much later in the war, and even then it was limited in its utility due to its scale. Our primary sources of information were people who knew of the area or those that had relatives in Khowst.

We spent the next few days planning and coordinating with a prominent warlord that held a lot of clout in the Khowst region. Most important was his access to soldiers that were extremely loyal to him. It was my understanding that he supported the United States primarily because he had no love for the Taliban. Later I learned that many Afghan people developed a deep hatred for the Taliban because of their ruthless and abusive rule over the people. After reviewing all the information available, we determined that we should proceed with our plan and we coordinated a meeting with the warlord in Khowst. The date was set for the first of January.

I woke up early on January 1st and I was tired; sleep had been difficult with thoughts of the new mission swirling. We performed our final checks and began the day's preparations for the mission. We would be inserting into Khowst by helicopter, so we thought a lot about insertion, as well as coordination efforts with the warlord and his people. As the day progressed into the evening you could see the excitement building in each of us, as this is what we had trained for most of our careers. We loaded our gear onto a jingle truck for transport to the airfield. Jingle Truck was our nickname for some of the cargo trucks in Afghanistan because of the decorative metal chains that hung from their sides which made a jingling sound. My thoughts were focused on what lay ahead for us. We were on our way to finding the enemy, and I couldn't help hoping we might locate Osama Bin Laden himself.

Raymond and I were looking out of the helicopter's windows as it circled the landing zone. As we began our descent, I could see approximately one hundred armed men waiting in the tree line. My heart was beating like a drum as I radioed the information to Raymond. "Switchblade, this is Rat, I have about 100 armed people, some with RPGs (rocket propelled grenades) on my side, over." I thought, *Holy shit! They have to be friendly soldiers or we'd be taking fire already.* He responded with, "Roger. I've got about the same number of guys on my side." His voice sounded much calmer than mine.

When the helicopter touched down, Raymond and I jumped out and posted ourselves on both sides to provide security as the rest of the team unloaded the helicopter. We all monitored the same radio frequency so we were able to communicate with one another and pass vital information. The other team leader made contact with our Afghan host, and that was when we learned that all the armed men were under his control. I was rather relieved to hear that.

There were about half a dozen small pickup trucks waiting to transport us to our host's home. We all moved to the trail of vehicles and began loading the gear. I was at the rear of the vehicles, making sure we didn't leave any gear on the landing zone when over the radio I heard a single word, "**Grenade!!**"

I hit the ground, anticipating an explosion. I could see other team members in the beds of the trucks loading gear, throwing themselves onto the gear, trying to find some type of cover to block the expected shrapnel. Our Afghan hosts were clueless to our actions as we lay on the ground or jumped on top of gear, waiting for a grenade to detonate. They must have thought we were out of our minds. A few seconds later another transmission came across the radio. "All clear. All Clear. Team leaders to the lead vehicle, over."

I made my way forward to the lead truck where I saw a lot more armed men. My sixth sense was telling me something was not right, I could feel tension in the air. I linked up with the rest of the leadership and learned that a rival warlord had arrived and surprised everyone with his soldiers. This was something of a Mexican stand-off between the two warlords, neither one backing down. Through our interpreter we tried to settle things down. Later we learned that the two warlords were fighting over who was going to host us. The team made arrangements with one warlord, and now the rival was trying to force his way onto the invitation list. Eventually the situation calmed, the rival warlord agreed to a meeting with us, the Americans, at his home after we were on the ground a few days. After the excitement we got on our way to a compound in the village.

As we departed, I could see that each warlord brought approximately two hundred fighters with him. It would have been an absolute disaster if the two groups had resorted to gunfire, we would have been right in the middle of it all. Once we cleared the landing zone and got on the bumpy road to the village, I was surprised to see that the road was lined with armed men. Apparently they were there for our protection. What was odd to me was the fact that these armed individuals were facing and pointing their guns at our vehicles as we passed. I'm guessing they wanted to catch a glimpse of the Americans as we went by.

We arrived around midnight at what appeared to be an abandoned school and were immediately led to the second floor, which was designated as our living area. The compound was dark but there was a faint light emitting from a room in one of the other buildings, which I assumed was our host's quarters. There was no electricity in the building, so we wore our headlamps to navigate while we carried our equipment in. After that, the leaders were summoned to a room for tea. The room was partially lined with blankets on the floor and a single kerosene lantern provided light. The first thing I learned about Pashtu culture was the importance of hospitality. Because we were guests, our host was responsible for our well-being. This included keeping us from harm.

The second thing I learned, and probably more important for us to realize, was the fact that nothing got done quickly in Afghanistan. We spent the first part of the meeting exchanging pleasantries over tea and cookies. It took a while before we discussed the particulars of our stay and what we wanted to do the following morning. As the meeting continued, the warlord estimated his army at approximately two hundred, and quickly added that he was able to summon hundreds more, if necessary. We weren't sure of his estimates, but we gave him the benefit of the doubt. The meeting was several hours long, and continued into the early morning. Then we finally hit the rack for some much needed sleep.

I was startled when Raymond woke me for my turn to pull guard duty, waking up in a strange new environment, immediately aware and uneasy. We were living out of our rucksacks, which meant we operated with minimal supplies. We carried mostly ammunition and communications equipment, with about a two weeks' supply of batteries and some warm clothes. Our host gave us some heavy quilt-type blankets to keep the January cold off of our backs. How I wished I had a steaming cup of coffee to help me stay awake. It was about four in the morning, and after about ten seconds I threw the blanket off and got up. I knew if I stayed under the blanket it would only get harder to get up. It is pretty typical for the guy on guard to wake up the relief about five minutes early so the new guard can be fully awake once he assumes his post. Afghan guards were assigned to us, but my team and I felt it would be in our best interest to pull our own guard, just in case.

I pulled my duty, a thirty minute shift, which in my experience is a perfect amount of time for one to remain alert and aware. We were lucky; there were nearly a dozen of us total, though Raymond and I were the only ones who consistently worked together. The rest of the element were individuals from other organizations. As I pulled my guard duty, I thought of the day to come and the tasks that lay ahead of us. I realized we had a full plate and would be busy. The first major task was to drive to the local airfield in order to do an airfield survey; we wanted to see what type of fixed wing aircraft, if any, we could land. We also needed to determine routes in and out of the village and to get a feel for the area. We promised to visit the warlord's security outposts to assess his troops, equipment, and capabilities. The biggest event was a meeting that was to take place mid-morning with our host and his junior leaders to discuss how they would assist us in locating terrorists in the area.

The next morning, the entire team was greeted with hot tea and cookies. I learned to love morning tea, and the green tea was my favorite. We were assigned an Afghan guard that spent most of his time with us, and that morning I tried to talk with him but found it difficult to communicate. Apparently, I was pronouncing the few words I thought I knew incorrectly. I resorted to hand gestures. With all the tasks needing to get done, we figured it best to first deploy a small team to check on the warlord's security outposts in the village. This would give us an idea of the number of fighters he controlled in the village. Plus, it also afforded us the opportunity to check some of their equipment, such as their tanks and technical trucks.

A small group with a handful of team members headed out at approximately 9 am. Raymond, Bruce, and I stayed at the compound. We planned to be part of the next team out, going to check the airfield because Bruce would be conducting the airfield survey and I needed to attend the meeting with our host.

Around 10 am I was summoned to the meeting with the warlord and his senior leaders. We sat around a small table outside and started our meet and greet over tea. I was sitting with my back to the main vehicle gate of the compound when I heard a ruckus and men yelling as a vehicle approached. The local guards at the gate were excited and agitated. A senior team member stood, rapidly grasping his weapon. I stood up and turned around, weapon in hand, and realized that the first team was returning and something was wrong. Very wrong.

The first team out was ambushed. Several people were shot and wounded. As the vehicle stopped in front of me, I realized a team member was severely wounded and was barely conscious sitting on top of some gear in the back of a truck. I called for the team medics, but quickly realized they were way ahead of me and already working on other wounded mates. I assisted the medics in moving the casualties to suitable locations for treatment. There seemed to be more wounded than medics available so they triaged them and got to work on those that needed attention first. I needed to separate myself from the hands-on treatment and figure out the situation.

Once the medics had a handle on the casualties, I grabbed my radio and set up a satellite antenna to make a radio call to our headquarters. I immediately dispatched a message requesting a helicopter medical evacuation to my boss. My radio call consisted of a grid coordinate for the landing zone, number and type of casualties, and then ended with, "Brick 50, be advised this is an immediate request. Over." He responded by informing me that the medical evacuation (MEDEVAC) helicopter would arrive in approximately one hour. The flight time was fifty minutes, and they still needed time to prep and move to the airfield.

I asked a teammate to man the radio for the next fifteen minutes while I moved to determine if all the injured were being helped. They were. There were two of our team members shot, as well as two Afghan soldiers. One team member was severely wounded and had lost a lot of blood. The medics were working on him as I tried to get a grasp on the overall situation. The other team member suffered a gunshot wound in the chest, but luckily he was wearing soft body armor, which slowed the bullet enough to prevent a through-and-through chest wound. I could see that the entry wound was large and oblong, meaning that the bullet tumbled after penetrating the soft body armor. Raymond immediately applied an Asherman's chest dressing. After this, we intentionally separated ourselves from tending to casualties and moved to work on our security perimeter. The real possibility that whoever ambushed the team would be headed to our compound next weighed heavily on our minds. We knew, based on our earlier assessment of the personnel within the village, that we could easily be greatly outnumbered and outgunned. If they came in a large group, we were fucked. We shifted gears and focused on preparing for a significant gunfight and securing a landing zone so we could get our wounded evacuated.

Raymond, several team members, and I gathered quickly to discuss the security of our compound. We really didn't know what to expect, so we addressed worst-case scenarios. The most pressing issue was that the enemy could be there any second. First and foremost was to ensure the enemy couldn't get a vehicle through the gate and inside the compound. We didn't have enough personnel to man a solid perimeter, so I moved with another team member to see how we could utilize the Afghan soldiers. We posted them in key security positions around the compound. Some we physically moved in order to show them where we wanted them because we were unable to communicate with them.

We knew we needed to have a vantage point for observation that afforded us the ability to see the enemy at distance. Unfortunately, the height of the walls around the compound made it difficult to easily see the surrounding area - they were too tall. Raymond volunteered to post himself on the second floor of the main building and manage security from a perch that overlooked the only vehicle gate into the compound. Bruce positioned himself on the roof of the building and was making radio calls to aircraft overhead. He prepared and provided the aircraft with a situation update and gave them preliminary target locations in case we found ourselves in a serious gunfight, which is what we all expected. To say that I was glad that Bruce was present would be an understatement. Once we established our security perimeter, we waited for whatever was going to happen.

After nearly forty-five minutes passed, the expectation of an immediate attack began to subside. That's when I learned that one of our team members died. The team medics worked hard to save him, but he lost too much blood. I couldn't believe the medics kept him alive as long as they did, which was a testament to their skills. Approximately one hour from my initial MEDEVAC call we heard the sound of rotor blades in the distance. They flew low to the ground to avoid taking enemy gunfire, which meant they would have to fly right over the landing zone to see it. As the noise got louder I caught sight of the helicopter and the ground team signaled the helicopter into the landing zone. The casualties were loaded, and the aircraft departed.

When the sound of the rotor blades disappeared, the medics focused their attention on the Afghan casualties, which were not as life-threatening as the American casualties. The more seriously injured man was shot in both legs, one bullet entering just above the ankle, shattering the bone, with another injury to his other calf. He also had a through and through gunshot wound to his upper right leg, luckily it didn't hit the artery or the femur. I asked their leader if he needed any assistance transporting his men to the local medical facility. He explained that they would be taken to Pakistan for treatment, as there were no medical facilities in the village capable of treating them. *Holy shit!* I thought. *Why didn't I get them on the aircraft so they could be treated in Kabul?*

From that point forward, I made sure to have a plan for all the casualties on the ground, both American and Afghan fighters. My justification for this was simple. If the Afghans were willing to fight alongside us, with the understanding that their lives could be lost, then I wanted them to have the best medical treatment available, just the same as our guys. Later that evening, the warlord transported his casualties to Pakistan. This was the norm, since the border was close and not protected by either side. It was especially easy to cross for those with strong ties to the tribes that live along the border.

Dusk fell upon those of us who stayed behind, and it weighed heavily on me that our small team had just gotten smaller. We lost a teammate. That loss was profound and is impossible to adequately describe here, words like sadness and responsibility aren't enough. I wondered how my injured teammate was doing. I thought about these things as we mounted our night vision goggles and waited for the fight that never came that night. Bruce stayed up all night communicating with the support aircraft, which he kept overhead the entire time. For a while my thoughts focused on my earlier decisions, and I wondered if I could have done anything different or better. In the end I realized that the war just hit me in the face, and now it was time for me to see if I had the internal resolve to stay the course. My focus shifted and I concentrated on what needed to get done next.

As one of the leaders on the ground, I was faced with the decision to stay or pull my team out of the area. Our command was waiting for our input and my final recommendation. This particular fight just got personal. With the loss of our teammate (who was the first soldier officially killed in action during the War on Terror) nobody on the team wanted to dishonor him or his level of commitment by quitting and retreating. We all wanted to stay. Ultimately, that decision would not be ours.

As night came, so did all the questions about the events of the day from those in pay grades way above ours. We passed the information along, with the recommendation to remain at our location. I requested additional forces to bolster our numbers since the current element was so small. Headquarters quickly went to work and within twenty-four hours they informed us that we would be getting a squad of Army Rangers to help us out. This was good news. More guns manned by Rangers would be a welcome addition to our team.

"Brick 53…you are cleared to remain on the ground and continue your mission, anticipate receiving your Ranger support within 48 hours, over." After receiving the approval, we were busy making arrangements to move our base location to the nearby airfield. As a leader I knew it was my responsibility to figure out how to guide these guys in the right direction. I learned firsthand that we were in a true war and our leaders displayed their resolve by allowing us to stay. I questioned my readiness, especially in light of the ambush, casualties, and the loss of a teammate. Was I the right soldier for the job? Initially, my confidence was a bit off kilter, but I was determined to stay the course. I had the distinct honor of not only being part of but leading an elite group of fighting men in the War on Terror. Some of the best in the world. This is what I wanted. It was time to get to work.

***

My joint team and I had been in Khowst, Afghanistan, just over two weeks, and the scars of our first engagement with the enemy were still a little raw. Like a lot of people who experience war and the rigors of combat, we found ourselves still mentally fighting (and critiquing) that fight. There was little action to distract us from the experience, and we were mentally stuck in the mud without even realizing it.

We moved from the compound owned by our Afghan host and established our own tactical outpost at the local airfield. The promised squad of Rangers arrived, followed shortly thereafter by a platoon of Marines which allowed the Rangers to get back to their unit. The Marines' primary mission was to assist us with base security. During this time we received a visit from some of our bosses. One of the visitors was Jimmy Rase, an officer that I served under in the Rangers. When I was first assigned to the Ranger Regiment, then First Lieutenant Rase was serving as the company executive officer and left a few months after my initial assignment. Now Major Rase moved up the ranks in the officer world and was serving as the second in command overseeing the teams on the ground.

His visit to the outpost was a welcomed one. He came with a new armored Suburban for us to use and provided updates on issues outside of our outpost and the war. The day after his arrival, we sat down for a talk. "Well, Rat, looks like you've got the ball rolling here, establishing your new camp."

"Roger that, it was good to get out of the middle of the city. Now we have some decent fields of fire. We just have to finish setting this place up and we'll be rockin'" I said.

Jimmy continued, "Hey, I want to let you know about something I've noticed since I got here. You guys are in a rut and you need to get out of it. Some of your guys have bunker syndrome, brother."

I was surprised at what he said. "Really? I'm not sure what you're seeing, but we're staying in the fight here. I'll try to identify and stay on top of your concerns."

"Don't get me wrong, Rat, you guys can run this place by yourselves. This is a small issue I know you can fix, I just wanted to make sure you are aware of it."

Had we lost our aggressiveness and gotten bogged down? Clearly, he trusted me enough to bring this to my attention. Unfortunately, I didn't return that trust, and I let my anger get the best of me. I got pissed and then, thankfully, I bit my tongue. I left the immediate area at my first opportunity to gather my thoughts before I said something I'd regret.

I found a quiet spot outside of a dirt wall near the parked vehicles, sat down on the ground, and sifted through all my thoughts and feelings. *How the hell can he question anything we did? He wasn't even on the ground when we fought the enemy. Who the hell was he to Monday morning armchair quarterback us? Leaders shouldn't second-guess the guys on the ground! This was a lesson the unit learned many years ago and re-learned during the battle of Mogadishu. A good leader listens to the guy on the ground and takes what he says as gospel.*

As I kept thinking about the issues, I finally realized he wasn't second-guessing our actions during the fight. Major Rase cared enough to inform me of what he currently observed of our team. He was simply trying to advise me of a problem he was seeing so I could fix it, and here I was being defensive rather than listening and trying to improve. Damn it!

My anger turned to embarrassment. As one of the leaders, I was responsible for establishing the tone for the team, and the outpost as a whole. As I thought about the problem, I began to feel that I failed the team by allowing us to feed off each other's emotions and remain in the mental quicksand of our first engagement. As the leader, I needed to have the ability to mentally and emotionally remove myself from the team and view things from a different, unbiased perspective. The current environment was one of group think, where some atmosphere of collective negative thought developed, and I needed to make changes immediately.

Major Rase's visit was the best thing that happened to me as a young leader. He taught me a hard lesson that I never forgot. Leaders are responsible for creating a good work environment. To be a good leader, I needed to learn how to create a new environment for the team and allow them to process and learn from their experiences without getting bogged down in them. It had to start with me - subordinates can and will take your view on the situation, especially if you are a respected leader.

The most impressive angle of the whole encounter was the manner in which he expressed his observations to me. There is not a good leader alive, or in the past, that would ever do something to demean his or her subordinates in front of others. Major Rase's manner was non-confrontational, and his timing was like clockwork. He approached me away from the men, when there was no one else around. Once I got over my defensiveness, I took his concerns to heart and worked to fix the problem. I felt like I had failed my team, in part due to my lack of combat experience. This was my first time as a leader in an unknown and unpredictable, dangerous environment, and I learned a lot from it.

On a personal level, I vowed to never allow the enemy to affect me in such a way again. I promised myself that I would always err on the side of aggressiveness when dealing with my adversary. I realized the enemy would capitalize on any form of weakness. Looking back at my combat experiences I know I kept true to my promise. Depending on who you ask, some might say I took this notion a little too far at times. As a leader I knew I had to show courage in action, as well as moral courage on and off the battlefield. I needed to demonstrate through my actions because I knew people would follow leaders that do. As the old cliché goes, talk is cheap.

Over the next few weeks, we developed a strong relationship with the newly formed Khowst Regional Afghan Army element. This army was created by a recently arrived Special Forces team. Sometime during the third week after the Special Forces team's arrival, the senior Afghan Army leader's vehicle convoy was ambushed in an area northeast of Khowst. Four of his soldiers were killed, and the Afghan commander narrowly escaped being killed himself. When he arrived on base he was extremely angry, and explained that he was ambushed by members of the Naim Kuchi tribe.

With our American contingent of leaders present, we were briefed on the situation by the commander through an interpreter. The first order of business was trying to determine if this was a tribal conflict between the two tribes, or possibly Taliban or Al-Qaeda fighters looking to attack a weak target. We continued with questions, and the commander was adamant that members of the Kuchi tribe were responsible and that they were allied with the Taliban. The leaders determined that any next course of action should include the use of the newly formed Afghan Army. The final decision was unanimous, we were moving against the enemy.

My team's first priority was to formulate a plan of action. The plan called for Raymond, Bruce, Scott (a Special Forces medic) and me to lead the entire force in our Toyota hi-lux pickup truck. This was no easy task for any of us, as this was going to be the newly formed Afghan Army's first time conducting an actual mission. The simplest of tasks were going to prove monumental and it was difficult for us because we had never conducted a mission with a force this large and inexperienced. Coordination and communication were critical. Unfortunately, communication would be hampered by the language barrier (we only had two translators). The Special Forces team chose approximately forty Afghan soldiers, loaded them onto their trucks, and we moved out.

Raymond, Bruce, and I knew this particular area and terrain well. I wanted to be in front so we could find a vantage point from which to view the enemy's position in case Bruce needed to call in air support. We found a good piece of high ground, and the Afghan Army, with the guidance of the Special Forces team, began their movement forward. Our initial maneuver force spotted the enemy and quickly got a fix on their location so we moved to link up with the forward team. We made our way to a hilltop closer to their position to get a bird's eye view of the situation.

We could see approximately fifteen enemy fighters on top of a large hill. Their location was definitely key terrain because it had a commanding view of the entire area and they knew where our maneuver force was located. We could see them posturing for our advance by preparing RPGs and machine guns around their positions. I used the laser range finder to determine the distance to the enemy and was surprised to learn that they were four hundred and fifty meters away. We wanted to use air assets, if feasible, since we knew we would be fighting uphill. This was an important issue because the aircraft over head were carrying two thousand pound JDAM bombs from which the minimum safe distance for our force would be eight hundred meters.

I made the decision to call in fire support only if the maneuvering force was able to get behind some form of solid cover. Something that could stop bomb shrapnel. They found and moved behind some terrain that would block the blast and its effects. To my surprise, a few enemy fighters advanced their positions and attempted to engage those of us that they could see, a mistake they would soon regret. Once I received confirmation that everyone was in position I told Bruce to contact the aircraft and let the pilot know that he was clear to drop his goodies.

"Thunder 41 this is Brick 53, you are cleared hot... over."

Bruce radioed the aircraft overhead, received an initial response and was then given a countdown from the pilot after he released his ordnance. We all watched and waited for the explosion. I actually saw the bomb in its entirety for a split-second as it impacted the ground, before it detonated. It looked as big as a car, and was absolutely unbelievable.

Unfortunately, the first bomb landed short. Because of the terrain, the bomb had minimal effect on the enemy, although it landed within seventy five meters of the position. The hilltop had approximately a thirty square meter area of walkable terrain before it dropped almost immediately to nearly a forty-five degree angle down the mountain. Because of the severe angle, the bomb wasn't as effective, as it landed on the steep downward slope. The bomb didn't kill any of the fighters, if you can believe it. It landed close, but it would have to land directly on top of the hill in order to kill those that manned the position.

Bruce radioed the pilot and brought him in for another run. Several minutes later, the far side of the enemy's position exploded, followed by a large mushroom cloud. By this point, most of the enemy fighters elected to abandon their post, so we cleared our maneuver force to move up the hill. As the maneuver element pushed towards the enemy I saw a small group of enemy fighters approach us from a flank, through a saddle in the terrain. As they closed the distance I could see they were carrying a white flag and waving it in the air. It was the leader of the tribe that occupied the position, and he was requesting a meeting.

We moved forward anticipating a ruse, and when we arrived we set up security positions. The Special Forces team commander and I moved forward with the interpreter and the leader from the Afghan army element to meet with the Kuchi tribal leader. Introductions were short, and the first thing the tribal chief requested was to stop the bombardment. We agreed to stop and our discussion then focused on the sequence of events that started the fighting. After a few minutes it became obvious that we were in the middle of a tribal conflict. One thing was clear to me early in the dialogue; neither side had any love for the other. As I listened I surmised that the Kuchi tribe had no formal alliance with the Taliban or Al Qaeda.

After about fifteen minutes of discussion, the leaders on both sides agreed to establish a truce and we advised the rest of our forces to prepare to move back to camp. When our Afghan soldiers heard this, they stopped what they were doing and started ransacking the belongings of the Kuchi tribe. I saw this and thought to myself, *This cannot be happening.*

It began quickly and within seconds our Afghan soldiers were in a looting frenzy. It was a surreal situation and as I looked at the Special Forces commander we stated almost in unison, "We've got to stop this!" The Special Forces commander ran forward to link up with his guys who were trying to control the situation, but the Afghan soldiers were like sharks in water with the scent of blood.

I snatched up the interpreter and headed directly to the commander of the Afghan soldiers. In order for this to cease, I knew I needed to be aggressive with him so he would understand that I was serious. I ran directly to the commander and told him to stop his men immediately. The commander looked at me, clearly perplexed at my request, and somewhat indignant. I persisted with my request and I wouldn't give him a chance to discuss the situation, I simply kept forcing my request upon him and getting more aggressive with him. This situation was something straight out of the Special Forces training I received during the qualification course called Robin Sage; I never thought I would experience such a thing, but here I was right in the middle of it. The Afghan commander's attitude changed when the Special Forces team commander arrived and threatened to stop payment to both him and his soldiers. Our Afghan partner and commander looked perplexed, but he knew we were serious especially now that we were threatening to take his money away.

Within a few seconds, something strange happened ... it rained... and it rained hard. It was like divine intervention. That's the only thing that made sense to me at the time. We knew that it might rain, but we never expected the deluge that was coming down on us. Regardless, the rain came down so hard and fast that it made our Afghan soldiers slow the madness, which allowed our guys to get the situation under control. The heavy rain lasted nearly five minutes before it tapered off but it was enough time for the Special Forces team to grab their Afghan soldiers and physically pull them away from the situation.

Once the teams regained control of all their Afghan soldiers we made our way to our vehicles. It was time to get the hell out of there. It rained so much in such a short amount of time that the small creeks that we needed to cross swelled into rivers, which made getting back to camp risky to say the least.

After returning to our outpost we focused initially on the maintenance of our equipment. Later that evening we got together for a team after action review. We reviewed the engagement and identified some issues that needed attention. The majority of our issues were related to our team procedures for calling in air fire support. From a leadership perspective, I wanted to work on the coordination with the Special Forces team.

At the end of the meeting, after all the team members left, I stayed in our operations room and tried to make sense of the day's events. I needed to improve my knowledge of the various tribes and traditional fighting between our Afghan soldiers and other local tribes. The soldiers didn't seem to think they were doing anything wrong; I was told it was standard procedure, not only for our soldiers but for the Kuchi tribe as well. In our soldiers eyes they won the fight, and in the Kuchi's eyes they lost and it seemed like both sides understood their positions.

As an American soldier and leader of American fighting men, I had to ensure that we followed the rules of land warfare. It was my responsibility as the team's leader to ensure that our understanding of the rules that govern our actions was rock solid. I fully believe the enemy should die if the situation calls for it but I also had a responsibility to protect those on the battlefield that didn't have the means to protect themselves.

Knowing your team or people is of the utmost importance. I learned from this engagement that knowing any other entity you would integrate with, as well as those you would fight against, is just as important. Pasteur said that fortune favors the trained mind. Taking the time to study and know your enemy as well as your colleagues will prove beneficial on the battlefield.

This engagement did not unfold as smoothly as I would have liked; communication was hampered due to language issues, and coordination with Special Forces teammates was not as clear and efficient as it needed to be. I needed to improve my communication efforts with everyone on the battlefield. I needed to make sure that I effectively received and effectively sent the information needed to all parties involved. If necessary I would communicate face-to-face.

This mission was the largest joint operation I had led at that point in my career. In the unit I was used to working fairly independently, often relying only on internal resources to get our missions done. During this engagement our small element from the unit had to rely on a variety of external resources. I gained an appreciation for working with colleagues from a variety of other entities; indeed, we could not have completed our missions without them.

I've seen leaders of units that care only about their own people and their own equipment, or ask *"What's in it for me or my organization?"* It's a form of professional selfishness. As a leader, it was essential that I endeavored to help others whenever and wherever I could. You never know when you or your people will be the ones needing help.

***

In late February and early March the snow came to Khowst. One snowstorm shut down the air operations on the airfield, and severely restricted activity in the surrounding villages for a couple of days. Afghan locals told us that it hadn't snowed that much in over ten years, and some believed that the Americans brought the snow. If we did, I didn't request it. The snow made work twice as hard, making mud as it melted that stuck to our boots and added another few pounds to pick up with every step. Vehicle mobility was limited. The snow and weather also grounded all helicopter and fixed wing flights in and out of our camp, limiting our resupply capabilities. So we made do as best we could.

During this downtime I reviewed my notes, trying to determine the next step for the team in preparation for a large scale operation that was in the works. We had been collecting information from the locals on Al Qaeda fighters and forwarding this information to our headquarters. We discovered that one location kept surfacing. Shahi Khot. There was a large contingent of Taliban and Al-Qaeda personnel in that area. This meant that the worker ants were near the mound. Finding a large number of the enemy concentrated together would make the task of capturing or killing them easier.

We immediately commenced route reconnaissance missions around the Shahi Khot area. The region was rough. The terrain was extremely mountainous and all the mountain passes were covered with snow. Our major obstacle was the mountain range that separated the villages of Khowst and Gardez. Additionally, a Special Forces team also told us of overtly placed landmines on the main road leading into the Shahi Khot valley from the north. Apparently, one of the Special Forces teams drove near the Shahi Khot valley during a route reconnaissance mission. The team stopped short as it was getting late in the day and decided to return the following morning to drive into the valley. When the team returned the next day they found the conspicuously placed mines. What the hell ever happened to traditional 'No Trespassing' signs? All the indicators were telling us that the area appeared to be a hornet's nest....that was full of hornets.

Word came down that there was going to be a planning session for the operation, so a helicopter made the rounds to all of the outposts and retrieved key personnel for the meeting. As a team leader I was considered key personnel and I was excited to be involved. After the helicopter landed at Bagram I exited and was taken to a series of tents that were utilized as a make-shift tactical operations center (TOC). All in attendance entered and proceeded to circle around the terrain model of the Shahi Khot valley. The lead planner introduced himself and immediately began what I thought was going to be a planning session.

He stated, "The planning for this operation has already been done so we don't need any good ideas, at this point. We're going forward with the plan as is, we've put too much work into this to make changes." I was surprised, to say the least. I stowed my notebook filled with information that my team and I had collected through months of hard work in the region and listened to the brief. I held my composure externally, but internally I was furious. At the conclusion of the briefing there was no discussion, and the planners were not taking any questions. Those of us standing around the terrain model knew that the ever-present Murphy was going on this operation with us (as in Murphy's law: what could go wrong, would go wrong).

The plan was decent, at best, given that the individuals planned the operation in a vacuum. The biggest issue I saw was the landing of the assault helicopters in the middle of the village, especially if the information we had gathered was accurate regarding the number of enemy fighters in the area. I felt as though each outpost had more to offer the planners in creating a better plan and that our team skills were not going to be properly utilized.

Based on their plan, my team was to partner with our Special Forces Team and provide a blocking position to the southeast of the valley.

Raymond, Bruce, and I would not be participating in any of the reconnaissance efforts prior to the operation. This was insane to me, as I knew we could get our team into the valley and into an observation post that would be beneficial to the operation. For the life of me I could not understand why they weren't using our team for reconnaissance. That decision must have been made way above my pay grade. In addition to poor planning, the lack of listening to others in attendance reflected poorly on the leadership.

The helicopter flight back to Khowst was uneventful, and the entire time I thought about the operation and my team's assignment. I knew my guys were going to be pissed about it, but I also knew that these decisions were out of my control. For the past three months my team and I had been self-sufficient in daily operations. But I remembered that I was in the army and soldiers must do what they are ordered to do. Regardless, as the team leader I still felt a responsibility to immediately voice my concerns to my superior upon my return.

I could see the snow-covered mountain peaks as we flew back through the mountain range that separates Bagram airbase and the Khowst valley. The mountains seemed super close as we passed, as if you could jump off the helicopter and survive. I had spent enough time in the Khowst area that I knew the roads and layout of most the surrounding villages. I retrieved the mental map in my head and confirmed the terrain features and village layouts with what I could see from the helicopter.

The wheels touched down at the dirt airstrip at Khowst and I bailed off. I cleared the rotor blades and headed directly for our operations room, which doubled as my bedroom. After I removed my kit, I sent a situation report along with some of my personal concerns and observations of the planning session to my superiors. Afterwards, I sat on my bunk and mentally planned our mission. I also kept in mind that the enemy always had a vote in what we did and this operation was going to be no different. Operational security and secrecy were crucial to our success. The prep work for Operation Anaconda began for our team.

On March 1, 2002 our entire force made our way to our blocking positions located southeast of the Shahi Khot valley, which was situated on a key road intersection that connected the villages of Gardez and Khowst.

The movement went well and our blocking position was established by mid-afternoon. Bruce, Raymond, and I along with twenty Afghan soldiers climbed a nearby mountain with the hopes of establishing an observation point overlooking the blocking position. Once we located a position, we did a short reconnaissance of the immediate terrain around us, which was rough. The mountains were extremely steep and unforgiving. At the end of the day we sat in our observation point looking at the mountain range between our position and the Shahi Khot valley. The operation was set for dawn of the next day.

The next morning, the entire team was glued to one of our tactical radios as we listened to the battle develop. We all felt a little helpless, holding our position and anticipating a flood of bad guys coming our way trying to escape the battle. Ultimately, that didn't happen as most of the enemy fighters died in the main battle. We moved our position several times in support of the fight, occupying two separate hidden observation posts in the high mountain tops, with the responsibility of providing intelligence regarding enemy movement. We found that the enemy fighters intentionally blended in with the local populace, which made identification that much harder. When the battle subsided, we realized that we were fortunate just to be a part of the operation. However, our involvement was in no way, shape or form, what we were capable of and had hoped for. We all wished we could have done more to help the fight.

When a leader allows rank to get in the way, for the sole purpose of feeling that others respect that rank, then this can have serious and even deadly consequences for his or her subordinates. Being a true leader does not necessarily mean there is an insignia or patch on your sleeve or collar. Being a good leader means knowing exactly when to step aside and allow those that know the opportunity to do, even if they are subordinates to the rank.

***

My small team and I called Afghanistan home for four months in a small outpost with even smaller living quarters. Because of the long distance from military support we had to maintain some form of radio communications with our headquarters twenty four hours a day. We conducted numerous missions primarily in an effort to gather information on the whereabouts of terrorist fighters, especially after the battle in the Shahi Khot valley. Our outpost was occupied by my team, a Special Forces contingent, and a platoon from the 10th Mountain Division that had replaced the marines. Even though the enemy had a fix on our location, we were now staffed with a larger assault element for any direct action missions that might arise.

I was the senior person for the JSOC element and I spent a lot of time in the planning and operations center. I needed to be there to maintain radio contact with my headquarters but also to be around the leaders from the other elements at the outpost. I established a great working relationship with each and every element in the area; we had to rely on each other because external support was far away. Specifically, the relationship with the Special Forces contingent that shared the outpost with us was second to none. There was no convoluted command structure, which allowed for great lines of communication.

One evening I was awakened to the sound of heavy machine gun fire from the top of my building. I could hear the assistant machine gunner communicating enemy locations to the gunner. Raymond burst into the operations center as I grabbed the radio and called headquarters.

"Brick 50 this is Brick 53, over."

Shortly thereafter my boss answered and responded, "This is Brick 50, over."

"Brick 50, be advised, our outpost is under attack. I request the helicopter pilots be made aware of our situation in case we need a MEDEVAC. Nothing further to report at this time, over."

My boss responded, "Roger, Brick 53, is there anything you need, over."

I responded, "This is Brick 53, we could use an AC-130 gunship, over."

I could hear him talking on a separate handset, requesting the aircraft before he released the handset that he was using to talk to me. Raymond could tell that I was busy so he advised me that he was going to check the security perimeter to ensure that the folks were aware of the situation. I knew he also wanted to get a firsthand look at what was happening. I was envious of Raymond because he got to stick his nose in the fight while I was stuck in the operations center.

The squawk box on the radio crackled. "Brick 53, you have an AC-130 en route. ETA twenty minutes, over." Twenty minutes was an eternity in a fire fight so I asked about something else. "Roger Brick 50, are there any other aircraft in the area than can assist, over?" Headquarters replied, "Brick 53, this is Brick 50, there are two F-16s inbound to your location, they should be there in a few minutes, over." That made me feel a little more warm and fuzzy. I replied, "Brick 50, this is Brick 53, thanks, out".

I went next door amidst the snapping sounds of bullets flying overhead to check in with the Special Forces team commander. As I exited the operations center, Bruce, my air force combat controller, was already on the radio with headquarters attempting to determine which aircraft would be inbound so he could communicate with them and coordinate their efforts. Bruce was extremely efficient and effective in his role, which allowed me to focus on other issues.

Approximately ten minutes after the attack started we heard over the secure radio frequency that the enemy was now attacking from two separate locations. I quickly jumped on my handheld radio and informed Raymond that the enemy had moved into an L-shaped attack formation. We had anticipated this type of attack and our forces were arrayed in a manner that facilitated defense against it.

My position as a senior leader had me tied to the inner perimeter coordinating efforts to defend our outpost. Even though I held my M4 in my hands I felt like I was only partially involved in the battle. When functioning in a leadership role there will be times when the situation dictates circumstances that create a feeling of uneasiness or unfairness within you. I wanted to get my ass involved in the battle, yet I had responsibilities as a leader. A good leader knows to intellectually maintain control and do what needs to be done, even if it's not what they want to be doing at that moment.

After I finished my face to face meeting with the Special Forces commander I grabbed a few guys in the immediate area and assembled a small reaction force. The small group was kitted up and standing by, behind cover, near the entrance to the planning area where I manned the radios and received updates from the perimeter and my headquarters.

I heard some yelling and a commotion just outside the door to the planning area. The platoon sergeant from the 10th Mountain Division suffered a gunshot wound to the upper arm and was being attended to by a Special Forces medic. The medic determined the wound was non-critical, therefore no immediate need for a medical transport by helicopter. The last thing we wanted, at the time, was to coordinate a helicopter landing in the middle of the fire fight.

Approximately twenty minutes into the attack there was a lull in the action. The Special Forces commander and I left the planning room and made a quick stop to check on the platoon sergeant. As we entered the room the platoon sergeant was sitting upright while the medic worked on his arm. We spent several minutes with the sergeant and then exited the room. We were lucky he wasn't critically injured. The following day we heard from members of his platoon that when the platoon leader initially went to assist the sergeant after he was shot, his first words were, "Sir, they got me." This continued to be a running joke for the next two weeks, especially by those he led in his platoon. His men trusted and liked him a lot.

The lull was suddenly broken by a large explosion just outside our compound walls. Approximately two minutes later there was an even larger explosion and I realized we were taking indirect fire. Based on reports from Raymond, this accounted for the enemy's stalled maneuver. There was going to be more indirect fire. Fortunately, the security perimeter was built with dug-in fighting positions and overhead cover. Our inner perimeter consisted of mud-walled shacks that would provide some cover. None of the positions would be able to survive a direct hit.

There was a third explosion off in the distance. The first few rounds were inaccurate and it appeared as if the enemy was uncoordinated or untrained in the utilization of their weapons system. The AC-130 gunship's pilots, with their birds-eye view, advised us that there were three separate groups of enemy fighters surrounding our camp. Ordnance would be inbound shortly and I really wanted the enemy to feel some pain.

I could tell the guys I had on reserve were getting antsy. One of the least experienced members spoke up and said, "I really feel like I should be out on the perimeter and not just standing here."

I stopped what I was doing and explained, "Hey listen fellas, we've planned for an attack and we have to allow the base defense plan to work. If we go out there right now we might make matters worse by mucking up the situation." I continued, "You guys are providing a vital function as both an aid and litter team and a reaction force. If part of the perimeter takes serious casualties we will have to go and get the casualties and bring them back to the med shed and help re-establish the perimeter." Once those on the reaction team were reassured of their purpose they all seemed to settle down. Luckily for us we never needed our reaction force.

The AC-130 unleashed some hell on the enemy positions around our camp. They initiated the engagement with fire from the 40mm cannon followed by several rounds from the 105mm cannon. Pieces of earth and enemy terrorists were flying everywhere. After the initial pass, the gunship made some adjustments and began their fire again. The gunship continued to engage the static enemy positions until they began to flee. Our rooftop machine gunners and guys on the perimeter were also getting in on the action, we were giving some good news to the bad guys from all angles. Our security personnel and sniper elements chased the enemy with direct fire until no enemy targets remained. The gunship picked up the chase and fired until there was no enemy activity. The AC-130 checked the surrounding areas and then resumed its orbital reconnaissance overhead. Bruce redirected the aircraft east of our location where we thought the indirect fire came from, attempting to locate the crew.

The assault on our outpost lasted approximately sixty minutes, and the platoon sergeant was the only person injured, which was a testament to our security platoon's preparations. Regarding leadership, there were three things that really stood out to me during that fight: positioning, information pertinent or applicable to the situation, and communication on all levels.

It was tough to resist the temptation of wanting to join in on the fight. But a good leader will always understand the important differences between wanting to and needing to, and only entering the melee if absolutely necessary. When coordinating the actions of others, especially while under duress, a leader needs to understand that physical positioning can make all the difference in the world. Being located in the physical middle or center can be the most advantageous position for a leader, but not always. For me in this situation it was best, it allowed for a full three hundred and sixty degrees of observation of the situation. It also provided me with short lines of communication to all members of the camp.

There has to be a solid communication conduit that allows incoming and outgoing information to flow smoothly. A good leader has to have the ability to digest all incoming information and prioritize that which is pertinent to the situation. The leader can then use that information to make a smart, informed decision. In a fire fight there is no time for any bullshit. I couldn't imagine being bombarded with tons of useless information and having to sift through it all before making a decision. So it helps when your crew knows what information you need. Subordinates can then provide clear, concise, specific information, and a good leader trains their team to do so.

Finally, I learned that communication across all levels was not just important but critically necessary. I was in contact with every element on the ground, which included the security platoon leadership, the Special Forces team commander, and my team members, as well as headquarters, and the aircraft overhead. This may seem like difficult task, but a good leader can definitely walk and chew gum at the same time! Integrating these three pillars of 'boots on the ground' leadership with the ability to understand the reality of any given situation and then confronting it decisively is what separates the true leader from the pack.

***

The plan entailed a long distance helicopter assault utilizing Chinook cargo helicopters (CH-47s). My team was responsible for clearing two lone structures approximately eight hundred meters outside of the main target location and we were to be inserted after the main assault force. This meant my team would lose the important element of surprise. We discussed the issues and contingency plans based on the most probable and dangerous courses of action. When we finished briefing our commander we moved back to our tents to prepare for the night's mission.

This was the first mission that I was executing with my original stateside team in combat...the team that I spent a lot of time working and training with at home before the September 11th attacks. My initial combat experiences were unique in that I deployed prior to my team, as part of a pilot element. The night's mission was a big deal to me. I was comfortable with my position and my abilities to lead my team, and I relished the opportunity to confront the enemy with them. I was ready.

Our sergeant major and his medic were supporting my team for this mission. We boarded the aircraft first because we would offload last, once the main assault element departed at the primary objective. Once the entire element loaded, the aircraft pulled up and we sat back and got as comfortable as we could for the nearly two hour long flight. I dozed off and woke about twenty minutes prior to our arrival. I could see out the front cockpit window and an amazing number of stars were visible through my night vision goggles. I thought of the mission and what might happen, and decided to try and relax and take in the sights and listen to the thump of the rotors as they split the air. Before I knew it, the pilots were passing back time signals and I echoed them back to my mates. Shortly thereafter, the one minute call came and we all held on to the aircraft or grabbed a cargo strap anticipating a hard landing. The bird hit the ground hard, so hard that I thought the landing gear hit a ditch.

Everyone regained their footing after the hard landing and the main assault element departed. After they left, my team moved toward the center of the helicopter for the short ride to our target. I looked forward into the cockpit and saw the pilots putting one hundred mile per hour tape, commonly known as duct tape, over the instrument panel in front of them. After the mission I learned that the pilots were taping over the warning lights that came on due to the hard landing. The aircraft engines whined as we lifted off and flew toward our helicopter landing zone.

We felt the helicopter slow for our insertion. The entire team tried to get a visual of our target buildings as the Chinook started its descent into our landing zone. Out of nowhere, it felt like we hit a mountain. The impact sent the entire team forward in an instant, and I could sense that the aircraft was pitching forward. Either the bird struck something or we were taking enemy fire. I looked out the rear of the helicopter and all I could see was the starry night sky. I felt helpless as hell, since I was not in a position to control anything other than my thoughts and emotions.

The rear crew chief dropped the tail gun as the helicopter rolled forward and I thought to myself...*this is it!* I knew the front rotor blades were close to impact with the ground. My team and I braced ourselves for a crash.

The engines whined and whistled loudly, and to our surprise, the pilot pulled it up and out. The rear crew chief moved off the gun and deeper into the aircraft, so my team and I moved towards the rear, took over the gun, and tried to get a look out of the ramp and windows to assess the threat. I connected my headset to the intercom system and conversed with the pilots, who stated they wanted to try again to get us in. I agreed. I worried about the mechanical structure of the helicopter and asked if the aircraft was capable of landing. The pilots couldn't be sure. All they could promise is that they would try to get us as close to the ground as possible. After inserting us they'd have to fly back to the support base to assess the damage. We'd be on our own after insertion.

After several failed approaches, the bird finally hovered and then slowly descended to within five feet of the ground. Several seconds later the rear crew chief cleared us to exit. My team jumped the hell out of that helicopter and immediately moved to covered positions near the exterior wall that surrounded our target buildings. Our plan was to breach the external wall that surrounded the residences with explosives. A teammate, Smooth, found a place where he could see over the wall and had eyes on the primary exterior doorway.

Smooth was actually working in our research and development section when he volunteered to deploy with our team. He had spent a lot of time in the unit that was tempered with operational experience, and he was senior to me by a number of years. He was a former successful team sergeant and his attachment to the team was a welcome one.

"Hey…I have a door, I've got security on it. You can climb here." Smooth kept his weapon oriented on the doorway as he spoke to us. I decided to climb instead of using our explosive charge. The wall was approximately six feet in height, so we made a team stack to get over it. Squirt, who was my second-in-charge, was first over, followed by Dingo, Lucky, and Buck. As the team sergeant, I was near the end of the formation, and I watched as the guys in front of me disappeared over the wall.

As I climbed up I realized the wall was crumbling and was about to fall over. It was unstable for further climbing, so Keebler and I pushed and pulled on the wall and the top portion fell to the ground on the other side. What we didn't know was that there was roughly a nine foot drop on the far side of the wall. Unbeknownst to us, the guys had had difficult landings on the other side.

I also didn't know that one of our teammates got his foot stuck in a small ditch on the other side and was trying to free it. As Buck tried to free his foot, part of the wall that Keebler and I freed from the top fell over and hit him in the center of his back causing him to be vigorously thrown forward. He grunted in pain as the wall knocked him down and forward; how he managed to keep from yelling I'll never know. The only thing I heard him say was a whispered, "*Motherfucker!*" as he crawled forward.

Buck continued to crawl forward, he knew the rest of us were behind him trying to navigate the terrain. Some team members moved up to help him. We needed to keep moving forward to clear our area before the enemy saw and fired at us. I directed Squirt to keep moving but he was a step ahead of me. Buck was in the capable hands of our medic and troop sergeant major. We moved forward to hunt the enemy.

As we moved to clear our target structures, we moved deliberately, knowing the enemy would be waiting for us if they were still in the area, especially after three failed helicopter insertion attempts including a near catastrophic initial insertion. We approached the first building, made entry and cleared the entire structure without incident. Then we made our way to the second building. During our approach I asked for air support to check the roof tops of the structures for any enemy movement. No bad guys on the roof tops. We moved on.

Through the front door we flowed and cleared the building like running water. Immediately thereafter, we began an external clear of the area. It was obvious that the enemy had departed, but regardless, we weren't about to drop our guard. I contemplated their absence and thought they may be lying in wait in the immediate area to ambush us.

With the exploitation of the area complete and the information we collected secured, my team moved back to our original infiltration area where our mates were waiting. Our main assault element was still at work on their location and would finish shortly. We moved Buck by litter to the landing zone and were informed by the command that the first helicopter inbound would take him straight to a medical facility. After Buck and the team medic departed on their bird, a second helicopter came in and picked the rest of us up. The flight back was uneventful and after a short time I was knocked out, asleep, on my knees, listening to the thump of the rotors, and feeling the vibration of the engine.

When the wheels of our helicopter touched down at our operating base I moved a bit to get the blood flowing back through my legs while we taxied to park. The rear crew chief lowered the ramp, and I could see the glow of night vision goggles in front of me as we exited and headed toward our staging area. Back at our team tent we wasted no time replenishing our expended flashbangs and checking gear, making sure that we were ready in case something popped up. I checked in with the command group to obtain the time for our AAR. We had approximately thirty minutes before it started. I took this opportunity to discuss the night's events with my team prior to the meeting.

Collectively, we discussed what went wrong and what we needed to amend at the team level, as well as identifying other issues that would have to be solved by those above our pay grade. I informed the guys of how the large piece of the wall had fallen off and struck Buck. While his back was OK, he did have a severe injury to his ankle. We attended the main AAR and at the conclusion we all retired to our respective tents.

When I hit the rack that night, I laid in my cot and thought a lot about what happened to Buck. I didn't get much sleep that night, knowing I was responsible for injuring my own teammate. I was mentally prepared for someone on my team getting hurt due to the actions of the enemy, but I was not prepared for someone on my team getting hurt due to my actions. I felt so bad about Buck's injury that while I thought I could keep my feelings from my team, I realized that they could sense something was amiss with me. I was granted a wide berth by each; I think they wanted to let me process my own emotions and concerns. I had a hard time accepting the fact that my actions were not intentional, and that it was not a lack of skill on my part that caused his injury, but simply a lack of awareness of conditions on the other side of that wall. I felt so guilty, that seemed like a cop-out.

Several days later I was talking with the guys about the night Buck got injured. Keebler knew I was upset about causing Buck's injury. He stopped, locked eyes with me and, in his matter-of-fact way said, "We all understand the risks of what our job entails. It does not matter if we get shot in the face or a wall falls on us. We make the decision to go ourselves, so you shouldn't feel responsible for anything. It was an accident and accidents happen in this kind of work." That night I got the best night's sleep I had had in four days.

Looking back at my first five and a half months at war, I must admit that it was one of the more rewarding leadership journeys in my career. I was exposed to, and learned to harness and develop many characteristics of battlefield leadership. Nearly thirteen years of training prior to my first true wartime deployment helped me immensely. At the same time, I learned that training was nothing compared to the actual experiences. After my initial deployment to Afghanistan, I took a brief break at home followed by a second deployment. There was much work to be done, and I was eager to be in the fight. Battlefield experience is incomparable. It also allowed me to solidify my confidence in my ability to lead people in difficult times and while under duress.

***

In March 2003 I had the distinct honor of leading my team during the invasion of Iraq as part of the initial invasion force. It was believed at the time that Iraq held weapons of mass destruction and was supporting terrorism. I felt lucky to be part of the overall effort, not to mention as a team leader with the best group of fighting men in the world. Preparation began months earlier, with planning and rehearsal for what we thought our mission might be based on past experiences and the foresight of our commander. Our commander's vision of our role in the invasion was incredibly audacious, accurate, and just plain awesome.

Many of us felt as if this was our generation's D-day; obviously not nearly as large as Operation Overlord, but the largest military operation since the first Gulf War. It was definitely the largest engagement most of us in the unit had participated in. Our preparation was extensive. We knew that we would be part of a small force operating in a large, open desert environment. The unit had operated successfully in the same environment during the first gulf war. We knew the Iraqi Army had the weapons and capability to be a formidable enemy. As we reviewed the information about the enemy that occupied our sector, we realized that if Saddam's army wanted to fight us, we would have one hell of a fight on our hands. That said, we were banking on their inability to fight at our level, especially at night. The intelligence briefs painted a picture that kept most people on the edge of their seats with anticipation. The equipment alone that stood in front of us was formidable. We were really going to have to be on our game if we were to accomplish our missions.

At this point in my career, I was a senior team sergeant and only one or two other team sergeants had more time in the unit than I. Because of my position, I knew that people would listen to whatever I said, whether it was about mission planning, equipment, or other matters. This was a serious responsibility, and I knew I had to watch not only what I said but how I said it. Because of my time in the unit and experience, I wanted to use my position and influence to help the commander, but I also knew I still needed to stay true to my perspective. Junior leaders must support their leadership if at all possible, even if there isn't complete agreement with all of the decisions being made. Mutual respect between junior leaders and their superiors is critical. It makes for a much more functional working relationship and successful organization.

During the planning for our operation, I continually reminded myself that there are many different ways to get something done, all of which can be correct. Some people have a hard time letting go of "their" way and looking at new approaches. This may be due to inflexible thinking, insecurity, a controlling personality, or simply experience - somebody has learned their way the hard way. A good leader educates their team to think flexibly, integrate experience, and consider new approaches to problems, as this fosters growth and innovation.

***

After a tremendous amount of planning and preparation, the day came for us to cross the border into Iraq to initiate the war - this was it! On the evening of our departure we gathered in our staging area for pictures and our commanders' final address to the entire unit before we headed into battle. It was a momentous occasion, and we were feeling that perfect mix of excitement and readiness. The first person to address us was the Joint Special Operations Commander and the only thing I can remember him saying was, "You probably won't make it into Baghdad." The rest of his speech was lost in the gloom of his forecast of failure.

Here was an opportunity for greatness - inspiration, motivation, confidence building - and I expected more. This issue bothered me and some of the guys, especially a few days later when we heard of Commander Tim Collins, Commander of the 1st Battalion Royal Irish Regiment and his eve of battle speech to his people. It was an incredible speech, and my team and I found strength in some of his motivational words: "If you are ferocious in battle, remember to be magnanimous in victory," and "As for ourselves, let's bring everyone home and leave Iraq a better place for us having been there - our business now is north." I carried his words with me. Leaders need to make an effort to understand who they're addressing and the message they want to convey, especially on important occasions.

Later that evening, my team and another sniper team headed to the border crossing point ahead of the main body of our unit. After our engineers breached the berm on the border we drove our vehicles across and began our journey into combat. Our first mission was to go down within the next twenty four hours.

Our movement into Iraq was incredibly arduous with long hours of driving during the cold of the night. We didn't want to encounter a large enemy force with our small element, so we would travel at night and hide during the day. If we were going to engage the enemy, we wanted it to be on our terms, so we tried to choose the best terrain possible when we hid during the day.

We worked hard to avoid contact during our movements and focused on getting to our designated targets on time, but didn't shy away from an opportunity to engage the enemy if the situation called for us to do so. It was a great time to be a warrior in the greatest unit in the world. As you can imagine, there were some stressful situations but we all, to a man, considered it normal for war. Approximately three weeks into the war, I could see that I, personally, and we as a unit were getting tired. We were starting to feel the effects of our environment; working only at night and staying continually vigilant were taking a toll on everyone. One of the challenges of being a leader is keeping your people motivated when the situation is unclear, especially during stressful times like combat.

We knew that we could only hide for so long before someone would find us or bump into us by accident. We had a lot of close calls with the normal Iraqi wandering the desert or moving to cut some time off their drive with a shortcut while crossing the desert. We rotated the responsibility of finding a suitable hiding spot for our force. We drove in our vehicles to preplanned locations that appeared suitable based on map reconnaissance. During the process, it was up to the leader of that reconnaissance element to determine if the area was acceptable for hiding in and potentially fighting from if we got busted.

In one particular case, my element was responsible for conducting reconnaissance of a possible hiding location. The sun was coming up and we were about to turn into pumpkins, so we made the decision to locate the entire element in three different locations that were within a few hundred meters of each other. We couldn't tell for sure initially, but once the sun was completely up we knew we lucked out because the positions were mutually supporting. This meant that we were able to cover each other's dead space with our direct fire weapons, like our .50 caliber machine guns and 40 mm grenade launchers. Once in place we hunkered down and prepared to get some much needed sleep. We had finished a mission the night before and drove a long way to get to our new resting spot. I was lucky my guard shift was in the middle of the day, I would get a few hours of sleep before waking up to pull duty. I tossed my sleeping pad on the ground, pulled my sleeping bag out, and quickly crawled into my bag with my boots still on my feet.

I was out as soon as I went horizontal - immediately in a deep sleep. I awoke to the sound of my teammate's voice. He was posted on our vehicle pulling security and manning the radio. He said, "Hey, the guys on the hill said they just got busted by a goat herder, they are trying to keep an eye on him to see what he does." I was struggling to wake up. I can't tell you how much sleep I got, but it was still morning so it wasn't much.

Approximately twenty minutes later we received another radio call from the guys on the hill informing us that roughly one hundred armed men were approaching our position in seven vehicles. This was something we never wanted to hear. We all immediately jumped up and prepared for the inevitable. I grabbed my sleeping bag and pad in one swoop and tossed them into the bed of our truck, as did the rest of the team.

We hopped into our vehicle and drove approximately 75 meters to the high ground above us. As we moved I could see Dahmer, a sniper from our sister team, in front of us, running with his sniper weapon in both hands. Once he reached the crest of the hill, he dropped to the prone position and immediately began firing - the bad guys were nearly on top of us. We moved on line with Dahmer and supported him with our forty millimeter vehicle-mounted machine gun. Our top gunner (the guy manning the gun mounted on top of the vehicle) began firing at multiple targets, including dismounted Fedayeen fighters and vehicles approaching our position. We managed to stop their advance. Fortunately for us, we were prepared and able to respond so rapidly that the enemy didn't have a chance to maneuver on any of our positions. We stayed mounted, meaning that we stayed in our vehicles just in case our commander gave us orders to move to a different location or to break contact.

At some point during the fight, our commander's voice came over the radio, breaking the radio silence. "All elements, this is Arrow 06, we're staying where we are. We have the terrain and we are holding our positions, over." This was the best decision our commander could have made. We would have had a running gun battle on our hands if we had tried to break contact and move away. After hearing this, most of our force dismounted our vehicles and assumed covered ground positions, leaving only key personnel on the vehicles such as gunners, ammo bearers, and people manning radios. I dismounted my HK-21 belt-fed machine gun, grabbed four hundred rounds of ammunition, and ran forward on line with the rest of my team. My top gunner was still engaging the enemy as we moved forward.

After we set up positions behind cover, we waited. Shortly thereafter, we could see several pickup trucks full of enemy fighters trying to find our positions. They didn't know exactly where we were located, so we got the drop on them. All of the top gunners and those of us on the ground opened up on the vehicles and dismounts, killing them all and disabling the vehicles.

We continued to hold our positions as more enemy fighters came to the fight. We fought them to a standstill. We were greatly outnumbered, but we had the terrain and most importantly, the will to stand and fight. The enemy fighters thought they could overwhelm us with speed and get us rolling back on our heels, but they were completely wrong. I believe they expected us to break contact and attempt to evade them. When this didn't happen, they were stuck in the low ground approximately 300 meters in front of us and they couldn't move anywhere without being engaged. They were using the terrain that they had to their advantage and were able to bring additional fighters in by vehicle from a nearby town without us seeing them. Fortunately, we had fighter jets supporting us. The jets were dropping bombs on vehicles approaching the area, but they could only drop bombs on targets a safe distance away from our positions. Most of the enemy fighters were too close to our positions for the jets' large 500 pound bombs.

We fought back several enemy attempts to assault our positions and multiple suicide assaults that left scores of dead enemy fighters in front of our positions. At some point during the fight, I looked to the other positions and realized that the medics were working on a fellow mate who was shot through the chest. We didn't know the extent of his injuries so we just hoped for the best. The commander called in a medical evacuation for our wounded, but we were so deep into the country that we waited hours before support could get to us.

During a lull in the fight, I came off the assault line to talk with my immediate commander who was monitoring radio traffic in my vehicle. As I approached the vehicle, I realized that Jay, our Air Force combat controller was shot in the chin. Smurf, our medic, bandaged him up. Luckily his condition was stable, his injury relatively minor. He used white gauze on the wound and wrapped his head with a white cotton wrap. My boss said the ground force commander wanted to leave our location shortly after dark, and had found what appeared to be a suitable location on the map to hole up through the night. The location would put us within striking distance for our next mission the following night. It all sounded good to me. Heading back to link up with my team, I couldn't help joking with Jay, "You doing okay, Q-Tip?" We both laughed as I ran back to my team's position.

The medevac helicopter came in and picked up our wounded, and behind them was a sortie of attack helicopters, hunting for enemy positions. Their initial flight over the battlefield yielded a gold mine of bad guys. They were stuck in the low ground in front of us and now they couldn't hide from the helicopters either. After the first attack run, some of the enemy personnel tried to make a run for it and they were met with direct fire from most of our positions. For the next run the attack helos came in hot and gave the enemy a taste of metal and high explosives. The bad guys were in a bad way and that's how we wanted it. After a few runs the helicopters were supported by a single A-10 Thunderbolt Attack Airplane. The A-10 was incredibly awesome! The pilot worked in between each helicopter run and the coordination between all of the air elements was outstanding.

Approximately an hour later all the aircraft were Winchester, meaning they had expended all their munitions, and they departed the area. It was roughly an hour before sunset and we knew the enemy had lost their will to fight today. But we didn't drop our guard as we prepared for movement to our next position; shortly after sunset we got the call to get out of dodge. This was our first major fight of this war and for me, it solidified my resolve in our mission. This fight got personal for everyone that shared the battlefield that day, and we needed to see the mission through the end.

The biggest lesson I learned during this battle was how well we could perform with minimal but appropriate leader guidance. Our commander made one decision that set the tone for his subordinate leaders to get the job done. My immediate supervisor gave minimal direction to me and his other team leaders. As a subordinate leader that day, I gave input to my team and my leadership on one issue. We knew we couldn't leave our location at dark without clearing the low ground in front of us because we anticipated the enemy chasing us. My platoon's leadership got together and I recommended that we wait until the attack helos arrived and let them do some work before we tried to push the enemy out of their hole.

This one recommendation was agreed upon by all at the time. Aside from this single piece of input, there was nothing significant that I told my team or the leadership told me. If you allow your people to make their own decisions, they will do the right thing more often than not. If you pick good people, train them well, and allow them to work with minimal guidance when possible, they will make you successful.

***

After our work during the invasion we redeployed home. We knew this was the start of what would be a long war effort on the part of the entire army and our unit. We started a rotation cycle, and elements from the unit would be in theatre as long as there were Americans on the ground. A few weeks after arriving home I was informed that I needed to move out of my team leader position and move up the ranks. It was time for more self reflection.

Experience is a great teacher. I learned a lot from looking at other leaders and understanding what I wanted to take away from all of them: developing the good traits and avoiding the bad. Reviewing my own performance, I could see many successes and plenty of failures. Here's what I believe I excelled at, things that I could have done better, and important things I learned from this stage of my career.

I believe I did a good job training my guys. I don't think proper training can be emphasized enough. We trained constantly to the highest level possible in order to master the skills we endeavored to use. Developing individual skills and working and training as a team made us the best in the world at what we did. I believe I did a good job training my team and others that I worked with.

I worked hard, and in hindsight I might have worked too hard at times. Looking back, I think I should have dedicated more downtime for my guys. At the time, I didn't want my guys to feel that I wasn't dedicated to my job, my unit, and most importantly them. I wanted to show them that I didn't take my responsibilities lightly. The best way for me to do that was to be the hardest working member of the team.

I think small teams need to do a lot of things together, as a team, in order to work well together. I could have done a better job in this area. I needed to schedule fun things to do as a team as well - not just training, training, and more training. We all must have some balance in life and work. More balanced training probably would have built better cohesion.

All forms of communication are important, not just talking with your people but also speeches, e-mails, and briefings. Continuous communication is needed throughout, not just to those you lead but to those that lead you and those that work around you. Communication goes both ways - you must ensure that you receive information just as well as you convey it. As a team sergeant, I realized that if I had the time, I needed to give most everyone an opportunity to voice their concerns or opinions on team decisions and issues. They all understood that I, as the leader, would make the final decision. This gave way to a personal lesson that I learned about myself: I learned to become decisive.

Anyone can make a decision, but making a good decision is harder. Stressful environments lead to hasty decisions. Uninformed decisions can be disastrous. Bad decisions compound themselves. I learned to solicit information from those around me in a timely manner, so I could make good, informed decisions that I was confident in. That, to me, is the difference between just making a choice and being decisive.

People can easily get caught up in their own world of who gets credit for whatever situation, mission, etc., and may be inclined to hoard important information to ensure they get the credit for it. I tried not to do this. When you're in the business of saving lives, catching bad guys, or killing or capturing terrorists, you must share information. You cannot allow ego to affect your decision to share information. The end result outweighs your personal agenda. Letting go of a desire for recognition frees your mind of tons of unnecessary stress.

From a military perspective, I learned early on and accepted the fact that there wasn't a terrorist waiting for me at every corner. The omnipresent fear that a bad guy might be waiting in ambush for you can and will drive people into a corner with little room to get back on track. There is nothing wrong with knowing that you may be engaged and preparing for it, as long as you keep it in the proper perspective. Do not allow being prepared to cause you to live on the defensive. If fear is driving you to make decisions that do not allow you to exploit opportunities to take the offensive, then you will find yourself constantly on the defensive.

At war you may find times when the enemy has the upper hand, but you must push forward with a winning attitude and fight to win. If you venture into battle with only the will to survive, then you have already assumed that you will fail.

I didn't have to convey purpose or resolve to my guys, they didn't need it, I was lucky to have some seriously dedicated people around me. I know it is important for leaders to share their purpose often. I saw similar defensiveness and fear in soldiers that did not believe in what they were doing or whose leadership didn't support them and their mission. In war, there must be purpose behind all decisions, especially when the loss of life is a potential outcome. Lack of clear purpose affects a soldier's resolve.

All leaders, at every level within an organization must share the same amount of resolve: they must believe in what they are doing and they must share this with those underneath them. If you, as the leader, do not fully believe in what you are being asked to do and you still intend to do said task, you must not share your personal beliefs with those underneath you. Do not bitch down the ranks.

I tried to have some seriously thick skin. I knew that I didn't have all the answers and I trusted in the idea that working together with colleagues to solve a problem was much better than my little bean head alone. Being a leader is never easy and I learned that leaders cannot and will not make everyone happy. But, I tried to take feedback from my mates and worked to improve myself. A good leader works to recognize their faults and tries to improve them. Remember, your responsibility is to your people and not your feelings.

My team leader time was extremely rewarding. I was fortunate to have the opportunity to lead some of the best fighting men in the world. I grew professionally and personally. At the end of my stint I can say that I stayed true to my team leader values, my list of things that I felt were important for a leader to be and do. I have always been a reflective person, looking back on things and reviewing my experiences. In doing this, I realized that I needed to think about what I wanted to do with that information.

First I wanted to make sure I analyzed the aspects of the situation that I knew I could change. I tried not to waste a whole lot of time thinking about issues that were out of my control, like the planning session for Operation Anaconda. Second, I decided that in order to become a better leader I needed to make a good plan for changing the things that were within my control. Regardless of what anyone tells you, good leaders are made, not born. With hard work, we become great.

Quick notes for aspiring leaders or those already in leadership positions...

- **When you become a leader, you are no longer "one of the** guys"

- Never fear trying something new for the right reasons
- Do NOT become the leader or person you do not want be
- When in doubt, focus on improving and fine-tuning basic skills
- Truly have an open mind and encourage independent thinking
- Great leaders must be able to mentally and emotionally remove themselves from any situation in order to have an unbiased perspective with clear judgment
- The enemy has a vote, but don't let the enemy drive your actions
- Err on the side of aggressiveness if able
- Communication on all levels is key to great leadership
- Know when to step aside and allow those that "know" to move in and work
- Military leaders must continually remember these three areas in a fight:

    Leader position - should be influential

    Information - clear, concise, and specific - train your subordinates on what you need

    Communication
- Great leaders support their superiors as best they can
- There is often more than one correct way to do things - sometimes your way isn't the best way
- Prepare carefully for important messages, and communicate purpose and resolve
- Have thick skin and know your weaknesses
- Information shared is far more effective than information corralled
- Be audacious and tactically disciplined

6

SENIOR LEADER TIME

Nearly ten years after first meeting Shawn Langston, our paths crossed again. I was walking down a hallway at the unit on my way to the computer literate folks, as I had inadvertently locked myself out of my computer. My head was down, buried in my notebook as I reviewed my to-do list for the day. Through my peripheral vision I saw someone approaching, and looked up to avoid a collision. Lo and behold, it was Shawn! I knew he attended the selection course, passed, and was in the middle of the operator training course, great news to me.

Like most candidates in the course he was moving with purpose, obviously on an errand for himself or his teammates. I instantly smiled and greeted him with his old nickname, "Dirty Shawn!"

He smiled back, we shook hands and he replied, "I can't believe you're bringing up that old name." I knew he was busy so I kept it short, and gave him my phone number in case he or his family needed anything while he was in the training course. As he walked away, I could tell that

Dirty Shawn had matured into Sergeant First Class Shawn Langston. Like all the hellions of our young Ranger days, we had all grown personally and professionally. I was excited for him to join us in the unit and hoped that we would have the opportunity to work together down the road with some time for a couple of brews (maybe our young hellion days weren't *entirely* over).

***

In the spring of 2005 I was deployed to Iraq, where I functioned as the operations sergeant major for the maneuver elements in my unit. In this role I worked in the headquarters element and my primary function was to support the troops on the ground. I had progressed up the ranks to the point that I was no longer on the battlefield as a fighter, and this was the tradeoff for stepping on the next rung of the leadership ladder. If successful in this new role, I could then be assigned to lead one of the maneuver troops, which would place me back on the battlefield. I couldn't wait for that opportunity!

I was in our Tactical Operations Center (TOC) tracking the actions of one of the maneuver elements in the western part of the country as they conducted a daytime mission. When the assault force reached their target they were greeted with intense enemy gunfire and a large firefight ensued, resulting in several members being wounded, two of whom were seriously wounded. We were informed that one of the team sergeants sustained a gunshot wound to his hip, and the sergeant major was shot in his leg. The assault force completed their mission, evacuated their casualties and were preparing to move back to their base when my command sergeant major approached me. He said, "Rob, you need to pack your bags. You're gonna replace the sergeant major that just got wounded."

"Roger that, sergeant major, I'll be ready to move as soon as I get a break from the current operation," I replied.

When the mission was complete and those of us working in the

TOC were able to take a short breather, I quickly packed my gear. The word to get on an aircraft could come at any moment. After packing, I returned to the TOC and continued to help coordinate efforts to assist the guys that just finished their mission.

The next day, I loaded my equipment onto a helicopter and flew to a forward operating base in Al Asad, Iraq. Members of the force there greeted me and we offloaded my gear into a small truck and drove to the operations center. As the senior enlisted man on the ground, I would be taking responsibility for all of the common items on our compound. Once I reviewed and confirmed that each piece of equipment, such as computers, matched the receipts, I signed my name on the dotted line and assumed responsibility for everything. After the administrative tasks were finished, I gathered the team sergeants for a meeting.

I wrote down a few things that I wanted to say to them. The first thing I wanted to ensure they knew about me was my dedication to our mission and to them. I knew I didn't have to say this to these professional team sergeants, but I felt it was important for them to hear me say it. I also wanted them to understand that it was honor to work with them in a leadership position, especially in time of war. This was important to me because I recalled, as a junior team member, that I held my leaders in high regard. I wanted them to know that I was extremely dedicated and passionate about my position and my responsibilities.

Now it was time to get re-acquainted with my boss, the officer in charge, Captain Dan Thomas, call sign Carnivore. He was a great operator, leader, and former teammate. Dan had a bubbly personality that went well with his size - he was a big, strong man, and definitely a meat eater. Then again, everyone was big compared to me. Like the vast majority of unit members, he was extremely talented. He was a former NCO in our unit before he elected to move over to the "dark side" and become an officer. Dan was my team sergeant when I was a newbie in the unit. I knew we would work well together, we trusted and respected each other on all levels.

In military units, there are usually two leaders - a commissioned officer (CO) and a non-commissioned officer (NCO). The CO is one hundred percent legally (in terms of international laws of warfare) responsible for the successes and failures of the organization, whereas the

NCO serves more as an advisor to the commander. The NCO is not legally responsible for the unit. The CO can elect to delegate as much or as little of his authority to his or her NCO counterpart as he or she chooses, but with the understanding that the responsibility for the unit cannot be delegated.

In my case, Dan delegated nearly all of his authority to me as his senior enlisted advisor. This rarely happens in the military but in our organization it happened more often than not and proved to be extremely effective. Just because we weren't legally responsible didn't mean we acted irresponsibly; quite the contrary. I was fully accountable for the actions, failures, and successes of those I led.

***

It was hot and pitch-dark. One of our teams was fast-roping onto the rooftop of the target building and I was running as fast I could from a block away, as the lead person of my four-man element. When we reached the team in front of us I stopped and tried to catch my breath. I watched the team in front of me breach the security gate of the target location and immediately enter and clear the courtyard. They moved quickly and with purpose to the side entrance of the building. My team held our position and pulled security outside the wall and into the courtyard. To say that our night vision goggles provided us with a definite advantage would be an understatement. Two teams orchestrated simultaneous breaching of second and first floor doors and initiated entry.

My guys and I immediately moved to make entry into the structure. As I approached the threshold, I was met with the strong smell of sulfur in the air from the explosive charge. I announced our presence before entering, and was provided with acknowledgement and permission to enter the room. The team in front of us had detained a few fighting-aged men and were in the process of putting flexible handcuffs on them when we entered. My headquarters team and I took control of the detainees and I told the assault team, "We've got this. Keep going!"

I kept my M4 trained on the head of one of the detainees as Jay searched his body for weapons. As Jay patted down his abdomen, he yelled, "I feel wires!" The hairs on the back of my neck stood up. This usually meant a wearable bomb or suicide vest. As an organization, we were encountering an increasing number of suicide bombers during our missions. Sometimes we'd find enemies were wearing suicide vests and other times we'd find them stored, ready for wear. This detainee was being combative and aggressively keeping his hands together near his belly button, and I was contemplating putting a bullet in his head.

I called out, "You need to get his arms behind his back right now or he's dead!" Jay, a strong man, forcefully pulled the detainee's arms behind his back. Once he was cuffed, we finalized our search and realized that Jay mistook a pair of flexible handcuffs that was left on one wrist by the assault team as wires to a suicide vest.

Our detainees were moved to a safe location as the teams continued to clear the building. The structure was cleared within minutes and I then requested a back clear, which is a more thorough and methodical search. Upon completion of the back clear, I requested an external clear of the target structure. Our belief is, the structure is not one hundred percent secure or safe until both the interior and the exterior of the structure are cleared. That meant searching vehicles, outbuildings, nooks, crannies, or any other place someone could hide, looking for bad guys as well as caches of weapons, ammunition, or explosives.

I jumped on the radio, "External clear complete. We are all secure. Continue with post assault procedures. Roger in sequence. Over." All team leaders radioed that they understood that we were all secure and they immediately shifted to their post assault responsibilities, which consisted of searching rooms for enemy information or intelligence. We questioned the detainees and catalogued the information and intelligence we collected. During our questioning we determined that we had captured the target individual.

We had to do our jobs in a thorough but quick manner. Our small force typically operated in the middle of bad guy country, so it was extremely important that everyone clearly knew their responsibilities. We were two years into the Iraq war with great experience, which made us super efficient. Our training prior to the war and current combat experience created an extremely well-oiled machine.

During the post-assault procedures, I was contacted by one of my teams informing me that they had located a wall-mounted safe. The structure we occupied was similar to a duplex. I had one part of my assault force in one side and another part of my force occupied the second side. We initially were uncertain if these residents were associated with our target individual, but became more suspicious when the occupants refused to open the safe. The team sergeant attempted to pry the safe door open with manual and mechanical tools but was unsuccessful. He elected to utilize explosives.

Prior to setting the explosive charge, the team sergeant moved the residents to a safe location inside the house. Since I hadn't heard from him, I decided to walk to the other side of the structure and have a face-to-face meeting. As I was walking, a single word was dispatched over the radio, "lighting!" This meant that the breacher just ignited the firing system and we all waited for the explosion.

BOOM! The walls shook as the charge detonated and subsequently caught the room on fire. As I entered the area I was approached by my team sergeant and my interpreter, both of whom were incensed, with different qualms. My team sergeant was dead set on opening the safe, and my interpreter was worried about the family members inside the house, whom I knew were in a safe location.

As the fire spread, so did the chaotic nature of the scene. Without hesitation I yelled at both men, "Quiet!" They both were surprised by my tone. After I had gotten their attention, I followed calmly with directions to each. We needed to completely evacuate the family from the building, and I requested that the team sergeant split his element into two groups. One would assist the family, and the other would suppress the fire and open the safe. The men quickly moved to complete these tasks. Once the safe was open and the contents secured, I consolidated the entire assault force at the main target building and had a quick meeting with all the leaders.

There was no information or intelligence that indicated a second target, so my boss cleared us to leave. I passed the command to the team sergeants, "Prepare to exfil." They moved to their respective teams, ensured they were ready, and radioed in sequence, "Rat, ready to exfil. Over."

After all the teams reported, I dispatched a net call to the leaders, "All elements, this is Rat. Exfil Exfil Exfil. Over." We moved with our detainees as a large element back to the designated helicopter landing zone, established security for the area, and called the helicopters in for transport. After they arrived, we boarded the aircraft and headed for our base.

Upon arrival at our base, we processed the detainees and then gathered for an AAR of the mission. We discussed all aspects of the mission, positive and negative. At the end of the meeting I was approached by the team sergeant that breached the safe. He looked me in the eyes and said, "You really got our attention when the fire was getting out of control."

I replied, "Really? Why do you say that?"

"You never yell. So when you raised your voice at us we knew you were serious."

Later that night I reflected upon the words of my team sergeant and felt a bit proud of his acknowledgement that I do not typically yell. Theodore Roosevelt once said, "Whatever I think is right for me to do, I do. I do the things that I believe ought to be done. And when I make up my mind to do a thing, I act." At that point in time, I needed to raise the tone of my voice to get their attention. It was what needed to be done, so I acted. I have always wanted to be a calm leader because I have seen too many individuals in military leadership positions that were "screamers." These individuals not only displayed little control over their emotions, but their over-aggressive style ultimately affected their judgment. Intimidation might get people to obey, but it's no way to lead.

I always wanted to follow the leader that was calm, even under duress. The type of individual that could reason through a problem because his or her mind was clear and free of emotion and whose focus was on controlling themselves first and then, the situation. Calm can be contagious.

***

It was about one o'clock in the morning and we were conducting another mission in the far western part of Iraq in search of the senior terrorist in the region. Intelligence placed the high value target at one of three neighboring houses in a rural farming village. Swooping in by helicopters, we landed as close as we could to the front doors of the homes. We rapidly breached them in our initial assault, clearing them within minutes.

After thoroughly searching the buildings and consolidating the bad guys into the largest of the homes, we learned through questioning that we did not capture the high value target we were after. *Shit. This guy is savvy*, I thought. One of our detainees had identified some secondary structures in the local area that might be of interest to us. I decided to move to assault and clear them looking for our HVT. I coordinated this with my boss, Carnivore.

I decided to split our element in half. I left a part of our force to maintain control of the bad guys we detained while the rest of us made quick work of the secondary structures. Once we exhausted the list of potential locations, unfortunately still not finding our high HVT, we made our way back to the primary target buildings to link up with Dan and the rest of the guys.

The team leaders, Dan, and I gathered to discuss our options. There was no more intelligence to lead us to another target in the area, so we made the decision to leave. As a small element it was critical for us to be out of the area before sunrise to avoid being located by the enemy and providing them with an opportunity to mass their forces against us. Speed also equated to security for us. Get in, get busy, and get out. No time for lollygagging. Functioning as a tactically surgical force, we never worked with the large numbers that the conventional military utilized. Coordinating a small element was much easier and better for the types of missions we conducted. After being on the ground for over two hours conducting our mission, it was obvious to everyone in the neighborhood that the Americans were in town, it was time to go.

Dan mentioned that he had seen some "peek-a-boos" - someone peeking from behind a curtain in a window of a house located approximately one hundred meters away. This was odd behavior in Iraq, as most Iraqis paid little attention to our actions and rarely, if ever, looked out of their windows to watch us. Maybe they were hiding. Perhaps they just didn't care as long as we weren't bothering them. As the helicopter landing zone was just outside the back door of the peek-a-boo house, Dan was a bit concerned and wanted to err on the side of safety. He made the decision that we should clear the structure before requesting the helicopters for extraction. We all understood and agreed with his decision.

It was my responsibility to clear the two story house and I decided to take two teams and my medic, Mike Rayes, to move to the structure and assault it. I quickly briefed the two team leaders and they went to work orienting themselves and their teams. Because of the experience and extremely high level of training of each and every operator on our teams, we could quickly react to any given situation and conduct assaults on a moment's notice and without detailed planning sessions. We operated from clear tactical principles which helped streamline our actions. Within minutes we were in our order of movement and headed to the target building.

We approached the house from the rear and realized that there was no back door into the home, so the teams made their way around to the front. Our medic and I held positions in the rear and pulled security on the back of the house just in case the occupants tried to escape through the rear windows. I watched as the lead team navigated the corner at the front of the house, preparing to make entry through a doorway. The second team bypassed the first and looked for an alternative entrance.

As Mike and I scanned the rear windows and bushes looking for any movement through our night vision goggles, the silence of the night was broken by machine gun fire from the front of the building. I jumped up and ran to the front of the structure. As I made my way around the corner, I could see two team members taking covered positions by and around the front door of the house. I could see one of my guys laying on the ground outside the doorway, wounded, not moving. Instantly I knew who it was, Dirty Shawn, and my heart sank. The rest of the team members were in the house, engaged in an intense gun fight with the heavily armed enemies inside. The second team was split by the cone of enemy machine gun fire coming out of the house focused at the doorway. They were occupying positions on both sides of the door where the lead team entered. They held their positions, looking through windows trying to get the drop on enemy fighters inside.

As I moved forward, the machine gun fire became so intense that Mike and I became pinned down behind some cover near our teammates. I could see the team inside the house retrograding out and taking up covered positions near the entry point. Several mates were injured. Once outside they moved to the windows near the doorway and tried to kill the enemies inside. They didn't have enough manpower to move the injured and engage the enemy so they focused on the fight first, casualties second, as we are trained to do.

Mike and I fought our way forward as best we could, trying to get to our fallen and injured comrades. During a lull in the enemy fire we were finally able to put hands on Dirty Shawn and quickly tried to pull him out of the doorway. It was a relief to finally get to him but that feeling would be short-lived. The terrorists in the house began throwing grenades out the door and windows at us.

Enemy fire erupted again, the rounds slapping the metal door near me like an automated hammer hitting tin. Without thought, Mike and I dropped and rolled out of the way, landing on top of each other. This was one of a handful of times where I thought for sure my ticket would get punched. To this day I don't know how Mike and I didn't take at least one round.

We laid there, making ourselves as small as physically possible near the front door, in hopes of avoiding the enemy's bullets. There was another lull in the fire. *The enemy must be reloading*, I thought. So we sprang to our feet and pulled Dirty Shawn behind solid cover where Mike could address his injuries. I knew it, but I didn't want to accept it…our teammate and friend was dead. Mike was working on his wounds and looking for signs of life, doing anything he could, trying to will him back to life. I know how helpless and sad I felt at that moment and cannot even begin to fathom what a capable and experienced medic like Mike was feeling. Try as he might, I knew the fight was over for our brother.

We were in a dangerous situation and I had other injured mates, so I forced myself to clear my mind and think about the fight. We needed to get the remaining teammates out of the building and bring something a little bigger to the fight, like our forty millimeter grenade launchers. From their covered positions outside the windows and doorway, the guys were able to keep the enemies at bay while Mike and I moved casualties and the rest of the teammates got out of the building. The enemy was heavily armed and not holding back - they were not going to let us leave easily.

We continued to dodge intense gunfire and grenades as we moved the injured and quickly prepared for movement away from the building. A few seconds of complete silence broke the chaos when I was told something that nearly stopped my heart: "Mitch is still inside!" The team leader of the lead team was still inside, fighting the enemy, by himself. He didn't make it out of the house with his team, enemy gunfire kept him from reaching the doorway and getting out with his guys. Luckily for me, I was next to his assistant team leader who was the first to realize that Mitch was not with them and then told me. Our mission immediately changed to a rescue, we needed to get inside and get him out.

I shifted mental and physical gears, deciding to press the fight and take it to the enemy. All of us fighting there that night would have loved to back off and use something a little heavier than our M4 rifles on the enemies inside, but this would have to be done a bit more delicately and with the equipment and guys immediately available. Several mates were too severely injured to walk or fight. Time was of the essence.

I gave the order to make entry into the structure. We identified a secondary entryway, breached it and immediately moved into and through the house. We encountered a series of gunfights in small rooms, and killed every enemy we met. We found Mitch lying on the ground in a room near the front of the house, he was severely injured but still alive. A few team members took security positions around him and started medical treatment as the fight went on. We continued to work until we had cleared the entire first floor of the structure and killed all the bad guys we could find. I made the decision not to clear the second floor. Our small force had sustained too many casualties and I didn't want to get decisively engaged in the stairwell and sustain more. For all I knew there were ten more heavily armed terrorists upstairs, or perhaps there were none. I chose not to chance it. The second floor had no windows facing the landing zone.

We cleared the area outside of the building to ensure a safe landing zone for helicopters as Dan radioed headquarters for a medevac. Those of us that were lucky enough to avoid enemy bullets and shrapnel carried our mates out to the medical evacuation helicopters as they landed.

This location was clearly an enemy safe house - each individual we found was heavily armed and willing to die fighting for their cause. After loading our wounded comrades onto the helicopters the remainder of the force and I waited for the exfil helicopters to extract us from the battlefield. The situation was somber for those on other teams that could only watch what was happening from a distance, unable to join the fight because of the dangerous approach to the house, which would have been over open terrain with no cover. They would have happily moved to assist us, but I felt it was too risky because the second floor of the building wasn't cleared. Any guys moving to help us would have been easy pickings for bad guys on the second floor with a machine gun - my guys wouldn't have been able to return fire without risking fratricide.

I could hear the chop of rotor blades in the distance. We waited until the helicopters were very close before moving from our covered positions to the landing zone. Loading quickly was a necessity. As the helicopters were touching down we prepared for the gusty blast of sand, dirt, and pebbles caused by the windy force of the rotor blades. Once the helicopter tires contacted the ground we quickly loaded our detainees first and then we loaded.

"Echo 56. This is Hawk 11, up. Over." The radio calls were received from the team leaders informing me that they were all accounted for and on board their birds. "Hawk 11. Echo 56, Roger. Out." I responded to the team leaders and then reported to Dan, advising him that all were aboard and ready to roll. I could hear the helicopter engines whine and the sudden rush of movement as the bird lifted its weighty load off the ground. The pilots were monitoring our radio frequency and the crew chiefs always tracked our numbers; they knew we were ready to skedaddle.

It was a short flight back to the forward operating base that we were using as a staging point for the mission. The med shed (field hospital) was also located on the base. Once the helicopters touched down they informed Dan and I that they needed to refuel before we could move to extract our sniper team from the battlefield. The snipers had inserted two days prior to the mission and were supporting us as we conducted our assault. Dan told me that he was going to walk to the med shed to check on our guys and instructed me to take the rest of the force to extract the sniper team.

The guys were quiet as we waited. Just the slight sounds of people on the airfield milling around, working to keep the war machine moving along. No one said a word for almost five minutes until John broke the silence, asking a fellow teammate to check his side for blood. A quick check with a flashlight confirmed that he sustained some type of injury, so I told him to go to the med shed to get checked out. As John walked to the med shed, the rest of us waited for the helicopters to return and when they did, we boarded them and flew to extract the sniper team.

Upon our return to the base, we dismounted the Blackhawks with the sniper team and proceeded to our staging area. I walked directly to the medical facility to check on our casualties. I was greeted by Dan and Mike. Mike immediately took me to see Mitch, the team leader that was severely wounded. He was conscious and alert, which was surprising to me, especially after seeing him on the battlefield and the extent of his injuries. When we extracted him from the battlefield I wasn't sure if I was going to see him alive again. Words cannot adequately describe the pure and absolute relief and elation I felt when I saw him alive.

"I'm sorry, I fucked up. I shouldn't have moved into the house. How is everyone?" These were the first words out of Mitch's mouth to me, and a testament to the type of people I had the honor of working with. Mitch, literally on death's doorstep, is thinking about his actions and how they affected his people and not himself. I reassured Mitch that he did absolutely nothing wrong and deliberately avoided answering his question about his guys. We talked for several minutes and I left him to rest. He was severely injured and needed to conserve his energy. I did not discuss the topic of his teammates as I felt it would have affected his condition at the time. He was definitely in bad shape. I briefly checked on my other wounded guys, and they were all stable.

As I left, Mike, our medic followed me until we were out of ear shot from Mitch. He leaned over and whispered into my ear, "I'll show you where Shawn is." I followed him out of the medical facility and over to a large walk-in refrigerated cooler. Mike said nothing to me as he pointed to the door indicating that Shawn was inside. He turned and left me alone. I entered and said goodbye to Sergeant First Class Shawn Langston, knowing my words were falling upon ears that could no longer hear. I was not going to walk in, look at him, and leave, as I felt the need to honor and respect Shawn, not just as a teammate, but as a friend. That June morning a brave man fell while under my leadership, and saying goodbye was one of the hardest things I have ever done. It was an untimely end for a great man.

I often thought of how I would feel, act, or what I would do when I lost a friend. Nothing that I imagined prior to losing Shawn was close to the reality of that experience. That doesn't mean one shouldn't think about worst-case situations and try to prepare for them. Everybody must come to terms with the reality of their chosen profession, and in the military, especially during wartime, you have to accept that death is a possibility. We did everything right that night. Mitch did his job correctly. The team executed their mission correctly and most importantly, we were there for the right reasons. We lost Shawn, but I didn't lose my resolve for our overall mission. His sacrifice solidified my determination to chase our enemy to the ends of the earth.

***

Some soldiers question their purpose in war. Rarely, if ever, do they truly question their purpose during training or in garrison. But when there appears to be insurmountable odds, the situation looks bleak, or an unexpected negative outcome occurs, soldiers may ask themselves, *"Why are we doing this?"* If they begin to question their own personal resolve, their purpose, or whether their mission is proving beneficial, then it is clear that their leaders are failing by not providing guidance, and most importantly, purpose. Once the seed of doubt has sprouted it will grow rapidly. A leader must stay engaged with his or her people, constantly reminding them of their mission and goals. People need the positive reinforcement of knowing that their work is making a difference.

The September 11th attacks gave many American soldiers purpose and resolve. Since we first went to war after those attacks, each soldier that enlisted in the military did so with the understanding that deployment to a combat zone could be in their future. The men that I shared the battlefield with on the night Shawn was killed all understood the risks of their profession. Our resolve was beyond reproach because each one of us carried a commitment to each other and our mission. Simply, we would not fail each other. I considered myself lucky and truly honored to lead men of that caliber. That night we fought with a purpose and resolve totally dedicated to God, country, and Shawn, as well as all other Americans and those that made the ultimate sacrifice.

After losing Shawn, I contemplated our tactics and the role they may have played in our casualties that night. I had one question at the forefront of my mind. Would we be able to modify our tactics, just a little bit, and still accomplish our mission? As I reflected on this, I remembered back to when I was brand new to the unit, at the annual information sharing session being briefed by some of our guests about a similar mission. They elected to not enter and clear the structure. When I asked why, their commander replied, "We've lost too many guys chasing low level bad guys, and we feel like it's not worth the risk."

They completed the mission without any unnecessary risk to their men. They really focused on utilizing their brains as opposed to their tactics and they were successful. This got me thinking on an even deeper level. It was my decision and plan to clear the house the night Shawn was killed in action. We did everything correctly, but how could we fight smarter, not harder? I didn't want to become excessively risk averse or overly defensive, but maybe there were some improvements to be made in how we operated.

A full day later we were still processing the fact that we lost Shawn and quite a few teammates had gotten hurt. I was still grappling with my leadership role, our current tactics and how we could balance risk and aggression when we received some intelligence placing a senior terrorist in our region.

Capt. Thomas and I evaluated the information and looked at the location; it was in the same general area as our last mission. I brought the team leaders into our operations center to review the information and area as well. We agreed that the information wasn't rock solid, and after a brief discussion with the team leaders Dan looked at me and said, "Well, what do you think?"

"Let's do it" I said. "Tell your teams what's going on and meet me back here in five minutes for a quick planning session." Two of the team sergeants were new, stepping into the leadership roles of the injured. They all moved without hesitation.

I sat at our small planning table and studied the terrain for potential helicopter landing zones. As the team sergeants came back in we discussed the particulars of the mission. The unit's planning process gave the team leaders the lead on planning, this gave them ownership of the plan. I delegated a majority of the authority to them, while still maintaining overall control and responsibility. They would be the ones executing the plan, so common sense, which is not so common at times, would suggest that it was best that they develop the plan.

As the responsibilities of each team were discussed, one of the team sergeants said, "I think we should land the helos here, at this field and move slowly toward the building. We don't have to take the helicopters to the front door." For years we planned, trained, and operated on the assumption that it was always best to insert as close as possible to the doors or entry points of our target location. This was the first time anyone suggested a change from the norm when inserting our assault force by helicopter. The thought process was that we could still accomplish our mission without being engaged at the entry point(s) of the structure. I loved it!

The team sergeants continued to plan and I offered minor suggestions here and there. They had the authority to include or exclude those suggestions, even though I was the senior leader. By the end of the planning session we had developed a helicopter assault plan that would allow for complete containment of the building while providing cover for the teams moving forward to their assigned breach points. The plan also supported our contingencies superbly. This was a new undertaking for us as we were going to execute different tactics that were driven by the team sergeants on the ground.

At the end of the brief the teams moved to don their gear and head to the helicopters. The pilots and crew chiefs were out conducting their pre-flight checks. I retrieved my intelligence products and maps, put them in my pockets and moved to throw on my gear. It was already laid out and prepped by my medic. He knew I tended to get wrapped up in final mission planning and leader huddles.

For a moment I stared at my armored vest with my combat equipment in front of me. We were about to head back to an area where we took a beating several days earlier. I grabbed my body armor with both hands, stared at it and said, "We have to do this." I said this out loud, as if speaking to those around me, but I knew it was pretty much just for me. I kitted up and made my way to the helicopters. It was approximately nine o'clock in the evening and it was dark as we boarded the helicopters. We were not headed back with vengeance…we were headed back with modified tactics and this gave me a feeling of excitement.

The sun was up when we landed back at our support base after a busy night of chasing terrorists. When the helicopters touched down we took our detainees to the in-processing area, the first step in the detention system. We had found improvised explosive device (IED) making materials, weapons, and tons of ammunition in the residence they occupied. After finishing with the detainees we moved into our command center and prepared for our AAR.

I sat with Dan and we discussed the particulars of the mission while the team leaders took some time to talk with their teams and run their own team internal AARs before attending the group AAR. When the entire assault force was seated in our small planning room, we got started. We discussed how the mission unfolded and decided that our plan was sound and successful. We had not taken any casualties. That mission taught us a lot of valuable lessons and I realized I had a ton of work ahead of me for the next one. If we were going to utilize the same mission profile for future operations then I wanted to make sure that we kept all of our ducks in a row.

I sat alone at the planning table reviewing my notes, trying to determine how I would follow through and correct the problems we identified. Two of my team sergeants came in and sat next to me. One of them looked at me and said, "I'm glad we did this mission tonight. And you were right, we did have to do it." He had heard me, talking to myself as I looked at my gear prior to that mission. It was a good feeling knowing that my guys trusted and respected me enough to talk with me about this issue. I knew I was making the right leadership decisions.

Over the next month our operational tempo remained the same: beyond busy. We were executing at least one mission nightly and many times we conducted four or more. During this time I learned one important concept relating to my philosophy on conducting direct action missions: the most significant factor in the assault equation was the element of surprise. I informally reviewed the missions where unit members got hurt or where we took significant enemy fire to try and understand what we could fix. The vast majority of time it was directly related to the loss of surprise. We gave it up by landing the helicopters too close to our intended targets or as a byproduct of how we conducted assaults. I knew from this point on it was imperative for us to achieve and maintain the element of surprise as long as possible, all the way to the decisive point, if feasible.

I also decided we needed to develop more tactical options for situations in which we lost surprise. This was critical for me. I did not want to default to conducting business as usual with the same tactics for all missions, so I worked to develop them. My focus was on operating smarter. Smarter meaning that I wanted to provide the enemy with every possible opportunity to reveal his intentions so that we could respond with counter tactics that he was not anticipating.

For example, if I knew individuals within a structure were armed, intending to do us harm, anticipating that we would make entry into the structure through the front door, then I wanted to enter the back door or a window. I also felt I didn't have to lead with one of my team members first. I wanted to lead with something more aggressive, like throwing a grenade or dropping a bomb, especially if the occupants had already fired at us. I wouldn't initiate such action without sufficient provocation that met rules of engagement. But there was nothing keeping us from deploying a flashbang, or two, or three, or something different to keep the bad guys on the defense. I wanted to be unpredictable to the enemy, varying tactics and keeping our enemy on their heels.

It was not worth losing a team member while chasing another terrorist. The same terrorist, who, in my personal opinion, legally and morally just needs to die. I was going to be happy if he died when I pressed the trigger several times on my M4 as I followed him to the ground, or if he died after he looked at the grenade rolling and stopping at his feet, or if he died as a result of having a five hundred pound bomb detonate on top of him. The end result was the same. The way we accomplished it was growing a little different: smarter, with more tactical options, less exposure and risk to us.

This shift in tactics was the genesis for a cultural change within my organization. Over the next couple months those of us on the ground began modifying and fine tuning tactics to offer us more options during missions. We were solidifying them and creating standard operating procedures for them. This was important work, and we were evolving and improving exponentially. I wanted us to operate like our enemy. If you were to ask any soldier that fought in Iraq about the terrorists' tactics they would say something like this: these guys are smart and hard to track down. They're fluid and change often and they are hard to fight because they are always changing their tactics. They operate in cells, and are constantly on the move.

I wanted the enemy to feel the same way about us. I wanted them to be afraid that we would be there when they least expected it and to know that there was no safe place to hide. Our tactical improvements were making a real difference on the battlefield. Still, change can be hard for some people to accept.

There were team leaders underneath me who believed that we should not change, stating that traditional tactics worked for years. Then there were those that accepted the new tactics wholeheartedly. An even smaller group was on the fence, not knowing exactly what was right. At the end of the day, I, as the leader, had the final say. Much to the chagrin of some...we were changing!

One thing I learned from this: leaders cannot satisfy everyone all of the time. Leaders make tough decisions and sometimes the culture cannot and should not be a democracy. I decided that Shawn's death would not be in vain and I was going to be a catalyst for change. Fortunately, or unfortunately for me, depending on your perspective, I was in a position of influence at the time and able to make the changes happen.

After about two months in my new leadership position, things seemed to be going great, or so I thought. I was having a joking conversation with some of the guys in the gym one day, talking about how we could fix the world's problems and what we needed to do to win the war. Out of nowhere a seasoned operator and friend of mine, Bill, jokingly said, "I think I can fix the problems. All I have to do is get out of here alive first." I knew he was joking, but there was also a bit of truth in his statement. I stayed with the guys for a while and then I disengaged myself from the conversation and ventured back to my room to gather my thoughts.

I thought long and hard for several days about Bill's choice of words, and I realized that I was somewhat out of touch with the state of mind of my own people. I had made the mistake of focusing on my own perception of what was happening to us in the war, and not really looking at how my guys were feeling. We were doing our part and I truly believed in and was comfortable with our actions and overall mission. But I failed to see that some of the guys were not dealing with the situation as well as I. There was no question that my guys were good with our mission. What I simply forgot was that everyone is human and we are all different in how we mentally and emotionally approach and process things. Even though we run in packs and share similar thoughts, values, and beliefs, we still have our differences. I needed to stay more in touch with my guys and pay attention to their state of mind. I also needed to be more proactive in dealing with significant or traumatic events.

I decided to manage my schedule in order to spend some quality, non-working time with my guys. I was a bit of a loner and tended to focus on my work. I really needed to change some of my ways so that I could get closer to the people around me. The end result was the establishment of a closer personal level of communication with and understanding of my guys.

We were scheduled to rotate out of the country and end our deployment around mid-July. As the senior NCO I created our out-brief for the incoming element from the unit. The guys coming in to replace us were professional, accomplished, no bullshit soldiers. I thought long and hard about the context of the briefing and I wanted to make sure that I shared all of our mistakes and lessons learned with our brothers arriving to continue the mission. I looked through my personal collection of AAR comments and began compiling them for my brief.

While conceptualizing the brief, I realized both the importance of the information and the need for it to be presented in a professional, non-confrontational manner that could be digested and accepted immediately. There would be no chest pounding on my part. I was going to be presenting information that contradicted some past practices and traditions, and I wanted people to see the changes as an evolution of tactics and also to see how successful the new approach had been for us.

If any of the incoming leadership demonstrated an inflexibility or rigidness toward new concepts or change, then I knew I was going to have something of an uphill battle. Good leaders are confident in their ability to do their job well. Unfortunately, some leaders take their confidence to the extreme (and at times it may be ego as opposed to confidence) and occasionally disregard useful information offered to them. Great leaders have a sense of balance and are willing to accept new information offered to them and then consider and apply it, as necessary, to help them become even better.

Those listening to my brief were talented, seasoned operators with many years of experience. I knew they had read our situation updates and understood what we were doing with our tactics and mission profiles.

I began the briefing by speaking about the facts of our missions, situations, and the environment, which set the stage for what drove our actions. Then I discussed the possible perceptions that people may have had at home about what we were doing, hoping to avoid any armchair quarterbacking by those who were not in our positions or in the moment themselves. While it's human nature to think of what you might do in someone else's shoes, a wise leader avoids second-guessing others.

The facts were undeniable, Dan and I led a small unit that sustained a significant number of casualties in a short period of time. That needed to be viewed with consideration of our operational tempo. When the incoming commander arrived he pulled me aside and talked with me one-on-one about the perception back at home. He wanted me to understand that he believed we were operating appropriately. However, the mere fact that a Lieutenant Colonel felt the need to talk with me one-on-one about this spoke volumes about the perception of our leadership back home.

This was less of a brief and more of an information sharing highway. I wanted the incoming leadership to know about the changes we had made to our tactics in response to current enemy trends and the threats we faced. We also offered our recommendations. It was important for them to see the facts and then make their own decisions. I did my best to explain that while we still maintained a traditional way of doing business, we had found that at times it was not necessarily the best way.

***

We deployed home a week after my briefing. It was awesome to be home with my wife again, drinking wine and eating pizza from our favorite joint, but the best part of being home was just being able to hug her again. After being home for several weeks I had the opportunity to review some situation reports from the guys who replaced us. I was ecstatic to learn that they took our concepts and ideas to the next level. There was a utilization and development of new methods and tactics that, as an organization, we never thought of or did prior. It was a great feeling to see this happen, not just because I was involved in the process at the start, but because we as an organization were evolving. We were operating smarter.

Our philosophies on conducting our missions were changing. This shift was the most significant change I saw or experienced during my time assigned to the unit. It wasn't a new piece of equipment or the acquisition of new people. This represented a change in our culture and mindset, a significant undertaking for an entity steeped in tradition! We were planning and executing missions more shrewdly. Couple that with years of combat experience that had forged battle hardened soldiers and we, as an organization, ensured we would continue to be the best military unit on the face of the earth.

***

Four months later I was the senior non-commissioned officer in charge of our sniper and reconnaissance elements and part of the surge of forces in Iraq. My teams were temporarily tasked to support and assist the numerous assault elements located throughout the country, which left me and part of my headquarters crew without a job. I asked my commander if I could serve as a liaison element with one of the Ranger companies located in the western part of the country. My commander did some coordinating and a couple days later my communication specialist (commonly known as the radio telephone operator or RTO) and I linked up with A Company, 2nd battalion, 75th Ranger regiment. I had the honor and privilege of working with my old company that I was assigned to nearly a decade before.

I didn't know the company commander or first sergeant but I did know one of the platoon sergeants, Sergeant First Class (SFC) Brian Stover. Brian was a young private assigned to the Blacksheep platoon when I was the squad leader of the Deerhunters squad back in the old days. Now he was the platoon sergeant of the Blacksheep. I didn't know him well back in the early 90's before I left the Ranger regiment, but we had crossed paths over the years and I was excited to work with him and his guys now.

After arriving and talking with the company leadership we determined that I would serve as an advisor to the company leadership and provide assistance wherever and however I could. The company was preparing for a mission that night, and the platoons were conducting rehearsals. My communications specialist and I weren't tasked to work with anyone in particular so we figured we'd try to fill in where it made most sense.

The Rangers were doing a full mission profile dry run rehearsal. As the rehearsal began I linked up with SFC Stover where he was watching his guys. "Hey Swede, what's up?" SFC Stover is a big guy and he earned the nickname Swede when he was a private in the Blacksheep platoon. He replied, "Sergeant major, what's going on you busybody?"

I laughed. "I'm trying to find some work and it looks like I'm doing a pretty good job of finding someone that might have some for me. I'd like to see how your rehearsals are going if you don't mind, brother." I wanted to see how they were planning to move to their breach points on their target building, as well as their overall entry plan.

"Heck yeah, sergeant major, help us out and let us know if you know a better way for us to do something" Swede replied.

"Sure thing Swede my brother. I'd like to run with the Blacksheep for tonight's mission if you don't mind. I'll make sure to clear this with the commander if you agree."

"Shit yeah", Swede said.

One of the squad leaders approached us and Swede introduced me to Staff Sergeant Eric "Bo" Bohannon. Bo said, "Hey sergeant major, you want to roll with your old squad?"

Holy shit, how the hell does this guy know I was an old Blacksheep guy? I thought. "Hell yes" I said, "I'd love to! How did you know I used to be in this platoon much less in the Deerhunters squad?"

"We all know who you are sergeant major, and it would be great if you joined us tonight" said Bo. What an awesome invitation.

Later in the day the Swede and I were talking and I asked how Bo knew who I was. Brian said that most of the guys that left a lasting, positive impression on the platoon were spoken of often. He said that I was one those individuals. He also told me how I had inspired him as he moved up the ranks. Incredible, there in the middle of a combat zone I was learning that my leadership and influence left a positive impression on subordinates. I had never realized that before. I couldn't believe it.

Swede and I talked about the good 'ole days and about the upcoming mission and how things in the Rangers and the war changed. After some reminiscing we left each other to prepare for the mission. Later that night we conducted the mission as planned. My RTO and I ran with Bo's squad. The entire experience was incredible and it was great to see how the Ranger Regiment had learned and grown professionally. Our mission went down without incident. Later that evening I thought of the significance of the day's events and how important leadership is, even when we aren't aware of it. This was an unforgettable experience for me, with the important realization that I had a positive impact on those around me as a young leader.

***

Six months later I was deployed to Iraq again, this time I was working with my sniper teams. My boss and officer counterpart, Major Jack Rowder and I also led and worked with a Ranger platoon and two sections of tanks and Bradley fighting vehicles that were part of our assault element. The Ranger platoon was the same platoon that I worked with during my last deployment. It was led by SFC Stover, Swede, and his platoon leader who was his officer counterpart. As in previous deployments, our entire assault force was responsible for tracking down senior Al-Qaeda terrorists and capturing or killing them. The mission was the same as prior deployments but the operational environment had changed immensely. The enemy had learned tremendously from our early punishing successes. They were joined by more and more sophisticated, dedicated fighters from other countries far and wide.

Vehicle-borne improvised explosive devices (IEDs) and instigating ethnic fighting had become the tactics of choice for Al-Qaeda in Iraq. This affected the battlefield for us in many ways. Communities were creating neighborhood watches responsible for protection. They would seal off neighborhoods, inadvertently making it difficult for us to move around to conduct operations. The enemy knew the areas where we were canalized and would scout the location for two purposes. First, to place sentries for early warning of our arrival. Second, to know where to place IEDs for us to drive alongside or over. Daylight operations became even more dangerous.

We were still part of the surge of forces into the country and the number of military personnel was at an all-time high, second only to the invasion force. Operations were conducted both day and night. My guys and I were responsible for conducting operations during daylight hours while another element operated at night. Our commander chose this division of labor because it allowed individual elements to focus their efforts and also have dedicated down time, amongst other reasons. It had the added benefit of keeping the enemy on their toes 24/7 - they never knew when we would strike with a fresh assault force ready to pounce. Daylight operations proved to be extremely difficult. We trained for and were comfortable with conducting missions at night. It was a lot harder to hide during the day. We needed to figure out how to get to the bad guys without alerting them first.

We were about three weeks into our deployment and all were feeling the frustration of searching for and locating the enemy. They continually moved and they knew that this frequent movement was key to their survival. Our window of time for operations was condensed and we were required to not only figure out where the enemy was, but where he would be in a specific, short period of time during which we could strike. Then we had to hustle to set up, to get "eyes on" them. We tried a myriad of methods only to feel as though we were spinning our wheels. I could sense the frustration in my team leaders and it was wearing on me as well. It was difficult work.

The missions were tough and ambiguous and no longer fit the template of assaulting a fixed structure. We learned to get creative and we actually tried to shape the battlefield somewhat, as best we could with our small element. We would place ourselves in an area, banking on the possibility that the enemy was there, and then we would try and force him to move or expose himself. This would provide an opportunity for us to capture or kill him.

We were busy, but we weren't capturing or killing a lot of bad guys, and I could sense that it was having a negative effect on the guys. We were used to executing missions nightly and confronting the enemy face to face, which allowed us to see the fruits of our labors first hand by placing flex cuffs on the guy we were after or by ending his life with our M4s.

We were fast approaching a month into the deployment and the frustration level was growing. We completed another mission without capturing or killing our targeted terrorist and we moved into our briefing room for our AAR of the operation. The mission was a success in part because we executed a mission plan that we had never done before, we were truly thinking and operating outside of our normal mission profile. I felt the entire assault force did well, although the bad guy failed to show for the party. When the leaders of the supporting units and all of my guys were present for the AAR I started the meeting with a brief summary of what we planned and what we actually accomplished.

Almost immediately I started receiving negative feedback from my guys. They questioned much of the process that led us to the mission, and most importantly they questioned my decision to execute the mission at that particular time. In my mind this was the last straw and I was pissed. Locating the bad guys was proving to be a daunting task and now I was dealing with the negativity from my guys. I did my best to keep composed and I addressed all their issues to the best of my abilities. At the conclusion of the AAR I dismissed all personnel except my crew. We were going to have a quick airing of grievances.

I was always honest with my guys and they knew they could be honest in return without repercussions. Without hesitation they let me have it! Most of my guys didn't agree with my decision to execute the mission and believed there was not enough information to support placing the assault force in danger. They wanted something a little more concrete. I immediately jumped on the defensive and explained to everyone that we needed to push the envelope a bit to catch the bad guys. Then the guys questioned the manner in which we were gathering our intelligence and that's when I lost my mind.

"If you guys are so concerned with how we're conducting operations, then be proactive and help me find these assholes and stop complaining about it!" I snapped back at my guys while raising my voice, which is something I tried to avoid at all costs.

"We are helping you!" one of my team leaders immediately yelled right back at me. At that point I paused and managed to gain some composure. I used this outburst and short pause as an opportunity to end the AAR.

After the guys left I sat alone with my boss Jack and thought about what they were saying. We both knew the situation was difficult and I felt like they didn't have any trust in my ability to lead them. I wasn't sure what to do and I was letting my emotions get in the way of finding solutions. Both Jack and I were staying up late, neglecting physical training, spending extensive hours sifting through intelligence reports and scratching our heads. We worked our asses off and I felt like they didn't care about any of that. All they seemed to care about was the fact that we executed a questionable mission with sketchy information and failed to capture or kill the terrorist we sought. Jack spoke up and said, "Hey, Rat, we're doing the right thing. We need to keep it up, continue to push harder and we also need to get the guys involved more in the entire process."

That evening I sat outside doing some soul searching with the hopes of figuring out what was going on with my guys. As I watched some of the guys walk to the gym it finally came to me. Jack was right, I was the one to blame. I failed to fully incorporate my junior leaders into the process of locating the enemy. I was making all of the decisions with the limited information I had and then presenting it to my guys. I never did this in the past. I had my reasons for doing this. I felt, in this unique operating environment, that it was my responsibility to do all of the leg work and to isolate my guys from the bullshit paper work so they were able to stay sharp and prepared for any mission. Regardless of my reasons, I failed to get them fully involved. It mattered immeasurably and I should have kept them more informed and involved. I couldn't believe I failed my guys in such a way.

I realized that when I asked my crew to do something different than our normal or traditional method of conducting business I needed to get my junior leaders much more involved in the process. First and foremost, I needed to equip my junior leaders with the appropriate information sooner so they could fully understand the operational constraints and their mission. People will operate better if they are part of the process of working towards a solution from the beginning. They will take ownership and feel responsible on all levels. I was asking my guys to do something different and expecting them to work with information given to them late in the game. I thought I was taking care of my guys, but I was actually constricting them.

This was a lesson learned the hard way: a leader should incorporate his or her people in the planning process, as much as possible and as early as possible. It helps create a great working relationship amongst all involved. Working together in this way will become the foundation for creating and building mutual trust, respect, and confidence. It helps a leader get to know and understand his or her people even better. When planning time is limited one might have to limit the amount of input. It is crucially important to provide an open environment for people's ideas, and be willing to change your mind if it makes sense. Ensure that at the end of the day you, as the leader, have the final say.

Several months later, my guys and I were back in Iraq for another deployment focusing on daylight operations, again. I knew how I failed last time and I wasn't about to let that happen on this deployment. So I made sure to keep all of my sub-element leaders not just informed but involved in the entire process. The primary issue with the last deployment was the fact that I was the only one that completely understood our constraints. The guys understood everything I was trying to accomplish, but it was crucial that I also exposed them to the difficulties in locating the enemy.

By keeping all of my sub-element leaders more involved throughout the process, I was able to ensure they clearly understood the situation and were involved in planning and executing all aspects of each mission. I also encouraged the teams to conduct supporting missions for other assault elements when they were able and wanted to. This made the teams and their leaders recognize that I would do whatever I could to make them feel appreciated and significant. Supporting your junior leaders can make all the difference in the world. When your junior leaders understand that you will support their endeavors, this demonstrates your care for them. In turn it creates an environment built solidly around mutual trust and respect.

While we continued to evolve and adapt our tactics, we didn't achieve results on the battlefield that were as satisfying as in previous deployments. We did however manage, with some evolution in leadership methods, to reduce our frustration all around. For me, as a leader, this was an important success.

***

What I learned about leadership from war

After many deployments, exposure to a wide variety of military leaders, and no small share of leadership responsibility myself, I found that my ideas of what a good leader should do and be had grown and developed. I grew...into a leader I was and am proud to be.

A great leader must be many things, but the most important skill they must possess is good communication on all levels. I knew I was required to communicate well with all of my people up and down the ranks. I delivered critical information clearly and rapidly in order to accomplish our missions.

I learned that almost all types of information can be important in leading. This included laid back sessions with my guys, which provided me with an unguarded look into what was on their minds or bothering them. Some may feel that informal contact is not absolutely necessary, but I feel it is and believe that it allowed me to take better care of my people and lead them more effectively.

I found that my mission briefs needed to be strictly professional and I needed to know our plans inside and out. It reflected on me as a person and as a leader. There is nothing worse than a military leader who briefs a mission plan without fully knowing or understanding the information being provided. A leader that is not invested or does not care is not a good leader.

In the early part of my career I led small groups of men by myself. Later I was partnered with officers and led multiple groups and large numbers of people. Even though it is not perfect, the military has a successful leadership model: two heads are always better than one when solving a problem.

Those partnered with me accepted complete responsibility for our elements with the understanding that I was armed with full delegated authority. These situations were great for me because my officer counterparts trusted me. Had they not, they could have pulled back on my reins and stifled my leadership. This was critical in my ability to lead in the manner that I was accustomed to and as a result, I returned their trust tenfold.

Because of our mutual trust for each other we were able to develop a division of labor. They were the true leaders and responsible for all our actions. Therefore, it was appropriate that they interfaced with our commanders and external units. In all military organizations, the commissioned officer is looked upon as the leader and I knew if I, as a senior enlisted soldier, tried to coordinate with other leaders (most if not all of them officers) outside of my organization I would not receive the same support I got from my own unit. My actions would most likely be frowned upon by other officers or leaders regardless of my accomplishments or potential.

The concept of leadership can be viewed differently based on your position within your organization. When I was a team sergeant my views on certain types of operational decisions made by my leaders at the time were different than when I made the same types of decisions as a troop sergeant major. My views changed based primarily on my position and the information I was exposed to at that level, along with the integration of my experience as a leader.

I learned that great leaders provide direction, make hard decisions, and solve problems. Leaders inevitably find themselves in difficult positions, with hard decisions on the docket. You must become comfortable with this, and the best way to prepare is by knowing your job, your people, and understanding your strengths and weaknesses. If you, as a leader find yourself in a position that may require making a difficult decision in an uncertain situation and you have not trained for such an instance, then you are setting yourself up for failure. When you fail as a leader, your failure will not only affect you, but your people as well.

If you are the type of leader that sticks your head in the sand hoping to avoid a bad situation then you must understand that you are failing those you lead. Leaders must be proactive in bettering their abilities to lead. There are a multitude of ways to improve upon leadership abilities, such as after action reviews of your past performance and reviewing other leaders' situations and decisions. If you understand your weaknesses and strive to improve upon them then you will at least be a step ahead when you find yourself in a tough spot. For those of us with a military background, although this may apply just as well to other environments, one of the best ways to become a better leader is to know your job and your boss's job just as well. There's an old military saying derived from wartime experiences: you're only a bullet away from taking your boss's job.

Leaders cannot do everything themselves. If you invest in your people and allow them to do what you ask of them without micromanaging them, they will most likely make you successful. A single person cannot accomplish what a group working together can accomplish. Great leaders must invest an enormous amount of their own time, which is never easy. In militarily circles this equates to time and sweat. On the civilian front, investing in your people begins with hiring practices: hiring the best people for the job. Just because an applicant is qualified doesn't necessarily mean they are right for the job. Traits like passion and personal motivation to do the right thing without being directed are things I look for in people with whom I want to work. Once you have the right people then you have the initial ingredients in the recipe for success.

Aside from the development of tactics and gaining true combat experience what really evolved was our mission planning process. Even at our higher headquarters the processes became more streamlined and easier to comprehend. This was an early byproduct of having to move quickly out of necessity to confront the enemy (our standard time line was thirty minutes once we obtained a location on a targeted terrorist). We also understood that behind the vast majority of our successful missions were solid plans. Nearly every plan was developed by the team leaders that would actually be conducting the missions. Even our larger missions that encompassed outside units were driven and heavily influenced by the team leaders. I feel that we were (still are) the masters of bottom-up planning.

This bottom-up planning process was something that I believe separated the unit from other organizations that conducted the same kind of business. How were we able to do this? The command relationship was based on mutual *trust* and *respect* between the commanders and their junior leaders. They respected our abilities to get the jobs assigned to us done, and they trusted us to follow their command instruction and any other specific guidance they provided for each specific mission. Conversely, we trusted our commanders to support us and our decisions, which in turn fueled our desire to work harder in developing the best plan for the mission. Like most organizations our commanders were still in charge and had the final say. We junior leaders understood that and knew that our suggestions or methods could get redirected.

Our use of after action reviews (AARs) was critical to our success. It was and is the most important tool that the unit uses to fix problems. I still remember conducting my first training mission in the operator training course and then rounding up the entire class to conduct an AAR. We didn't spend a whole lot of time patting each other on the back. Our purpose was to identify problems and find solutions. The majority of the errors were made by the operators themselves and those individuals were expected to "man-up" and take ownership of their mistakes. Failure to do so was frowned upon, even more than having made the mistake in the first place.

This was difficult for some folks to handle, especially for those that were afraid to admit an error or face potential embarrassment in front of their colleagues. It was clear to everyone that the purpose of the AAR was to improve all aspects of the mission, not just the individual. It was also utilized as a tool to identify and support things that were done correctly. I have worked with many different military, law enforcement, and private organizations around the world and haven't seen anybody conduct AARs the way we did.

The AARs in the unit are professional, no-holds barred discussions about an event or training. They have a specific format and are managed by the senior enlisted person in charge of that section or unit conducting the AAR. The environment is open for any and all input from the most senior person to the newest team member. Everyone is expected to participate.

When I became a leader in charge of several maneuver elements in combat I took an aggressive approach to collecting and reviewing data from our AARs. It was my responsibility to conduct the AARs and take action on the issues that were discussed. As the senior NCO I was in charge of cataloging all of the information in my AAR notebook. I would reference the notebook periodically so as to avoid making the same mistakes repeatedly. I also used it to identify any equipment shortcomings and ideas for improvements on our gear. This benefited everyone in the command, especially those of us on the ground who needed a particular piece of equipment.

We functioned under a set of standard operating procedures (SOPs) that encompassed the entire spectrum of our operations. We developed SOPs for planning, preparation, our actions on the targets we assaulted, post-assault procedures, and intelligence analysis. These SOPs became living documents, constantly evolving in efficiency and effectiveness due to one simple thing, our AARs. The importance of the AAR cannot be overstated, and if properly utilized can provide exponentially successful improvements.

When my senior leader time ended I felt like I was leaving my family. I poured my heart and soul into our mission, my job, and the organization. Looking back at that leadership experience, I've come to realize that it was the people above, around, and below me that I really worked for. Most people treat their leadership position as a job because that is what it is. But if you can find a place in your heart to work for your people and not yourself, to serve others, you will be more successful.

Quick notes for aspiring leaders or those already in leadership positions...

- **Learn the difference between leadership and management**
- **Learn to become a better person in order to become a better leader, let your character guide your judgment and it will never fail you**
- **Be reflective - evaluate your performance in order to become a**

better person and leader, and make a plan of action to improve

• Leaders provide clear direction, make hard decisions, and solve problems

• Leaders delegate authority (not responsibility) to give subordinates ownership and to help with time management

• Arm your people with the skills and training to do their jobs to the best of their abilities - they will make you successful

• People will follow competent leaders - know your job well

• Guide your people well: tell them what they are doing right and how to improve their weak areas

• The after action review (AAR) is an excellent tool for leaders to improve their organizations

- Have a good format, allow the input of all, and follow through with issues identified in your AARs

- Collect and maintain data from your AARs

7

WHERE'S MY WEAPON

About a year after retirement I reconnected with a former squad mate from the Rangers who was living in the same town in Washington. We decided to meet and catch up over a couple of tall cool frosty ones. I drove downtown to meet Mark at the Viking Tavern. I was happy and a little uneasy as I pulled into the parking lot and parked my truck. It had been nearly fifteen years since we had seen each other.

Mark arrived early and was waiting for me at a table inside. I walked up with a smile as we greeted each other and shook hands. I ordered a fine Washington state microbrew and we sat down. We talked about our families, current employment, the good 'ole days we shared in the Rangers, and everything in between. After thirty minutes or so, Mark said he wanted to ask me a question.

"Sergeant Major, do you happen to remember your three general orders?"

I responded, "Mark, call me Rob, and yes, I do remember my three general orders. Do you remember them?"

Mark answered, "Yes, sergeant major. By the way, I can't call you Rob, it isn't right. I remember your three general orders. Do the hard right over the easy wrong, seek responsibility and take responsibility for your actions, and hope for the best and expect the worst."

Mark continued, "I've gotta tell you, I think about those rules a lot. Do you still follow them?"

"Yes," I said somewhat surprised. "And actually, my list of rules has grown."

Now Mark looked surprised and said, "What do you mean?"

I explained, "I used the rules as a foundation for a leadership document I made for myself. It lists my three general rules and more for me to follow. The rules helped guide me when I was a team sergeant in the unit. To this day I still try to follow those three general rules, if you can believe it."

Mark smiled as I spoke and when I finished he raised his voice, slammed his hand on the table and said, "I knew it! You haven't changed one bit. This is incredibly awesome!"

"Hey Mark, do you mean you've remembered my rules all these years?"

Mark looked at me and said, "Yes, I've tried to live by those rules most of my adult life. They've guided me and helped me become the person I am today."

I couldn't believe what I was hearing. I was humbled and proud to have helped someone that I led and to find out that I had been a positive influence in his life. What more can a leader ask for?

About a month later I got a call from Mark, and he said another friend of ours, a former squad mate, was coming into town and he wanted all of us to get together. I agreed and a few days later the three of us met at the same pub. Mark, Mike, and I talked for hours about nothing and everything over a few beers. It was great to catch up with these guys and see how well they were doing with their lives. After a few hours we left the bar and went our separate ways.

The following day I received an email from Mike talking about the previous night and how cool it was reconnecting after so many years. He ended the email with a statement that I will never forget: "I learned more from you than any other person in my life." These guys humbly reminded me that my guiding principles were not just useful in the military and in leadership, but in life.

***

Do you have a desire to obtain a leadership position or are you currently in a leadership position and looking to improve your skills? Some final thoughts on leadership for you:

There are many reasons why individuals aspire to lead others. Being in charge of other people should not be one of them. In my experience, having authority does not necessarily make a person a leader.

Some people do it for money, especially in organizations outside the military. Some people do it for the prestige of the leadership position. Others seek leadership for different reasons, what I believe are the right reasons: to help others and to serve the greater good. The type of people that seek leadership for the right reasons also tend to be the people that have the integrity and character to be good leaders. The rank on the sleeve or the title plate on a desk tend to have little meaning for these individuals, as they seek leadership for deeper reasons.

In the military rank is typically a natural progression of time in service. At some point you will have the opportunity to move up as long as you didn't seriously screw something up, have legal problems, or perform extremely poorly. The military has an extremely rapid leadership progression. It is not uncommon for soldiers to move from one position to the next level in just two, three, or four years. When you move up the leader ladder, remember to take a step back and put your new position into perspective. Strive to educate yourself and improve your leadership skills. If you fail to do so you will not be as effective at leading. Be prepared to make mistakes and get back up and dust yourself off. At some point in your life, there was someone in a leadership position that impressed you and inspired you. Try drawing from that experience and emulating some of the leadership qualities and characteristics of that individual. It will help you form a starting point in your new position.

Regardless of the reason you find yourself in a leadership position, you must remember that the responsibility of the position is not for you, rather it is for the people that you lead. The earlier you recognize this concept, the earlier you can create an environment in which you can become a great leader. No one expects you to know everything in order to lead people. You have to be decisive, have a clear vision and be full of determination and initiative to see your vision put into motion. Working well with your people will provide you with an opportunity to be a great leader. Things will not get done if you try to avoid the help of others, especially subordinates. Subordinates must know that their leaders have their back. If you ever hang a subordinate out to protect your own ass then I guarantee that you will fail at being a leader. Great leaders not only support their people they also promote an environment in which their people make them successful.

I have been inspired by what I have learned of American leaders throughout our country's history, especially by what many leaders accomplished with what they were given. Just as some of them came from humble beginnings and overcame great obstacles, so did I and I felt a certain kind of connection to them. Great leaders throughout history worked to better themselves at every opportunity.

I have always felt a need to help others, and this was the most fundamental driving force behind my desire to be a leader. My parents and early life experiences instilled in me the importance of helping others, no matter how menial that assistance might seem. I love the challenge of leading others, but I truly relish the challenge of helping others. I feel the same need to help someone in one of my tactics or leadership courses as I would to help a stranded driver on the side of the road with the hood open. You never know where people are in their lives and a little assistance may be just the inspiration they need to get through a tough time. Everybody at some point in their life will need some help.

Being a leader is not a job

Being a leader is a way of life. It does not mean that you have to have rank, or in the civilian environment, a title. Those that can lead, do so when it is necessary, when those around them are in need of guidance and a sense of purpose. It is also a way of life that can be all-consuming for those that lose balance and totally focus on their leadership. To be a great leader one must be mentally, physically and spiritually well balanced.

To be a great leader, one must start with a foundation of solid principles, high ethical standards and good character. You should also understand that your people are what actually make you a leader. It is imperative that you have the ability to comprehend the thoughts and attitudes of those you lead. Always keeping their best interests on the front burner and providing for them before yourself. This will result in your people running into the fire on a moment's notice for you without ever asking why.

You may find yourself becoming more persistent and results-oriented. It will be difficult to put off an assignment or finish the job tomorrow. Set goals for your subordinates, motivate them, and watch them work together to achieve the goal.

The mission or task comes first and foremost

The mission comes first, and great leaders ensure their people are prepared for the mission or tasks assigned to them. Nothing is worse than just assuming your people are ready because they've attended this training or that schooling. There must be sustainment training in order to maintain an acceptable level of preparedness and proficiency. Even though the mission comes first, a balanced leader supports his people as well. Fight for them. Don't just talk about supporting them, you must do it. Remember, the best way to take care of your people is to ensure that they are ready and prepared for their toughest mission or task.

Know your weaknesses and be honest with yourself

To be a great leader you must be reflective and honest in your evaluation of your performance and decision making. Never become defensive or insecure when evaluating yourself and strive to determine your weak areas that need improvement. Then look to a true friend to help you evaluate your work without bias. Ask your friend to be extremely blunt in their assessment and to provide feedback, both positive and negative. Many times we have an idea of what our strengths and weaknesses are, but having a colleague provide their unfiltered opinion can be a huge eye opener. Find your weaknesses and work to make them strengths.

Know your people well

One great thing about knowing your people well is that it allows you to manage them effectively and individually. One of my team sergeants was an extremely positive person and always took an analytical approach to everything. He would think through the problem, analyze it, and provide solutions based on his review. Another of my team sergeants was more of a Grumpy Gus and he would typically make me defend my position more often than not. He too was capable and talented but he would question me more than the other team sergeants. One of my team sergeants was a spark plug full of energy and always viewed things from a different perspective, which was positive and at times, negative depending on the circumstances. A great solider and leader, but I watched him closely because he was always leaning way forward in the saddle on issues that may not have bearing on the situation at hand. Recognizing a person's personality, strengths, and weaknesses allows you to tailor your approach in a way that is most effective for a given individual.

There are some individuals that do not aspire to lead. The military ranks are loaded with individuals that are content with their position and focused on getting by without additional responsibility, which is fine for organizations that need worker bees (not the unit!). Sometimes you have a complainer on your hands, one who is more interested in bitching than solving problems. These individuals should be reminded of their choices and decisions. If possible, put the complainer in charge of finding a solution to the problem, so they can learn to be productive instead of negative. Hold him or her accountable, this will help them understand the difficulties of leading and how complaining without solutions is often just having a sour attitude.

Learn to embrace change

Change is unsettling for most of us. Most people like routine, it makes us comfortable because we know what is coming and are prepared for it. If you've heard, "that's how we've always done it" as a reason for continuing in a direction with nothing else to back up the reason, then culturally, your organization is averse to change.

There are several things that I believe leaders can do to help build an environment supportive of change. First and foremost, allow your subordinates to solve problems at the lowest level. This alone can make a huge impact in the culture because instead of being told what to do, your people will be empowered to find the solutions for you. Incorporate your subordinates early on in the process. Take the process slowly and your people will embrace the idea and will take ownership.

Use facts to help sell the idea behind the change. No one can argue when the facts of the issue are staring directly in their face. Present your information regarding the potential change intelligently and systematically. Change is easier to consider when your subordinates see that you have done your homework.

If you know that making a change is the right thing for your company or unit then tell your subordinates exactly that. Look at the purpose for the change and ensure it's for your people and not for money, status, or to win a trophy. Finally, have a solid plan. If you incorporated your subordinates early on, then the plan will be driven by everyone in the organization. Give your people guidelines and authority to put your plan into action and let them make you successful.

Communicate your vision and guidance and review it periodically for relevance

Present your vision to your people, and inspire them to accomplish their tasks and to see your vision through the end. If you want to help your people or unit get to the next level or accomplish a goal, just pointing them in the right direction will not suffice. You have to guide them there and provide assistance along the way.

This can be accomplished by clearly communicating your vision in writing and then addressing the groups within your organization separately in order to provide specific guidance to each. Remember that you must follow through and hold people accountable once you have provided your guidance. Review your guidance periodically and amend it if needed, as this will keep it relevant and current.

Resolving conflict

Resolve conflict openly and quickly. This will help you and your organization grow and prosper. Attempt to have, dare I say, transparency. Great leaders know that winning a conflict over someone isn't the goal. The goal is understanding. You must understand the problem, then look to solve it. My experiences have taught me that you must not give in to the dominant personality every single time just because you want to avoid a conflict. This will empower that individual and will place coworkers and colleagues in a position to do the same.

The ability to manage your feelings and emotions can be a critical skill in processing the problem. Sometimes it might be better to just take a break, to stop yourself from acting irrationally, like I did when my team sergeants were hammering me about our unsuccessful mission. This can be an icy road because sometimes it is better to address the issue immediately.

If you disengage yourself from the conflict you must come back quickly with a resolution, don't take an extended period of time away from issue. Let your emotions settle down then get back to solving the problem. The worst thing any leader can do is avoid a bad situation, you must confront it as soon as possible with the intent of resolving it. Your organization's culture can have an effect on how you handle conflict. If people are not used to being held accountable, then it may be difficult to put someone in their place if the situation calls for it. Take this into account when you decide on a course of action.

A good leader must be able to compromise. There is more than one way to do a great many things. If you compromise without violating your character you will not lose much. You may actually gain a better ability to work well with those around you.

Try to be a good hearted person with a wagon load of courage

Strive to be a good person and always be truthful and fair with your people. No exceptions! The best way to show that you care about your people is to show them that you support them. Be good to your people and accept the responsibility of your position and take what comes your way. If one of your subordinates does something unintentionally wrong and you move to support them, then everyone will see that you are sincere. Try to handle the problem at your level and inform superiors of the situation and your intended actions to correct the problem. Then move to correct the problem based on the plan you have outlined. Always be courageous in what you are doing. You must have the moral courage to try to solve problems and do what you believe is right. Your integrity will be tested. Do not mortgage your integrity for any reason!

For those in the military, having moral courage is just as important as having physical courage. Your people will follow you in a hail of gunfire not because they are ordered to do so, but because they trust you. Once you've established this trust with them they will follow you without question. This is what separates great leaders from the rest.

Don't be the ostrich with its head in the sand

Taking the approach that things will be fine, when you know they may not be, is unacceptable. Facing the situation and failing is a lot more honorable then avoiding the situation all together and possibly laying blame elsewhere. It is not easy dealing with adversity and subordinates will definitely be paying attention to the actions of their leader when it counts. In practice, a leader should be anticipating the training and equipment needs of their people in order to provide the best preparation for success.

Your people know more than you think

We all have seen the leader that believes the leadership climate is cool and everyone underneath knows different. You must understand that your people know more about your weaknesses, shortcomings, bad decisions, etc. than you think. You might think you're doing well, hiding your troubled past, or painting a facade of a good leader. Make no mistake about it, your people know what kind of leader you are.

Here's the deal. Nobody is perfect. You already have a reputation based on your past performance. If your reputation is in any way negative, then there is only one way to fix the situation you are in and that's to change your path and break new brush. You must look in the mirror and decide to change. Your people will see your decisions and actions, and they will see you for the person you are. Make that person a good leader.

Never quit

Great leaders never quit their people. Period. No matter how bad the situation may seem or what is lost. When you discuss loss, nothing makes you question your leadership abilities more than losing the life of a teammate and friend. Trust me on that one. As hard as things may seem, that is the time you pull up on your boot straps, jump right back in the saddle and face the situation head-on. Do not try to do everything yourself. That is an expressway to failure. Look to your people for support and guidance, just as they are looking to you. At times, subordinates can offer explanations or answers that you just did not see. Defeat or failure does not mean that the fight is lost.

Decisiveness without intimidation

When you make a decision you must stick to your guns. Research the facts, consider alternatives, make sure that your final decision is consistent with your vision, and then be confident in your decision and stand by it.. See it through and amend as necessary to accomplish your goal or mission.

Being decisive does not mean being rigid, and you should never use intimidation to influence people. Allow yourself to be open minded and flexible, and let subordinates make suggestions or amendments along the way that may prove to be more efficient and effective. Never allow a subordinate to act upon your responsibility without consulting with you first. Delegating authority may be useful in some circumstances, but you must be clear about responsibility and limitations. Always remember…you have the final word on any matter.

Always find time

Even if you are working twenty five hours a day, always find time to meet with your subordinates when called upon. Meet with your subordinates in a relaxed, comfortable environment. Always make it a point to provide words of encouragement and let them know how important they are to the overall vision. Being an accessible leader builds strength, trust, and cohesion on your team. One of the attributes of a great leader is the ability to listen to those they serve.

Hire or select the best…Not necessarily the paper tiger

While in certain fields education and training are critical components of suitability for a job, it is hard to see some of the most important qualities of a person on paper: judgment, integrity, and character. Tailor your interview process to focus on these qualities, and remember that training can be acquired, but character is fundamental and critical to success.

Other important qualities are the ability to get along with others, emotional intelligence, self awareness, self regulation, and being able to connect with people and understand how they are feeling. Understanding how you are feeling and being able to do something about your feelings is a great personal attribute. I tried like heck to be decisive without letting my emotions get the best of my thought process. This can be hard to do.

Finally, personal motivation is what separates the worker that does the bare minimum from the one that goes the extra mile. Money and perks are great motivators but do not rely on money alone to keep someone motivated. This will make someone work just hard enough to not get fired. The best motivation is derived from support from your leadership.

Go on a walkabout

One of the best ways to gain a unique perspective on your people and information on the working environment is to spend some time with your people during the conduct of their job. See how they are working, what is bothering them, how you can improve the working situation and most importantly, listen to what they say. Try to incorporate some of their ideas into what the organization is doing, this will give them ownership.

As a senior leader, keep your subordinate leaders informed of any information garnered from your interactions. Meet with your subordinate leaders after your walkabout, share your information, and work together on actionable items. It's critical to ensure that your people understand that they can share information with you without repercussions from their immediate supervisors. It is your responsibility to create a positive and communicative work environment.

Avoid public transportation

One of the worst leaders imaginable is the one that throws his or her people under the bus, especially the one that is trying to protect their own position or self interest. An organization must support its people with education and training, but most importantly, support their desires to better themselves.

Over my twenty one years in the army I have heard the dreaded tales of soldiers wanting to transfer out of their current units who are met with friction at some level by their leadership. Some leaders feel any movement out of their organization is a violation of trust or loyalty and will not support that soldier's endeavors. This is absolutely the wrong attitude for leadership, and has a negative effect on subordinates. Support and trust are a two way street and leaders must realize that as long as your subordinate is progressing in a way to better himself or herself then you must support them in their endeavors.

Nearly as bad is the type of leader that hammers their subordinate for making a mistake, for no other reason than to exercise their authority. They promote an environment of dominance through intimidation and every subordinate knows that the bus may run over them at any time. This breeds an atmosphere of fear and negativity amongst the people. Definitely not conducive to a positive and productive work force.

Doing the right thing is contagious

It is human nature for people to want to do the right thing. The key is creating a culture within the work environment that supports this. It needs to be present at all levels and is initiated at the top and the bottom. The high level leader should get voluntary buy-in from their subordinate leaders before pushing downward. If you incorporate change through your subordinates then the change will feel as though it was driven from the bottom up. Provide your subordinate leaders with methods and guidance on how to lead people and not just manage them. Allowing your people to work through problems on their own is the best way to lead them but this can only be accomplished after you have properly prepared them.

Delegate some of your authority when appropriate. This will make your subordinates feel as though they are trusted, valuable, and have ownership in the overall vision. Provide guidelines and boundaries; spot check to help keep people on track, but be cautious not to micromanage. Doing the right thing is contagious, especially when the majority is committed to the vision. This will make the wrong-doer think twice before acting. Once you have decided to change for the better be aggressive and fight for what you know is right.

Be a lifelong learner

Keeping a child-like curiosity might not be such a bad thing. As leaders we must remember to keep looking forward as we review the past. Do not become comfortable with the status quo. You must also strive to understand the importance and differences between theory-based learning and reality-based learning, and incorporate both in your institution when possible. Educate yourself and support your people with applicable education and training that benefits both the individual and the organization.

One goal of training is to get your people to think through problems and make decisions. Those leaders whose decisions can lead to direct and immediate loss of life (such as soldiers, police officers, firemen, etc.) should practice decisiveness and problem solving under stress. The ability to think through a problem and solve it while under physical and mental stress is a priceless individual and leadership trait.

Do not forget that a leader also wears the hat of a teacher on many occasions. As Theodore Roosevelt said, "As soon as any man has ceased to be able to learn, his usefulness as a teacher is at an end. When he himself can't learn, he has reached the stage where other people can't learn from him." I firmly believe that deep within the recesses of every great leader is the latent desire to be a great teacher. Pass on what you've learned to those around you.

Navigating ambiguity

Leading and decision making in clear cut situations is relatively easy. When the situation is unclear or there isn't enough information, the decision making process is much harder. A great leader realizes he or she must make the best decision possible with the information available and allow for contingencies. One will never have one hundred percent of the information needed to make a perfect decision. There will always be information gaps. I've learned that making a bad decision is much better than making no decision at all.

For those of you in the military, at a tactical level you must focus on the basics. People get frustrated when the mission or tasks are unclear. Everyone wants to be able to focus their efforts toward a specific task but many times this cannot be done, especially in a counterinsurgency war. Basic skills are the foundation for everything that you and your organization will be asked to do. Leaders at all levels must ensure their staffs can plan and coordinate effectively and efficiently. War gaming, vertical and lateral communication, briefing, and coordination with multiple organizations are basic skills for a battle staff.

At the ground tactical level, all individuals must be masters of their weapons systems, have solid understanding of their unit's operating procedures, and communicate clearly and rapidly in times of crisis. All individuals must have an understanding of maneuver and how to move as a team or element. These elements must be able to do this with little coordination in order to operate under certain contingencies.

The platoon leadership must be able to control their squads in all areas including the field, garrison, and in a crisis. The leadership must be able to create a sound plan quickly, disseminate information rapidly, and coordinate seamlessly with their leadership. War gaming and understanding maneuver are critical to being successful. The platoon must be able to perform their primary tasks well and with little direction from leaders, allowing subordinate leaders to take control.

Outside of the military, any organization must similarly rely on training and communication in order to navigate ambiguity. All departments must be able to communicate laterally and vertically, and people should know specifically where to go to help them solve problems. Leaders must be decisive while providing support and guidance.

Care for those you lead more than you care for your professional self

Through my experiences, I've learned that the best leaders care more about their people than themselves. I believe this one distinction is what separated the great leaders from all the others. Caring, from a leadership perspective, should involve a strong desire to motivate, teach, influence, and assist whenever necessary.

Your care should be demonstrated more by actions than through the use of words. By focusing on your people and your organization, your priorities will be clear to those you serve.

Lao Tzu: "A leader is best when people barely know that he exists, less good when they obey and acclaim him, worse when they fear and despise him. Fail to honor people and they fail to honor you. But of a good leader, when his work is done, his aim fulfilled, they will say, 'We did this ourselves.'" I could not have said it any better.

Support on my "6"

Each leader has a family. Parents, siblings, spouse, children, close friends, or all of the above and more - they influence us. If the influence or pressure is negative, then it will negatively affect your professional functioning and leadership abilities. Alternatively, positive support facilitates our great journey down the leadership path. I have found that the majority of great leaders have enjoyed positive support from their families, and they also always made time for their families. Striving to be become a successful leader without the support of your family will prove to be an almost insurmountable task.

After retirement I am still learning and facing the hardest leadership test I have ever experienced: stay at home Dad. At times, I feel that it is was easier getting shot at on the battlefield than parenting small children! It has definitely provided me with a new perspective and admiration for my wife Leigh and my own mother. Like I said, I am a lifelong learner and I'm definitely learning patience.

I am deeply grateful for the chance be a part of my children's early years, and there is nowhere else that I would rather be. Do I miss the action and the camaraderie of the unit? Hell yes I do! That was my military family and home. But I chose to retire and focus on my family. I spent a lot of time at war, and lost some friends who couldn't come home to watch their children grow up. The people in my former unit are still out defending our country, sacrificing time away from their families. I am thankful and grateful every day for the opportunity to be here, with my family.

***

The guys were already headed out to the helicopter and I was still in the tactical operations center (TOC) getting some final intelligence on the target. I could hear the helicopter blades chopping the air, and as I exited the TOC heading to the tarmac I felt the hot August air hit me like opening a hot oven. It was hot, hot like only the desert can get mid-afternoon on a summer's day. We were reacting to time sensitive information, so we moved quickly. I ran to my aircraft and could smell the oily fuel and exhaust as I approached the rotors. I was in full gear and I jumped up and into the belly of the UH-60 Blackhawk and found my position inside. I connected to the headset as the teams conducted their final communication checks.

"All elements, this is Lima 6-2. Radio check. Roger in sequence. Over." I initiated radio checks with the team leaders. The teams responded in order and then I advised my commander that I had accounted for our people and the assault force was ready to move. The pilots were monitoring our frequency and as soon as the commander gave the word to move the helicopter engines whined and the pilots moved the bird like a roller coaster on an upward swing. The air flowing into the back of the aircraft felt like a hot hair dryer blowing on us. To take my mind off the heat I thought about the mission, trying to think through contingencies that might occur. My mind focused on casualties, squirters (individuals who ran out of the target location upon our arrival), overwhelming enemy personnel, breaks in contact, loss of leadership, losing my medic, mass casualties due to IEDs, etc. I couldn't think of them all, so I tried to focus on the ones that were most probable and I thought through my reactions.

"Ten minutes!" The first exit notification came from the pilots. It seemed like we had flown for just a few minutes. Shortly after that the one minute exit notification was given and I could feel the aircraft slow as we approached our designated fast rope locations. I could see the number one person grasping the rope in his hands, and when the aircraft settled over the target area the crew chief gave the signal to toss the ropes. The rope hit the ground and guys started to slide down. As I made my way towards the rope I could tell something was not right, intuition if you will. I looked at my gear and realized that I didn't have my rifle. I thought about my situation and realized I was going to be in a bad way once on the ground. I figured, or more realistically, hoped, that if things got real bad I would be able to pick up a gun from someone downed.......foe....or friend.

The next thing I knew I was on the ground and we were taking gunfire from several directions. I was the last person out, so the helicopter was already on its way out of the area as we pressed the fight to the enemy. The force of air from the rotor blades coming down on top of us was gone and so was the noise....suddenly it was so quiet. Everyone was off the streets. I could see small flickers of movement in the distance. Without a doubt, I knew the enemy was trying to maneuver on us. I looked ahead at the lead team as they made their way into the target building. Our daylight mission quickly turned to nighttime and all the guys were working in NVGs. The rest of the assault element made their way to the target structure. My headquarters element and I stayed in the rear to give the teams room to work, so we posted and pulled security as they isolated the structure. Within seconds they were inside and the target was cleared in a flash.

The guys with me moved into the courtyard. I could see someone approaching our location rapidly from the from the opposite street corner so I pointed the guy out to my mates as I drew my pistol. There was no response from my guys. The individual was approximately forty five meters away and closing. I could see an AK-47 hanging around his shoulder. I fired. I felt in my gut that this guy was a suicide bomber especially now that I knew his gun was not in his hands. Unable to stop him with my hand gun I yelled at myself, *"Where the fuck is my weapon?!!"* He was going to blow up my guys and I could not stop him. He was screaming as he sprinted toward us. I knew this was it and I told my guys to move to cover but no one moved. They looked at me with dark eyes behind the glow of their NVGs. Why weren't they moving?! I frantically tried to push them out of the way and shove them behind some cover.

I opened my eyes to a dark room, breathing hard and drenched in sweat. My heart was pounding. My sweet wife was laying next to me. I stayed there a minute to see if I awakened her before I got out of bed and headed to the kitchen to grab a glass of water. It was about three in the morning, and I had only gotten few hours of sleep. I needed to get back to sleep soon because my baby boy was going to be up before long. I sat on the couch and tried to elude my dream. I remembered that I had a similar dream the week before. The mission and situation varied somewhat, but I just couldn't find my weapon. I'm sure I'll have that dream again.

Significant traumatic events affect everyone. Some of us are hardened by our experiences, and even those that seem indifferent are affected on some level. Leaders must understand how their people are affected by what they do, no matter how tough they seem, and ensure appropriate resources and support are available without any stigma attached. Most former unit members and those that serve in other special operations units have developed an ability to close certain chapters of their life's history. This is a critical skill, especially when you have to keep operating. And we all have to keep operating.

ABOUT THE AUTHOR

Rob Trivino is retired from a long career in the United States Army. During his time on active duty he was assigned to several units; he spent the majority of his time in service assigned as an operational member of a United States Army Special Missions Unit under the United States Army Special Operations Command. Rob has extensive peacetime and wartime leadership and tactical experience, leading small teams and larger maneuver elements in combat at the ground tactical level. He has deployed on multiple combat missions to the Balkans, Afghanistan, and Iraq and has served as a Sniper Team Leader, Operations Sergeant Major, and both Assault and Sniper Element Sergeants Major. In his final assignment, Rob served as a senior enlisted advisor for a multi-service organization supporting the special operations community.

Rob's awards and decorations include the Silver Star, the Legion of Merit, 5 Bronze Stars (2 for Valor), and the Defense Meritorious Service Medal. In January of 2012 Rob created Evergreen Mountain, LLC, offering specialized training in various aspects of conflict and leadership. You can see what Rob is teaching at: www.evergreenmountainusa.com